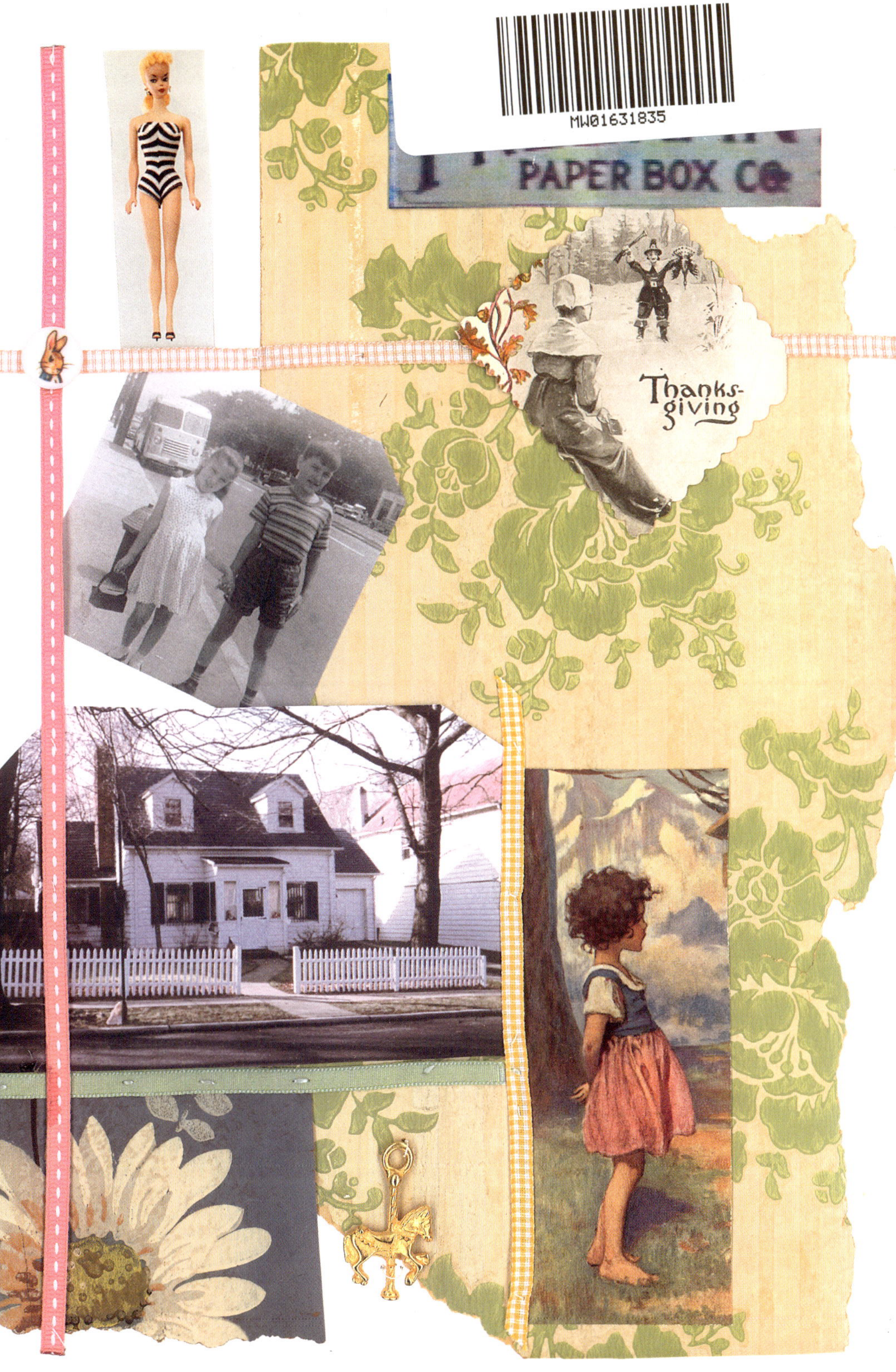
PAPER BOX Co
Thanks-
giving

Before We Met

A MEMOIR

BY

ELIZABETH G. UHLIG

WITH COLLAGES BY THE AUTHOR

To Bea—

MARBLE HOUSE EDITIONS

Published by Marble House Editions

96-09 66th Avenue (Suite 1D)

Rego Park, NY 11374

www.marble-house-editions.com

Library of Congress Cataloguing-in-Publication Data

Uhlig, Elizabeth

Before We Met/by Elizabeth Uhlig

<u>Summary</u>: The autobiography of a children's book author and illustrator that includes all the people, places, and events that influenced her creativity.

ISBN 978-0-9815345-0-3

Library of Congress Catalog Card Number 2008902720

Printed in China

In loving memory of my parents, and in celebration of everyone in my family and circle of friends.

Foreword

As I travel to schools every year to talk about the books I have written, I meet many children. I am most appreciative of their questions and insights, and it is my hope that some of them will gain encouragement from me in their quests to be writers, artists, and fully formed young people.

I was not planning to write a book about my life. I had covered a lot of my family's history in my first book, *Grandmother Mary*. But so many children have asked me about my childhood and what took place before they met me, that I feel it is time to share some of the stories from my past.

And so here, in these pages, is some of what happened...before we met.

Part One: Childhood

I am falling asleep on my father's lap. The room is dark and he is singing, *Little white duck, swimmin' in the water, little white duck, doin' what he oughta...* over and over with its repetitive verses...*little green frog, little brown worm*. Outside, the moon must be shining down on the night-cloaked neighborhood. We rock together in the chair, on this and every night. I am very tiny and sleepy, and my father is holding me. His voice and the melody are over my head. Night after night.

Then all of a sudden, I am four. I am part of a large household with a mother, father, and many children. I have a sister named Eleanore, who is almost a grown-up; one brother who is a teenager named Steve, and the two other brothers, Herm and Joe, who are just a little older than I am. Eleanore does not have a nickname, but Steve is called *Stevie*, Herm is called *Hermie*, and Joe is called *Joie*. We'll get to my name later.

The house is always full of life, movement, and voices. My mother is a constant presence, most of the time loving and warm, but sometimes loud and explosive. My father is like the strong oak tree in our front yard – grounded and protective. This is our home and I am the smallest person in it.

Where was this place? Not far from where you are, right in the middle of Queens in the early 1950s. We are a family of seven, all sharing the space in an enchanting white house, the only one of its kind on the block.

My parents, Mary and Henry Freeman, are rugged individualists who are in many ways well-matched and in other ways quite different from one another. Mom's background is Italian, but she is very proud of having been born in Connecticut and frequently refers to herself as a "New Englander." Dad is Jewish, of Russian/Polish descent, but thoroughly Americanized, identifying with the New England authors and philosophers Thoreau and Emerson, and embracing everything that is natural. He takes us kids walking in the wooded areas of Queens, which are now all gone and built over, singing, *I love to go, a-wandering, along the mountain track, and as I go, I love to sing, my knapsack on my back...*and we fancy ourselves some kind of hiking, mountain climbing family. He taught us to ice skate at Tilly Park, which we called Goose Pond. It is still lovely today, nestled at the foot of a hill and looking like an old Christmas card when the snow falls.

Mom is energetic and dynamic, full of life and new ideas. Dad is gentle and quiet, but fun-loving. And we children are a mixture of the two of them, their personalities, talents, and quirks, as you will see.

As I am growing up, my mother does not go to work but instead is home making breakfast, lunch, and supper. Dad walked in the door every night at precisely 6:00 and knew that supper would be on the table, or at least he expected it to be. There was always plenty to eat in the house, especially bread. In fact, in the kitchen, designed in the 1940s, there was a drawer just for bread. My father insisted upon having in the house every kind of bread, and if any one of them was missing, he complained.

"Why isn't there any rye bread?" he'd moan, noticing the *one* kind of bread that my mother has not bought.

She has a retort for this: "I can't have EVERY kind of bread in the house! I can't have white AND rye AND whole wheat AND cornbread AND English muffins!"

"Why not?" he'd ask, walking away and shaking his head.

When Mom is not cooking, ironing, vacuuming, or decorating her windows, she is talking on the phone to her own mother or one of her eight sisters. Somewhere in Brooklyn is the rest of Mom's family, the Italian side, a rowdy bunch of aunts, uncles, and dozens of cousins who provide an unending stream of gossip. It usually starts with a question like, "Tell me if I'm wrong..." or "Do you think it's right?" which is followed by a complaint about something someone did or did not do. All of the sisters are always on the phone with each other debating these questions.

This all happens while my father is at work in Brooklyn. On weekends he is at home, giving the house and family his undivided attention. He likes to tend to the grounds of our huge plot of land. He plants flower bulbs, but refuses to fuss over the garden. He has a belief that everything should occur naturally, so only hardy flowers like tiger lilies, lilacs, irises, violets, and lily of the valley survive. Dad does not bother with pansies or other flowers that won't come back next year. He uses no fertilizer and does not go around with a watering can. No, in Dad's garden, everything has to go with whatever nature is doing.

As children, we get along with each other and form bonds that change as the years go by. Sometimes we are bound by being two girls and three boys; sometimes we are closer because of our ages, and sometimes we are linked by common sentiments. These relationships and roles will evolve as we grow and change. But right now, at the time I am describing, we are just five kids living in the house with Mom and Dad, like a lot of other families in this time and place.

Our house sits at the bottom of the hill that is 168th Street. The property is surrounded by a sweet picket fence and a walk made of flagstones. There is a large front yard and backyard with plenty of trees, including a row of poplars in the back, which my father calls the Dancing Trees because of the way they sway when the wind blows. In the front, there are two dogwoods wrapped around each other. Borrowing from mythology, Dad made up a story about how they were two runaway lovers who disguised themselves as trees so as never to be separated. Dominating the front yard is a large oak that sheds an incredible number of acorns all during the fall. They rain down on our heads as we go to and from the house, and squirrels pelt the shells onto us as they go about their business. Year after year, my father rakes those acorns until the acorn season is over. One day, when Dad is no longer there, the rest of us will do acorn duty, right to the end.

In the winters of the 1950s, there is a lot of snow. Dad is out there shoveling all winter long. He loves it – it is one of those activities, like chopping wood, which makes him feel connected to the earth, as he imagines the Pilgrims felt. We all love the snow and we love the winter. In the spring, the front yard is adorned with puffy and fragrant lilac bushes that give off a sweet, evocative scent. We love that too.

Inside the house, in the dining room, are some framed pictures: the Good Shepherd, a benevolent Jesus holding the one lost lamb, and Jesus knocking on a door with no doorknob. This, Mom told me, is to show you that *you* have to open the door from the inside and let him in. Completing the trio is the illustrated song-poem "Bless this House," showing all the lyrics, as well as a painting of a most appealing English cottage nestled in a little lane.

There are two cars in the driveway, a black and pistachio-green Pontiac and a snappy yellow convertible that my mother drives. Before them there had been a solid, lumbering Packard and then a chubby, squat Chrysler that my mother hated. I loved the Chrysler because of the small pull-down armrest in the back that my father called "The Catbird Seat." As he explained, this was a seat for a little girl like me. Later, when cars of the 1950s got sleeker, we would trade in the Pontiac for a creamy Mercury which would bring us through to the late '60s when it would reach an undignified end in the junk heap.

The house, which plays such a large role in this story, has some special and unique aspects. There is a porch with two long windows that face the street; they always have some kind of display, usually motifs of the seasons or a family event – a marriage, a baby. If it is Easter, there will be bunnies; in March there are shamrocks; in October, pumpkins. These window displays, designed by my mother, are famous, not just for their content, but for the expression of the love of every passing day.

The inside of the house has a number of interesting features, which will become dearer to us over time, culminating in total worship of these when we finally sell the house decades later. There is a different wallpaper in every room, all hung by my father, who thought nothing of getting up on a ladder with a single-edged razor blade in his mouth, ready to slice off the next sheet of paper. Then there is the black cast iron door knocker in the shape of a sailing ship. We are really very fond of this.

The house also has various passageways and unexpected hiding places, such as a tiny closet in one of the upstairs bedrooms. Its little door makes it looks like someplace for a miniature person to stay. Over the years, this closet lends itself to all kinds of made-up stories for the younger members of the family. Some of us were told that if you crawled in there, you could get to a house that was three doors down. In my lifetime, it was used to store old toys, which were still in the closet when we parted with the house.

There was a cedar closet for my mother's "good" clothes, her velvet and tweed suits. It was large enough for several children to go inside and pretend they were in a rocket ship destined for outer space. Later, when Mom no longer went upstairs or made use of the closet, it became a haven for mice, squirrels, and raccoons, traces of which we found when we cleaned the house for the last time.

There is an attic over the garage, a mysterious, dark place. In the basement were a number of dusky corners that I did not have the courage to explore. One was a space under the stairs, another behind the knotty pine bar, and still another near an old fireplace. It was just so dark and full of cobwebs that there was no chance of my ever going near it.

About all these basement places we younger children heard tales of how life *used* to be. Eleanore spoke of parties she had there with her high school friends, of red and white checkered tablecloths and little curtains, and how the basement had once been set up like a little Alpine-style night club. I guess it had degraded seriously by the time I came along.

There were the secret places that really did not exist at all, but that my brothers *told* me did. One was an underground windmill that they said was beneath the front lawn. What an idea, *an underground windmill*. Just think about it. And this windmill had a macabre purpose, which was to make bread out of *me*, a threat always held over my head by Herm and Joe. I sometimes wonder why my parents did not intercede in this kind of terror.

Then there are some words associated with the house that we may have believed belonged only to our family, like *vestibule*, which represents that front porch where you stamped the snow off your boots. Another word is *cubbyhole*, a narrow area in the back hallway, divided into shelves for odd items, like single mittens or old hats. Then there was always the misuse of the word *pagoda*, which should have been *pergola*, because that was what Dad actually built – a decorative wooden structure in the backyard. Ever the dreamer, Dad probably envisioned it as a place for people to sit and talk. But it really just invited insects to build their nests there and spiders to spin webs from which they could dangle, which surely put off anyone who ever thought of sitting there. Another favorite word is *hammock*, which brings to mind lolling in the shade of springtime, or falling asleep under the bronze glow of the moon.

Around the property there are sometimes stray kittens in the bushes. Joe and I, who were the lowest to the ground, would be the first to spy them, their little bodies partially camouflaged by the shrubbery. That was the best – to discover wee furry creatures huddling under our forsythia bushes, maybe with their mother, all in need of a home.

This is the context in which I grew up, and how wonderful it was. Not all of it, of course. Some of it was hard – hard to get through, hard to understand. But as Dorothy says when she returns from her dream of Oz, "Most of it was *beautiful*."

* * *

Sometimes when people meet me for the second time, they are embarrassed that they don't remember my name. But I don't care. I think a person's name is the least important thing about them. I have been living with two names my whole life. Although my name is Elizabeth, no one related to me calls me that. In my family, my name is Mizey. This must seem unpronounceable to you because we don't have the letters in English to make the necessary sounds. The **z** is pronounced like the **s** in "vision." I don't think anyone else in the world has this name, but I can't be sure.

You are probably wondering where this strange name came from. My brother Joe invented it. When my parents brought me home from the hospital, my mother told little Joe, then two years old,

"The baby's name is Elizabeth. Can you say that?" to which he replied, "Mizhewizh." It stuck, but got shortened to Mizey. So I have lived with this duality my whole life – one name for family and another name for the rest of the world.

I and all my siblings went to PS 131, which was a short walk from where we lived. It was a great school and it still is. Like so many other schools in New York City, it is built in a well-balanced design and has that wonderful, clean scent that public schools have. Until recently, schools built in the middle of the twentieth century were fitted with graceful desks and seats that were nailed to the floor. Your seat was connected to the desk of the student in back of you, and it flipped up like a jump seat on an airplane. I always thought the whole thing was very cozy, all of us being attached to each other that way.

The teachers were all unmarried women. Everyone was "Miss" – Miss Fuller, Miss Herdman, Miss Zach, Miss O'Farrell. (There were no male teachers.) They all looked alike, too. They were old, with grey hair, and wore matronly clothes and sensible shoes. It was inconceivable that they might have families, drive cars, smoke, or even eat. They appeared to just live at the school, probably in the teachers' room, a mysterious place to students.

There were two teachers for every grade, usually one nice one and one mean one. As we five kids went through that school, some of us were luckier than others. My brother Steve had the misfortune of having Miss Herdman in the first grade. Miss Herdman, a hard-faced woman with straight, unstyled hair, was known to be serious and unsmiling, pitiless and humorless. This is hard to imagine in someone working with six-year-olds. Joe also got Miss Herdman, but somehow managed to escape her wrath, as he was so unbelievably bright that his brilliance must have won her over. On the other side of the hall was Miss Hallock, a benevolent, maternal woman with finger-waved hair. Herm and I were lucky — we both got her.

Eleanore, the oldest of us, had different teachers because she attended PS 131 long before we did. She had Miss Bennett, the tallest, whitest-haired, most serious, no-nonsense teacher. By the time I got to 131, Miss Bennett had retired and was working as a substitute. One day when Miss Hallock was absent, I had Miss Bennett. She distributed paper and asked us to write our names at the top. I wrote "Mizey Freeman." As she came around to check our papers, she looked directly down at mine, and, standing straight as a rod, peered at me and said in a grave voice, "*What* is THAT?"

"That's my name," I replied.

"That is NOT your name," she advised me. "Your name is Elizabeth." *That's impossible*, I thought. *I never heard that name before and anyway, how would I ever be able to spell it?* She wrote *Elizabeth* on the blackboard. "*That* is your name," she said sternly.

I looked at the long arrangement of letters. There was a **z** in there, just as there was in *Mizey*. I wondered how I was ever going to write this name and not get lost somewhere in the middle of it. *That* is what teachers were like when I went to school.

But I loved PS 131. Being the fifth in my family to go there, I was always greeted in September by the new teacher with "Oh, another *Freeman* child!" I guess we had a good reputation. I thought the school was beautiful with its polished floors and large, mushroom-shaped chandeliers of milky glass. Herm and Joe were there with me, but we rarely saw each other because apart from assembly, fire drills, and lunch, you just stayed in your classroom all day. I knew that Joe was somewhere on the same floor, but Herm was on the second floor, which seemed not only very far away, but unimaginable.

Of course, when I reached the third grade and had class on the upper floor, I saw that the second floor was identical to the first floor. However, there *was* a floor that remained unreachable, and that was the *third* floor. The stairway leading to it was blocked off by a gate that was always locked. Eleanore told us that when she went to 131, the third floor was still in use, with a cooking room, a sewing room, and other features that we could only imagine. It was a source of constant frustration, wondering about that floor.

I was shy and did not have many friends at school, but I loved the kids in my class, and went through kindergarten to sixth grade with all the same people. There were new students in the fourth grade, when integration began. Many of the kids in my class were very privileged, with fancy houses, clothes, and activities outside of school. It seemed at that time that everyone but me took piano lessons. We had a baby grand piano in our house, but whoever played it played by ear. In our family, we took it for granted that you just sat at the piano and "found" the melody on the keys, and we could all do that quite well. (My mother was still able to do it when she was eighty-eight.)

When I was about nine, I wanted piano lessons. It seemed so nice to go to Mrs. Mintz's house after school for the half-hour lesson, as other kids were doing. I wanted to be a part of that. Like so many things in life, piano lessons were not at all what I had imagined. The atmosphere was very tense and competitive, and the teacher was very strict. I felt nervous all the time and never showed up prepared. It was just no fun at all and I was not very good at it. But at least my mother let me try. She never said, "Oh, you won't like that," or "You can't do that." If one of us wanted to try something creative or adventurous, Mom was always in favor of it. What a wonderful notion to pass on to children.

In time, I stopped going to Mrs. Mintz and instead, had a kinder, gentler teacher, Mrs. Baumann, who came to the house. Again, I was never ready for the lesson. But somehow, because of the little bit of training I had in music, coupled with whatever natural talent was there, I can now play the piano fairly well.

In connection with this piece of my life, the most tender thought is this: my oldest brother, Steve, who was, at the time of these lessons, already a grown man who went to work, paid for my teacher. He doesn't remember this and I have no way of being sure it's true, but it's what my mother told me, and I like believing it.

* * *

There were the other activities in which most children participated: Cub Scouts, Brownies, ballet lessons, and Little League. Not all kids were cut out for these. You had to try them out and see. Some children were going to Hebrew school and summer camp, two activities unknown to us. But we did have our favorite pursuits.

I loved Brownies and Girl Scouts — the uniform, the little gold pins, and the sash with the embroidered merit badges, which I still have. I can't help but notice that if I were to earn merit badges today, they would be for the same things: art, music, childcare, collecting, letter writing, cooking, and sewing.

Being a Girl Scout was a lot to live up to because my mother frequently pointed out my shortcomings, saying that a *Girl Scout* should do better. She often implied that I was some kind of hypocrite, a young lady who claimed to live up to the standards of scouting, but did not want to hang the laundry on the clothesline. Somehow, she drew a correlation between these two pieces of my life. I knew this was unfair, but it did not dampen my devotion to the troop.

Years later, as an adult, sorting through the old books in my mother's house, I came across the *Girl Scout Handbook*. Its copyright is 1947, but its contents are still valid. There are instructions on safety, first aid, outdoor activities, sewing, hostessing, etiquette, letter writing, and other advice that is still useful today. Courtesy, prudence, safety, and cleanliness are never out of date. But best of all is this piece of instruction: *A Girl Scout directs her thoughts toward things that are worthwhile, so she will not stoop to words or deeds that would bring shame upon her or upon others. To make desirable thoughts rule her conduct, she fills her life with worthwhile interests.*

What good guidelines for anyone to follow.

* * *

I was only five years old when the film *Gigi* came out. My father had been talking about taking me to see it, and we anticipated this with great enthusiasm. I find this amusing, because *Gigi* is not a film for children, and yet it had an influence on me that my father never could have imagined.

Gigi is the story of a young girl living in Paris in about 1905. She is being raised by her doting grandmother and haughty great aunt. They are grooming her to be a cultivated Parisian woman who will win the affection of a rich and handsome man one day.

The film shows a Paris of long ago, with gracious parks and gardens, well-kept homes, and fashionable people. Gigi and her grandmother live in a snug apartment up a flight of narrow stairs. It is gently cluttered with lovely details of the time period – framed paintings and photos, lace tablecloths, colorful china, and decorative chandeliers. Of course, this is all the product of the set designer's romantic image of Paris. It was only a movie, but it would have a profound and lasting effect on me. As a young adult, I would go to school in Paris and look for those places I had seen in the movie. Yes, Gigi, both the character and the movie, would come up many times in my life, in different forms and for a variety of reasons.

* * *

I grew up right at the beginning of the civil rights movement, and PS 131 was one of the first schools to become integrated. African American children were bussed (I have always hated that term) to our school from South Jamaica and St. Albans, neighborhoods into which white people did not go.

Once upon a time, this racial tension was not so pronounced, and children were not even aware of the differences between *white* and *colored*. But with the deaths of President Kennedy and Martin Luther King, long-festering problems came to the surface. Race riots started breaking out in parts of New York, Newark, Detroit, and Los Angeles. Down South, blacks were fighting for their right to vote, and violence was rampant.

This was not a new problem, just one that was suddenly visible. The American South had long been living with Jim Crow laws, which made a clear difference between the rights and privileges of whites and blacks. In the late 1950s and early 1960s, the rumbling got louder and then there was an explosion. It had to happen sometime, and in 1968, it happened in the most violent way.

I was in the fifth grade when the first young African Americans came to our school. It was no problem for us children. We made friends with all these kids and they blended right into the school population. The same allegiances that had existed among white children were now created among black and white children. A photo taken at my birthday party in the sixth grade shows all of us dressed as American presidents and their first ladies, and there is my friend Keith, the only black boy in the class, in a dignified outfit mimicking the clothing President Lincoln wore. When I met up with Keith decades later, I showed him the photo and he remembered how his mother had made the top hat out of a Quaker Oats box.

We were the lucky ones. For us, the changes of the civil rights movement took place with minimal struggle. New York had some of the rioting, but it was little compared to that of other parts of the United States. What stands out for me was that there were neighborhoods you "couldn't go into." These were East New York, South Jamaica, St. Albans, Bedford Stuyvesant, Brownsville, and parts of the Bronx. My father had grown up in East New York, but when I asked to see the house he had lived in, he told me, "You can't go there. It's dangerous."

My mother was never perturbed by "bad neighborhoods." She used to visit her own mother, who lived in Bushwick, right under the elevated train, and never thought of herself as a target for crime. Perhaps this was because she had not grown up living in a dangerous city.

My grandmother's neighborhood was in the midst of social and economic change as it transitioned from German/Italian to poor black and Hispanic. These changes brought tension that erupted as fights, threats, and vandalism. When I would accompany my mother to my grandmother's house, I was always afraid because of the stories I had heard about gangs, crime, and muggings.

None of this disturbed my mother. I'd ask her, "Aren't you afraid, Mommy?" and she'd say, "There is nothing to be afraid of. *People live here*. It's just a neighborhood with people." I think these are very powerful words about her view of the world. To her, if you were dealing with *people*, there was nothing to fear. It's not that she was naïve. She simply did not see how people could present a danger. Birds, yes. Elevators, yes, but not people. And I daresay, in the thousands of visits she made to her mother in Brooklyn, no one ever approached her in any harmful way.

And so I grew up in a New York of contrasts – poor, middle-class, and rich. There were decades of unrest, of burnt-out neighborhoods, dangerous housing projects, drug-infested areas, and places that were off-limits. When I drive through South Jamaica today, I see beautiful white wooden houses with large porches that speak of a pre-civil rights era and I am in awe that they are standing there in good condition. They survived the upheaval and destruction of those years. As a child, I always appreciated old houses with their carved woodwork. I wondered why, even when they were in poor condition, they were so much more welcoming than modern houses. "Why don't they make houses like that anymore?" I asked my mother.

"Years ago," she said, "people used to take more *time*."

It is only now, as a traveling author, that I see that there are no more "bad neighborhoods" in New York – just poor ones. Since my goal is to reach as many children as possible, I never turn down a chance to visit a school, no matter where it is. Now I can explore these areas that were once shrouded in mystery. It is a privilege to be able to go anywhere in my own city. As a child, I witnessed the sudden and long-awaited changes in our urban society, and I am grateful that I was there when they happened. They are still happening, and I am still here.

* * *

Dad frequently entertained the notion of moving away from Jamaica. He dreamed of having a large Victorian house in the country, one with lots of rooms that could double as a hotel. I don't know where this idea came from, but it would cling to him his whole life. Even as he sat on the rocker, swathed in a bathrobe after his heart attack, he still mused about it.

He made several attempts to acquire such a house, and had a kind of hobby that entailed looking at ads in the paper, following through with a phone call, then with a ride up to the place. Sometimes he'd even put down a $100 binder, which he would later renege upon and lose. This daydream seeped into our lives as children and always threatened to yank us from the life we were so enjoying. But I commend my mother on letting my father indulge in this fantasy, even though it meant wasting precious family funds. Dad would play out the whole scenario until he himself would decide that the house was not worth the money or the disruption to life, and often ended the entire project by declaring, "They oughta put a match to it."

When he'd read the newspaper ad, the deceptive language would lead him believe that he might acquire a lavish house with all features he loved – verandas, pavilions, porticoes, willow trees. He pictured a new lifestyle in which he and my mother would have interesting, well-traveled guests who were literary and musical. He and Mom would serve them tea while someone else cut the grass, raked the lawn, and cleaned the kitchen.

Amazingly, my mother never said, "Are you kidding? This is madness!" which is what we kids were thinking. No, she used to volunteer to go riding with him to see the house in Long Island, Maine, or Connecticut.

And what did they usually find? A dreary, drowsy rooming house on its last legs, withered and pallid, with all traces of bygone splendor washed away by time and neglect. The rooms would have been long-deserted, their somber, chilly interiors poorly furnished with tattered curtains and ill-fitting bedspreads. The porch, which should have been restful and inviting, sagged and creaked. On the grounds, a dusty path or pebbly walk might curl its way through puddles and tufts of grass. But the ad had said "Paradise Found." *They oughta put a match to it.* Dad would go home, his fantasy unpinned.

It is interesting that my parents didn't fight over Dad's cockamamie scheme when there was so much at stake. Instead, they used to fight over nothing. Actually, it was Mom who started all the discord. My father had no idea what her problem was. Neither did we.

Sometimes when they'd argue, Dad would storm out of the house and disappear for a little while. He was not the type of man to go to a bar and drink away his troubles, so we wondered where he went to cool off. One day I asked him.

"Where do you go when you have a fight with Mommy?"

"I go to the diner and eat eggs," he said. He was referring to a small '40s-style diner, the Hilltop Diner. I can just picture Dad sitting at the counter with the Daily News, a plate of scrambled eggs, and a cup of coffee, trying to come down from the disturbing mood.

Once, well after my father's death in 1983, as I was heading back home from a visit to my mother, I too felt somewhat disturbed and looked for solace in the Hilltop Diner. I sat at the counter, as I imagined my father had done, and ordered a bowl of soup. I wondered if the gray-haired man behind the counter had been there in the old days when Dad was a patron.

"You know," I said, "years ago, my father used to come and sit here after he'd have a fight with my mother."

"Yeah?" the counter man said. "I've been here for many years. I bet I knew your father." Then he laughed. "So, they used to fight, your parents?"

"Yeah," I said. "Nothing serious, but my father was not a drinker, so he used to calm himself down with scrambled eggs."

"Yeah," the man said, "I bet I knew him."

It was odd to think of my father there, maybe on that very counter stool, maybe talking with this man or reading his paper. I wondered what he must have felt like back then when there was nothing but time that would make the pain go away.

* * *

"The House with Nobody in It" is a poem that I fell I love with when my fourth grade teacher read it to the class. Since I have always had an attraction to old houses, this poem struck a chord with me – the idea that someone else could feel sentimental about a house that was not theirs assured me I was not alone in my love of abandoned homes.

THE HOUSE WITH NOBODY IN IT

By Joyce Kilmer

Whenever I walk to Suffern along the
Erie track
I go by a poor old farmhouse with its shingles
broken and black.
I suppose I've passed it a hundred times, but I
always stop for a minute
And look at the house, the tragic house, the
house with nobody in it.

I have never seen a haunted house, but I hear there are such things;
That they hold the talk of spirits, their mirth and sorrowings.
I know this house isn't haunted, and I wish it were, I do;
For it wouldn't be so lonely if it had a ghost or two.
This house on the road to Suffern needs a dozen panes of glass,
And somebody ought to weed the walk and take a scythe to the grass.
It needs new paint and shingles, and the vines should be trimmed and tied;
But what it needs the most of all is some people living inside.
If I had a lot of money and all my debts were paid
I'd put a gang of men to work with brush and saw and spade.
I'd buy that place and fix it up the way it used to be
And I'd find some people who wanted a home and give it to them free.
Now, a new house standing empty, with staring window and door,
Looks idle, perhaps, and foolish, like a hat on its block in the store.
But there's nothing mournful about it; it cannot be sad and alone
For the lack of something within it that it has never known.
But a house that has done what a house should do, a house that has sheltered life,
That has put its loving wooden arms around a man and his wife,
A house that has echoed a baby's laugh and held up its stumbling feet,
Is the saddest sight, when it's left alone, that ever

your eyes could meet.
So whenever I go to Suffern along the Erie track
I never go by the empty house without stopping
and looking back,
yet it hurts me to look at the crumbling roof
and the shutters fallen apart,
For I can't help thinking the poor old house is
A house with a broken heart.

As a junior high school student, I won second prize in the school's oratorio contest when I presented this poem on stage. It was said that I recited with "great feeling and expression." Decades later, "The House with Nobody in It" comes up again and again; I use it in poetry workshops and discussions with students about memoir writing. Since my own family home had such value for me, I have often wondered if, at some future time, a passerby might stop and look at it. What would that wanderer imagine about our house, about what happened there, and who lived in it? Would he make up a story to ease his curious and sentimental spirit?

* * *

When I look at my elementary school graduation photo, I think of all the people I knew and the many homes I visited, either to play or to attend birthday parties. As I look at the faces in the photo, I remember the first and last name of every child, even those who were not in my class. Well of course, after seven years together, one would know that.

A classmate didn't have to be your friend for you to go to their house after school. Sometimes a quick decision was made and an invitation was offered: "You want to come to my house after school?" This meant that you went home with them and played for a few hours. It was not a "play date" because it had not been arranged beforehand. I wonder that my mother didn't worry about me not showing up at 3:20 at home. Maybe my brother told her I had gone to another girl's house. And how did I get home? I don't remember. Did I call home? Did I walk home? Did my friend's mother drive me? How could life have been so uncomplicated?

The school was fed by two adjacent communities – Jamaica, where I lived, and Jamaica Estates, where the wealthier kids lived. The houses in Jamaica Estates were among the most beautiful in Queens. They were built in the 1930s, and have cubbyholes, secret stairways (which, in days gone by, were for maids and butlers), stained glass, frosted glass, vestibules, breakfast nooks, dormers, finished basements, and bathrooms fully tiled in pale green and dusty rose. And luxury of luxury - the den. The idea of a den, a room completely dedicated to leisure, was so alien to me, because in my family we did everything in the living room. Some houses had a glassed-in "front room," which had piles of books and old magazines, games, and odd toys. Tiny panes of glass admitted the afternoon light as we played there.

Then there were the girls' rooms, with their glossy, matching furniture, the rugs, the vanity tables, and frilly curtains. My classmate Susan was one of three sisters, and her room and those of her sisters all had canopied beds. The family lived in a quaint stone house at the foot of Charlecote Ridge (the streets all had beautiful names: Aberdeen Road, Mayfield Road, Tudor Road). They had a white carpet in the living room — who has a white carpet? Could real people really live in a house with a white carpet?

Another classmate, Joanie, lived in an intriguing house on Mayfield Road. It was a three-storey Tudor house with two panes of fluted glass on either side of the front door. Joanie and I were not close friends then, just classmates, but we had something in common: we both had siblings who were much older than we were and were already married while we were still kids.

I loved Joanie's house, and later learned that I was more sentimental about it than she was. When the class of 1964 graduated and we all left PS 131, Joanie didn't go with us. She was so gifted that she was selected to go to Hunter High School. At the end of June we said goodbye to each other and blithely went separate ways. I didn't see Joanie again until forty years later, when my mild obsession with her house sent me looking for her.

I was driving around Jamaica Estates one nostalgic fall day and thought to myself, *I wonder which house was Joanie's*. I drove up Mayfield Road and parked the car in front of what I could best remember as her house — a Tudor with tall pine trees out front. I tried to recreate the feeling of going up the front walk by merely standing in front of it. Then I saw them – the two translucent panes of glass flanking the front door – and I knew I was there. I wanted to go inside. What or who did I think would be there? Surely the current residents would think it rather odd for someone to ring their bell and say, "Excuse me, I used to play here as a child. Can I come in and look around?" No, I couldn't do that. I *wanted* to, but I couldn't. So instead I decided to look for Joanie. If I found her, she could walk me around the house with words, with a description of it. And besides, I wanted to know what had happened to her after we left 131.

I knew I had to find Joanie. But how? I went on a long quest for her, calling Hunter High School, searching for her under her name as I had known it at school. Nothing. Then one day I was standing in front of my mother's house when a woman passed by. She said hello to my mother and introduced herself to me as Kathy. I had not known her as a child, but she had grown up in Jamaica and was still living there. She had also gone to PS 131, but not at the same time as I had. We chatted about our long-ago lives and I mentioned my terrible sentimentality, especially about houses, mine and those of other people. Then, of course, Joanie's name came up.

"I know Joan!" she said. "We work in the same field. I know where you can find her."

I was dumbfounded. Kathy gave me the name of the company where Joan worked, and the next day I called. Joan answered the phone. I told her who I was, and although forty years had passed, it was as if I were calling to say, "Can I come over to your house this afternoon?"

We arranged to have lunch and met near her office the following week. I was so excited and still am when I think of it. I waited in the lobby and then she came downstairs. She looked exactly the same, just a bit older. I felt a surge of warmth as I reconnected with my past.

We sat at lunch and talked for one hour without stopping. I learned that after the first year at Hunter, Joanie and her parents had moved into Manhattan.

"They sold that *house*?" I asked incredulously. *How could anyone have let go of it?* Then I learned that Joanie had none of the yearnings that *I* had for *her* house. In fact, she had gotten married and was living in New Jersey, and had never even gone back to see her childhood home! She had a fourteen-year-old daughter whom she had never taken to see where she had grown up. This was incomprehensible to me, but Joanie just laughed. *She* remembered *my* house very well, and a lot of other bits about our childhood that I had forgotten, but she was not weighed down with longing for the past. She was amused that I had such an attachment to the memory. How funny it must have seemed to her when I told her that I stood outside her former home and contemplated knocking on the door.

The following summer, when we spent some time together sitting on the beach, I asked Joanie to give me a verbal tour of the house.

"Describe it to me," I said, "and go room by room." And she did. She walked me in the front door, through the hallway, and around the ground floor. Then, with more words, we went up the stairs to her room and looked out the window onto the pine trees down below. Joanie had no problem remembering or describing it, and she delivered it all without any tremblings for the unreachable. Never, as I stood on Mayfield Road that autumn day, would I have guessed that we would be doing this exercise. It was a roadway into my past, and I was enjoying it tremendously. It was like looking through a photo album, but instead of pictures, there were words.

I found Joanie again, but she is a new kind of friend. It's good for me to have someone like her to remind me that we are living *now*. While I might use some of the childhood imagery for my books, life is really taking place now. Sometimes artists need to be reminded of that.

* * *

As students at PS 131, Joe and I used to meet on the street corner at noon, walk home (that took about 20 minutes), eat lunch, and walk back to school to be there by 1:00 p.m. School was over exactly at 3:00 p.m. That walk, which at one time included Herm, too, was a very creative part of life. We used our imaginations to *name* certain landmarks along the way – the roots of a gnarled tree, a creepy house, an old, rotting fence. These were milestones in the miniature city we constructed on our route to school. We even had a song that we composed to sing on our walk – kind of a traveling song, "On the Way to School," which was made up of nonsense verses.

In time, Joe graduated from 131 and joined Herm in junior high school, and I stopped going home for lunch. I wanted to be with the other kids in the cafeteria, so my mother got me a lunchbox. These were wonderful things in the 1950s. They were made of a particular kind of plastic that had a great smell and they snapped closed in a very satisfying way. But these memories of the lunchbox may simply come from the utter starvation we all felt at five minutes to noon, when we would be set free to eat.

I have been back to visit PS 131 since I began my work as an author. It is pretty much the same except that a lot of the mystery is gone. One day when I was between presentations, I went into the teachers' room. *So this is the teachers' room*, I thought to myself. *Whoever thought I would be here?* It was just an ordinary room which (of course) had been much better in my imagination.

The intrigue was also stripped from the principal's office. When I went to elementary school NO ONE went in that office unless they had been very, very bad. It was all lacquered, dark wood and polished glass, very serious, like a courtroom. Now it has been redone to be more cheery. When my first book came out and I was invited to make a presentation at 131, the principal invited me into her office and even offered me the use of her bathroom facilities. That was too much! The thought that I was in the principal's bathroom – could I have ever imagined such a thing as a student at 131? We did not even know that the principal *went* to the bathroom.

The principal back in the '50s was a solemn and serious woman named Miss Tobin. She was not mean, just very dignified. At assembly, she would read from the Bible's Book of Psalms, and who knows what anyone was thinking. Surely, we had no idea what the language of the psalms meant, but we never questioned anything. To this day, my brothers and I remember lines such as *Make a joyful noise unto the Lord*, and *...He who hath clean hands* *and a pure heart....* Not only did we not know what Miss Tobin was reading, but we never asked. This is much the same as the way we never questioned the archaic language of "The Star Spangled Banner" – *...the rocket's red glare...*, or *...what so proudly we hailed...* It is the rare child who will ask, "What does that mean?" Instead, children will assign a meaning to the words they don't understand, or even to pictures that they don't understand. Perhaps you do not understand some of what you are reading in this book. Will you ask? Probably not. You will most likely add your own meaning to what you read. This is why as we get older and read a book or see a movie for the second time, we derive more. Now as an adult, when I read the psalms, I take more meaning from their beautiful language. But as an elementary school student, I just sat and listened, as we were told to do.

* * *

At the time I was growing up in Queens, there was a large expanse of green countryside across the street from our house. It was a golf course, but little by little, it was changing, as St. John's University was being built.

One of the fascinations for Joe and me was to watch the huge derricks as they unearthed the trees and made room for the buildings. A narrow strip of wooded land provided us with a place where we could settle in and simply *look* at the machines at work. This was so exciting to us that one day we actually *planned* a visit (the place was only up the block) for the following morning.

For the derrick-viewing expedition my mother made us bacon sandwiches on Kaiser rolls. Early the next day, we took our sandwiches and walked up the street, finding a spot from which we could observe the derricks. We sat quietly, as though we might disturb the work in progress, unwrapped our sandwiches, and watched the spectacle.

There we sat in the woods like two tiny spies, observing the building of the university. Now, so many years later, the place is unrecognizable – except for that narrow strip of wooded land. I wonder whom it belongs to. No one has ever touched it. It is just as peacful today as it was when I was a kindergartner. How many places are like that?

Then there was the "picnic" ritual, which had nothing to do with food. I have always loved collecting, and still have many collections of miniscule objects. Joe and I collected charms. These were tiny plastic miniatures of furniture, animals, people, musical instruments, cars, and other amazing replicas of everyday objects. They came in various colors, sometimes with metallic finishes.

Charms were sold in gumball machines. You put in a penny, turned the knob, and three or four of these astonishingly detailed toys would tumble out into your hand. Joe and I had our own game, called "having a picnic." We'd take a few pennies and walk up to the corner candy store where the charm machines stood. We'd put in those pennies and let those charms slide into our little palms, but we would *not* look at them. When we had a fair number, we'd sit down, cross-legged, right on the sidewalk. We'd open our palms and let the charms drop onto the pavement. And just *looking* at them was the main activity of the picnic. Waiting until we had used all the pennies was important, because the delicious part was sitting face-to-face, looking at the charms together, at the same moment.

Then we'd pick them up one by one and examine them charm by charm. What had we hauled in that day? Perhaps tiny pieces of furniture, a colorful plastic rooster, a gold key. But then *chewing gum* started to insinuate itself into the charm machines, so that if you inserted a penny, you might get a useless ball of gum instead of a charm. Little by little, the gum replaced the charms altogether. How can one compare a piece of gum, which has a very short lifetime, with a collectible little piece of art that a child can hold?

In time, our ritual came to an end. Instead of holding charms in our hands until picnic time, we'd shrug with disappointment as we felt the cool, colored gumball roll into our palms. The penny, which had promised a handful of treasures, now only yielded a reward on every fourth or fifth try. It became depressing, and so the picnics came to an end.

* * *

The stores up at our corner used to be so appealing. The twin luncheonettes punctuated the two-block stretch and in between, there were little shops that now form a garland of memories. I remember a toyshop where my mother bought me a child-size sewing machine that really worked; the shoemaker, where I had large, professional-size taps put on my school shoes; the beauty parlor where my long, long hair was cut for the first time; the barbershop where my father and the two boys used to go, that is, until the 1970s when they stopped cutting their hair, letting it grow below their shoulders, in keeping with the current style. In the middle of one block was what would now be considered a rather quaint supermarket called Goldmark, where the store manager wore a white apron and knew everyone's name. The bakery next to it supplied all our birthday cakes, and there was Lowenstein's Deli, where Mom used to take Joe and me on Fridays for hot dogs and Cokes. Filling in the odd spots were a modest Chinese restaurant, an auto supply shop, and a privately owned pharmacy, which one rarely sees anymore. Those two blocks are totally different now.

Shopping in the 1950s was quite another thing. My father and mother had their own preferences and we kids benefited from both of them. With Dad we used to go to Macy's in Jamaica, a sand-colored building with a curved glass window. This was the reliable source for our Christmas presents. The beauty of Macy's was that you drove the car up through a tunnel at street level and parked on the roof. Then you went through a set of glass doors and glided down, down, down the escalator, which afforded you a panoramic view of the ground floor with all its colorful merchandise.

The alternative to shopping in Jamaica was shopping in Fresh Meadows. This little piece of Queens was anchored by Bloomingdale's, a posh, elegant department store, so unlike its modern-day counterpart, which is a windowless, noisy madhouse. Bloomingdale's in Fresh Meadows was a lightly scented temple through which you could stroll, like a visitor taking an afternoon walk. Even if you were not buying anything, it was just wonderful to look, because everything was beautiful and desirable. The salespeople were older women with impeccable diction and gentle manners. You just felt at home there.

As you walked about the store, light poured in through the large windows, allowing the shopper to glance outside at the early spring maple trees or the topaz-colored autumn oaks. In winter, you'd see the twinkling lights on the evergreens. The whole experience gave you a sense of being part of a community in which people were going about their business in a pleasant, purposeful way.

I have several memories of Bloomingdale's. In one, I am a very young child pointing into a glass case where rhinestone tiaras are displayed. Seven years old, I choose a sparkling crownlet and my mother buys it for me. It stayed with me my whole life, either on my head or in a cabinet at home. On another visit, I spy a small metal pillbox, whose enameled top is decorated with three tiny ballerinas. Their long dresses are flecked with sequins which, to this day, still retain a bit of metallic spark.

As an adult, I asked my mother why she spent money on these valuable items when I was so young.

"I figured that if a little girl could recognize and appreciate the beauty of those things, she had to have them," she said.

Next door to Bloomingdale's was Woolworth's, the Five and Ten, which sold everything from live turtles to men's slippers, cosmetics, and greeting cards. It had a lunch counter where you could have a grilled cheese sandwich or an ice cream sundae. The wide stairway in the middle of the store led to the spacious lower floor, of which I remember nothing but the mechanical horse at the base of the steps.

Between the two stores was a kind of a raised meadow, flowering in the springtime and adorned with a Christmas tree and reindeer in the winter. In the late '60s, the little meadow was subsumed into a larger building that was constructed between what had been Bloomingdale's and Woolworth's. Woolworth's disappeared completely and the whole concrete mass became a new, trendy Bloomingdale's with harsh lighting and no windows.

Now we just have to imagine it as it was before.

* * *

Nothing, not even the passage of so much time, has dampened my pleasure in collecting small things as I did in the days of the charm machine. In fact, I credit the charms with having sharpened my appreciation of the more valuable objects I now collect as an adult: gold lockets, antique cards, vintage buttons, old photos. Perhaps collecting charms and examining them in such a deliberate way has fashioned my perceptions as an artist.

Despite my parents indulging us in every creative pursuit, we were not spoiled, unappreciative kids. My mother was wholly in favor of "expressing yourself" and approved of this in any form. We had some fairly outrageous requests. Joe wanted and *got* a real printing press, Herm had a collection of guitars, Civil War memorabilia, and art supplies. I loved small things, shiny things, jewelry, lace, and old-fashioned clothes.

One winter, when I was about eight years old and was in bed with the flu, my mother wanted to get something to cheer me up. She thought nothing of sending my father out on a cold night to get it. Earlier that week, we had seen some "birthstone" birthday cards with imitation jewels stuck on them. Mom knew that any of these cards would delight me. My father, who had just come home, put his coat back on and headed out. He came back with the "July" card, with a lovely fake ruby planted right in the middle of the flowery illustration. The ruby, of course, was nothing more than a piece of red plastic with a sparkly background. Like all children, I had a plan to obtain the entire twelve-month collection (but I don't remember this actually happening).

With this memory, I see myself honing appealing images. I credit my mother for knowing the difference between the ordinary yearnings of a child and the light going on in a creative mind. And I credit my father for running the errand.

* * *

Sometimes Mom and I liked to take a ride to Glendale to poke around the appealing German shops and bakeries. At that time, the whole Glendale-Ridgewood area was German and Italian. The main street, Myrtle Avenue, was especially charming in snowy weather, which increased the European feeling.

Our favorite shop was Edelweiss, a German import store that sold carved wooden elves, candles with little colored flowers spiraling around them, and miniature houses sprinkled with a bit of fairy dust. They also carried imported cheeses, records of German music, and German magazines, all of which my mother loved. I don't know where she got a yen for them.

But in time, this neighborhood would fade, retaining only small remnants of its German-ness. Walking there today, if you're looking for it, you can still see the tiled threshold of what used to be a Five and Ten, some lovely curved glass shop fronts, and other bits and pieces of an old way of life. But the patina of Europe is gone.

Mom and I had a few of these fantasy trips to Europe. One day we set foot in the 1964 World's Fair and had a little adventure. Was there ever anything more beautiful and wondrous than the World's Fair? I smile when I think of those sweeping archways flanked by flags of all nations, the wind blowing, the fountains spraying plumes of colored mist.

On that first visit, Mom and I entered the large and imposing gates and headed toward the Germany pavilion. Looking among the lovely and tempting crafts for sale, Mom found a copper filigree bracelet, light and satiny to the touch. She bought me a petite cuckoo clock with little blue bird to tell you the hour. In the Japan pavilion we found a two-inch-tall geisha doll with every teeny detail of the wig, the sash, and the kimono perfectly replicated. Then, following our noses, we came upon the Belgian waffles – those hot, glistening rectangles topped with whipped cream and fresh strawberries. There had never been a dessert like that before. It was a brief visit, and lucky us, to have had that little taste together.

There would be many more visits to the fair. We lived so close to it that Joie and I, footloose teenagers, were sometimes able to go there on our bikes! On a family visit, we went to the Parker Pen Pavilion, where Mom got herself matched up with a pen pal in England. Finally, she knew a real person in England, a place with which she had long been enchanted. What would follow would be a seven-year correspondence between my mother and a little white-haired lady named Ruth Burgess, whose remarkable address I shall not forget:

Pembroke Cottage
Pilling-Near-Preston
Lancashire, England

No street address, no number, just all these names. *Our* address was all numbers: 81-38 168th Street. We really had trouble believing that a mailman could find Ruth's cottage. Country life in England was quite a bit different from our life in Queens.

Later, when I was in college, we would go to England and meet Ruth in person. And as often happens, the correspondence would evaporate once the two letter-writers had met, not because they did not like each other, but because the personalities they had on paper were so different from those of in real life.

If you go to Flushing Meadow Park today where the World's Fair once was, there is just windswept grass and open space. The Unisphere, that giant globe encircled by its satellite paths, is standing there, a dull, watery grey, with not one soul gaping at it in wonder. In its heyday, it was a luminous monument, a majestic symbol of a world on the brink of greatness. It is hard to believe that at one time thousands of people were strolling through that space, mesmerized by the colors, the sights, the foods, and the new things there were to see. There has never been anything like it since. It was not just a place. It was a *time* and, in a wonderland kind of way, a state of mind.

* * *

I have to admit that I did not like to read as a child. But my father was an avid reader and a great storyteller, too. Whatever he read aloud came to life as we listened. If Dad were just reading the comic strips to us on a Sunday morning, he created all the voices, accents, and personalities of the characters.

The "funnies," as Dad called them, were part of a routine that included a walk to the candy store on Sunday morning. It's a wonder that Herm, Joe, and I have any teeth left in our heads because we ate so much candy, sometimes before breakfast! We would go with Dad and pick out something from the selection – Chuckles, Nibs, Pez, Hershey Bars, or Jujubes. Dad would get the papers and we would walk home, perhaps singing something like this…

Peanut sittin' by the railroad track,
His heart was all a-flutter.
Choo-choo train came round the bend,

Then we'd sit in the backyard to listen to Dad read the funnies to us. I didn't understand a lot of what he was reading, but he'd laugh out loud and enjoy himself thoroughly, getting a kick out of Barney Google and Snuffy Smith, Miss Peach, Andy Capp, and Pogo.

He could also tell a true story the way an old-time storyteller would, using his expressive eyes and voice. You couldn't help but listen. He was so engaging, you just forgot all about where you were and you got caught up in the narrative. Dad was especially good at dramatizing the Uncle Remus stories, so very out of date now that they have been banned from library shelves. But in their day, before we knew any better, we loved them. The characters, Br'er Rabbit, Br'er Bear, and Br'er Fox, were such stereotypes of southerners, probably slaves. Were the stories not so disparaging to the people who actually lived in the Deep South, they would be valuable for their wisdom. The rabbit is clever and chatters quickly. The bear is naïve and speaks slowly, slurring his words. The fox *thinks* he is clever, but is always outwitted by the rabbit.

The neatly crafted stories of "The Laughing Place" and "The Tar Baby" were our favorites. I think that half the time we had no idea what Dad was reading about, but he used to laugh so much at his own lecture and so did we.

These stories were so popular in the 1950s that Disney made the cartoon version, *Song of the South*. In its day, everyone loved it, especially the song "Zippity Doo-Da." But now we know too much and have come too far to be entertained by such stories. We know it's all a myth about the slaves and their happy times on the plantation, and so Uncle Remus has fallen from grace.

Dad was a great fan of library visits, and frequently walked to the library by himself, as he had done when he was a young, single man. Mom told me that when they were courting, she often looked for him in the public library, knowing that he was a solitary, bookish type of guy. He continued this library habit, even after he was a married man with five children, rambling through the hills and dales of Queens, down to the main library in the heart of Jamaica.

I never went to that library. Dad used to take me to Windsor Park, a fresh, new branch. The children's room was on the lower floor, but admitted plenty of light. I knew exactly where I could find my only choice of a book: *Around the Year*, written and illustrated by Tasha Tudor. This was a picture book of rhymes about each month with illustrations showing an idyllic life in the New England countryside. Tasha Tudor, who is in her nineties, drew from her youthful experiences in writing and illustrating this book. I loved it, and longed to be living that life of country fairs, apple picking, deep snowfalls, and picnics on open meadows.

Each time I wanted to borrow the book, my father would say, "What, again?" But I insisted. It helped that my father also loved this imagined country life. So although he tried to discourage me from taking out *Around the Year* yet again, he also could not argue that this book was worth rereading.

Many years later, when I wrote and illustrated *Grandmother Mary*, I unconsciously incorporated the "look" of Tudor's book. I guess I did not realize the impact it made upon me, but then, this is what happens when we are very young.

* * *

Any adult will tell you that the toys they grew up with were better than yours. I remember how Dad used to talk about a box of clothespins that he played with as a child. He always said, "The box was the ship and the clothespins were the sailors." Somehow, with the image he created, I used to imagine that he grew up on the prairies and traveled in a Conestoga wagon, like a pioneer, instead of being a Jewish kid who grew up in Brooklyn. For sure, he wanted to convey to us kids that his simple, homegrown toy was more satisfying than any toy soldiers, dollhouse, or chemistry set that we had.

One toy born during my childhood is Barbie. Barbie has evolved only a little bit since her first appearance in 1963—now she comes in various ethnicities and has a wider array of career fantasies, but basically, she is the same – a glamorous, smart, capable woman with great possibilities.

When Barbie first appeared, she had a mystical quality. The dolls that we played with before her were either baby dolls with chubby faces and soft, lacy dresses, or Revlon dolls with fancy clothes, earrings, and long eyelashes. But Barbie was different. She had the tiniest feet, the longest limbs, and a facial expression that was hard to read. Her eyes didn't open and close and she did not look up at us lovingly, as Tiny Tears did. She didn't appear to need us doll "mothers." No, she could do everything on her own. We just had to supply the gorgeous wardrobe and accessories.

The real Barbie doll was expensive and appeared at a time when money was scarce in our family. I got the knockoff, *Mitzi*. In one way, Mitzi was even better because her name was almost the same as *Mizey*. She didn't have the fine features that Barbie had but she could wear Barbie's clothes.

Barbie's wardrobe was a remarkable work of art, spinning a whole world around itself. Each outfit came with a miniature catalogue, whose text conveyed something about Barbie's wonderful, socially satisfying life. The outfits had names, like Friday Night Date, Enchanted Evening, and Open Road. Each ensemble came with props. There were miniature combs and brushes, glasses of lemonade, road maps, and tennis rackets. There were suitcases and trunks in which to keep all Barbie's clothes and shoes, and even a case in which to keep Barbie herself.

As I look over my vintage copy of the Barbie catalogue, which my mother saved in a scrapbook, I relive the thrill of Barbie's adventures. I am particularly fond of her Winter Holiday outfit, which I would be happy to wear myself. Barbie is wearing black leggings, a striped, hooded sweatshirt, and the neatest white car coat. I *want* that red plaid tote bag she is carrying, but more than that, I want to go where she is going.

As any girl today knows, Barbie has grown into her own empire equipped with cars, apartments, and sets of furniture. But can Barbie influence today's girls as she did in the early 1960s? Like my father with the box of clothespins, I cannot help but wonder if we older girls have the advantage. We saw Barbie in her black and white striped bathing suit and gold earrings, and we experienced her enormous power.

* * *

It took me a long time to understand, as a child, exactly what my father did for work. When I'd ask him, he'd say "I make money," and I'd picture him printing nice green dollars. I wonder now why he answered me that way. He must have assumed I would not be able to understand the concept of work. It is interesting that he did answer that way, though. Those were the prosperous years, and I think his confidence came from earning a good living and providing well for the family. But here is what he did: he and two of his brothers were co-owners of The Freeman Paper Box Company, which they had inherited from their father. My Jewish grandfather, Herman Freeman, had come from Poland at the turn of the twentieth century and worked as a fare collector on the trolley. Dad told us that his father would come home at night with his pockets filled with nickels and that he used to say (about those nickels), "One for the company, and one for me."

Somehow, Herman Freeman got into manufacturing paper boxes and opened his own factory. Before the 1960s and the advent of cheap folding boxes, everything you bought, such as games and clothes, came in sturdy, solid boxes that were covered in gaily printed papers. The Freeman Paper Box Company manufactured these boxes and had prestigious clients, such as Ideal Toys and Lady Marlene Lingerie. My father really knew a good box when he saw one. In fact, we used to poke fun at him because whenever any of us received a gift in a paper box, he was always less interested in the contents than in the box itself. He would hold it at arm's length, examine it and then nod and say approvingly, "Good box."

As children, we used to love to visit the factory, which we called "the shop." Dad might come home on a Friday night in the Freeman truck, which he'd park outside our house. This was the signal that he was going into the shop on Saturday, and we could go with him. I am amazed that the three of us used to ride in the back of the truck, bumping along the streets of Queens and Brooklyn. What fun it was to sit on the raw wood floor and peer out the half door at the cars behind us. I cannot imagine how my father let us do this. When he was stopped at a red light, he'd get out of the driver's seat and walk to the back, look in on us and say "You kids all right back there?" I always thought this was quite risky and wonder that he was never stopped by a policeman. But in our journeys by truck, we never had any problems, ever.

The shop stood on Lee Avenue in Williamsburg, Brooklyn. To enter it, you had to step over a low partition, as the front door was "raised" off the sidewalk. The one-storey building was dark and cavernous inside, and once you stepped into its dimness, you were overtaken by the wonderful smell of cardboard and glue.

Most of the space inside the shop (which was not a shop at all) was taken up by gargantuan machinery and stacks and stacks of cardboard resembling a miniature skyline. There were also giant rolls of paper, like gigantic spools, sitting on top of one another.

My father would go into his office, where he did the accounting for the company, and the three of us were free to roam the premises. We used to climb on those stacks of cardboard and jump from one to the other, like three little Supermen bounding over buildings in an imaginary city. It shocks me now when I think of three small children running around a half-lighted factory that housed dangerous machines that cut things apart and glued things together. But we felt no danger at all. We loved all the colored papers in larger-than-life-sized books. I am certain that the exposure to all the printed papers and colored foils had a deep effect on us as we grew up.

We also loved the ancient, heavy machines, and the Coke vending machine that released, with a dry thud, a thick green glass bottle of soda. At the back of the factory there was the garage where the truck was kept. You could enter it from an internal door, and seeing that truck parked there in the darkness was the closest thing to sneaking up on a sleeping dinosaur. It was both terrifying and wonderful.

After a couple of hours at the shop, we'd go to Sam's, a corner luncheonette, where we'd order bacon sandwiches on rye toast. Maybe it was not so much the activity, but just being with Dad, that made it so special.

Years later, long after the shop was out of our lives, my brother Joe and I took one Sunday and went back to see what had become of the building. On the outside it was pretty much unchanged, except for the sign that read "Zion Pentecostal Church." We stepped inside and found ourselves in the midst of a gleeful service of believers wearing taffeta dresses, sharp suits, and amazing hats. Tambourines were thrumping and clinking and voices rang out. The sanctuary, which had once been filled with the whirring and clanking of machinery, was now filled with music.

One of the ushers asked if he could assist us. We explained that this church had been our dad's factory and we were making a sentimental journey.

"Feel free to look around," he said, which is just what we wanted to do. I guess we were looking for some vestige of the shop, a molding, a window perhaps. But nothing remained. It had been completely purified of its sootiness and was now fitted up for a very different purpose. Still, it was memorable to be in the building again.

I went back to the shop once more, years after that. By that time, the church had moved out too, and only the building remained. It had a "For Sale" sign on it. How tempting, I thought, to buy this place and do something with it. But I don't know what that would be.

* * *

My Jewish grandmother Lena came to America in the early part of the 1900s from a place she called Russia, which was probably a village in the harsh expanse of Eastern Europe.

"Where are you from, Grandma?" I would ask her.

"Russia." That's all she would say in her soft, gravelly voice.

When Dad visited Grandma he used to take us along to keep him company. Grandma Lena lived in a tiny little apartment skirting the Coney Island boardwalk. When we arrived, she'd always be sitting with the other elderly people who were sunning themselves on the benches. We'd stroll along, scanning the crowd, and then Dad would spot her. I never really understood how my father could pick Grandma out from the rest of the women. They all looked the same.

Dad usually gave us some pocket change to buy hotdogs and French fries. Then he'd take Grandma upstairs to her dusky, cloying apartment, where he and his brothers and sisters would visit. After our romp on the boardwalk, we too, would go upstairs, and that would signal the end of Dad's visit. It must have been very boring for him; there was no real kinship between the siblings — no laughter, no inside jokes. Nor did there seem to be any real connection with Grandma. Perhaps it was their generation. It all looked very unsatisfying to me.

When we were out in the sunshine again, we might wander down the boardwalk to Steeplechase, an amusement part that used to dominate Coney Island. There was a big slide there, a satiny, dark spiral of polished wood, and a merry-go-round. It was great. We were a foursome again, wild and free.

* * *

And what of my grandfathers? I did not know my father's father at all. He had died before I was born. But it was because of the book *Heidi* that I learned about my *mother's* father. I had read the Little Golden Book version of this enduring story and then saw the movie. Heidi is an orphan living in Switzerland in the mid-nineteenth century. No one in the family wants to raise her, so a distant aunt brings her to live with her grandfather, a hermit living on a Swiss mountaintop. Alm Uncle, as the grandfather is called, is a bitter old man who has cut off relations with the people in the town below. He is feared and disliked by everyone.

Heidi, being a pure soul, manages to creep into her grandfather's heart – she is so in love with the countryside, the goats, the flowers, Alm Uncle's sweet little house, and of course Alm Uncle himself. In time, the old man softens and the tender, loving person he once was begins to re-emerge. Just when the relationship between Alm Uncle and the little girl is becoming comfortable, that same aunt shows up to take Heidi away. The story is a terrible heartbreaker, but has a happy ending. I was so affected by this story that my father bought me a little wooden bank in the shape of a chalet, complete with snow on the roof, flowers in the window boxes, and a small pile of firewood on the side of the house. He called it the "Heidi House." But that was not enough. I began to wonder why I did not have a grandfather, as Heidi did.

As it turns out, I did. His name was Christopher Simeti, and he must have been in his seventies by the time I went looking for him. Mom had not seen her father for a very long time because her parents were divorced when she was a baby. But I wanted to meet him, and Mom arranged it for me.

Christopher, the oldest of seven children, left Sicily for America in the early 1900s. In New Haven, Connecticut, he met and married Lucy, my grandmother. They had three children, one of whom was my mother. Then World War I broke out and Christopher went to France to fight, leaving twenty-year-old Lucy with three children to raise on her own.

Because Lucy had to go out to work, she farmed her children out to other people who would care for them. My mother, just a baby, was given to Aunt Theresa, who was wealthy and childless. It was rumored that Lucy "gave" her children to other people because while her husband was at war, she fell in love with a man named Alfred, and wanted to be free to be with him. When Christopher came back from the war, he sensed that his wife's heart was elsewhere. They got divorced. He turned around and quickly married a family friend and settled in another part of New Haven.

Lucy then married Alfred, with whom she was deeply in love. They left New Haven and moved to Brooklyn. There, they raised eleven children over the next fifteen years. Meanwhile, my mother was growing up in New Haven with Aunt Theresa and did not have the benefit of either her mother or her father. She told me that as a child, she was aware that she had a mother somewhere in New York and a father somewhere on the other side of town, but she rarely saw them and did not know them. Later, when I would write my first book, *Grandmother Mary*, I would retell this story with more details, changing the parts that were not suitable for a children's book. The deeper part of this story I will share with you in a little while.

So when I presented my mother with the question, "Why don't I have a grandfather?" she revealed to me that I did. I was about eleven years old when we took the railroad up to New Haven. At the station we got into a taxi and went to what my mother *thought* was Christopher's house, a small garden apartment. We stood outside an arched alleyway where, in the shadows, a man was sweeping.

"Joe!" my mother called out. The man turned around.

"Mommy, how did you know the man's name was Joe?" I whispered.

"All Italian men are named Joe," she replied. (I shall never forget this little rule that she had.) Then she asked the man, in *Italian*, "Where does Christopher Simeti live?" This was astonishing to me, for I had never heard my mother speak Italian before.

The man replied, also in Italian, that Mr. Simeti was now living with his girlfriend, Emily, and gave us a new address. We got back in the taxi and continued our journey, arriving at a small yellow brick apartment building. We walked up the stairs and knocked on the door. Emily answered, and seemed to know why we were there.

We entered the little apartment, and there he was – a rather distinguished man in an armchair. He had a peaceful demeanor.

"Hello, Pa," my mother said.

"Hello, Mary," he replied in a friendly way. "Who is this little girl?"

"This is my Mizey," she answered. "And she wanted to know you."

I walked over to my grandfather and sat right on his lap. He didn't seem to mind. I was thinking how I was just like Heidi. I had a grandfather. He didn't have to do anything. Just sitting there being my grandfather was enough.

We stayed for an hour or so and ate an asparagus omelet, which I thought was dreadful. My grandfather ate a bowl of beans topped with ketchup. Now that I think about it, I realize they probably had very little money and were not prepared to receive guests. I wonder what we talked about, since there was barely any relationship there. We don't think of these things when we are children.

That visit may have been the only time I saw my grandfather. As the years went on, I would hear my mother mention that he was "in town," which meant he was visiting another one of his daughters. My mother never cared to join them. She really had no bond with her father, and so consequently, I would not have one either. But I did get the intellectual satisfaction of knowing that I had a grandfather. More important, though, is realizing the power that a book could have – if not for *Heidi*, I never would have opened this little chapter of my own life.

Another time I was able to connect to my mother's distant past was in the 1950s when we, as a family, drove through West Haven, Connecticut near where Mom had lived as a child. As we rode along a stretch of beach, we came to a tiny cottage, where, Mom told us, her godmother Michelina lived. This was hard for me to imagine. I had to visualize my mother as a child living in the context of a family, having parents and a *godmother*.

As Mom had predicted, we found Michelina, a wee speck of a woman with flowing white hair, sitting peacefully in her front yard, under a gnarled tree. We stopped the car and got out.

The tiny lady smiled affectionately at my mother, who bent down to kiss her.

"This is my godmother," Mom explained tenderly. "She was my mother's maid of honor." That was *really* hard to imagine. It meant that back in the far mists of time when my grandmother Lucy was a young girl in a white dress and veil, Michelina, this tidbit of a lady, was a teenager standing at the bride's side. It was all too far away.

Once, my mother explained, Michelina had nine sons, but lost two in the Second World War. Mom knew she was proud of this. "She's a Gold Star Mother," she said, indicating two gold medallions in the window that had been there since the 1940s. And so I learned this term for mothers who had sacrificed their sons to the war effort.

That's all I remember, but the feeling of the day would resurface much later, when I would pass that way again.

* * *

I am not a big fan of the early morning hours, and have never really liked the idea of getting up early. As a child, I found it painful to get up and get dressed at 7:00 a.m., and still do. But there is one memory that brings delight to my mind — the cool, fresh hours of the day when we all went on vacation in New England.

My father worked fifty weeks a year, and with the other two, he used to take us on a road trip. In the 1950s, families did this by driving to places like Niagara Falls, Vermont, or Quebec, an activity my mother called "breezing up the rocky coast." There were plenty of motels then, and great roadside places to eat.

There was no air conditioning in cars, so a chance to get *out* of the car was welcome. Stopping the car meant you were going to go to a "rest area" to have a picnic at the wooden picnic tables, or eat at one of the many diners along the highway. All grown-ups will tell you that the food tasted better then, the Coca-Cola was colder, tastier. Maybe it was. I can guess that everything tasted better because we were hungrier, thirstier, and hotter. We did not travel with bottles of water as we do now, so when you got thirsty, you were *really* thirsty. Of course a soda tasted great. Of course a hot dog was amazingly good. We hadn't had anything to eat or drink for the last three hours and it was hot outside. Of course an air conditioned coffee shop seemed like an enormous luxury - one did not always expect it or get it.

The souvenirs at the tourist shops were great too - those little pillows stuffed with pine needles, the cedar boxes that had such a dry, pure smell of the woods, the beaded items produced by American Indians — belts, the necklaces, change purses. And the real maple syrup whose cans were made to look like log cabins.

And the motels! Not all motels had pools, so to find one that did was terrific. Some of them allowed you to swim at *night*, which had an awesome, other-worldly feel to it as you floated under a star-dimpled sky. My parents loved the offer of "Continental Breakfast," orange juice, a donut, and coffee, and it was *free*!

Best of all was that early morning smell of the country in summer — a combination of grass, hay, country air, and a touch of flowers. Along with the smell is the background sound of buzzing of woodland and farmland insects, which is about the only way I like insects - unseen and producing an ambient hum.

In my book *Rainwalk*, which is about the seasons, the poem "Summerwalk" speaks of early morning in the country. The illustration shows a young boy enjoying the early hours "...before the world is wide awake..." on a meadow in a rural setting. The countryside is sweeping out in front of him as he races toward the rising sun. I guess that little boy is me, relishing the first hours of the day, one that holds promise and possibility. Would my father ever have guessed that with all the effort he put into all those family vacations, the strongest memory is of those mornings?

* * *

Dad always had great zest for Christmas, Christmas trees, Christmas presents, snow, ice skating, driving around to see Christmas lights, and the mood in the air at that time of year. Dad was ethnically Jewish, and so for him, and by extension for us, there was nothing religious about the holiday. My mother was Catholic, but she was a kind of "secret" Catholic, keeping her rosary beads and prayer book next to her bed, hidden in her night table. So even though we played the piano and sang Christmas carols, our Christmas was purely an American winter holiday that had absolutely nothing to do with the birth of Jesus.

It was my father who went out to get the tree just a few days before Christmas. He would place it in the backyard and it would sit out in the cold. Then, on the evening of December 23, he would drag it into the living room and set it in the stand. He always bought a large tree, so the first step was to trim the top. Then we'd all go down into the basement where we kept the dusty boxes of lights (which were all tangled together) and cart them upstairs. Next we'd help bring up the many boxes of Christmas balls and Christmas stockings, which were quite tattered. Since I am the fifth child in the family, the Christmas stockings with our names written in now-tarnished glitter already showed signs of age.

For the next hour or so, Joe, Herm, and my father would wind the lights around the tree. This involved a lot of turning, balancing, untangling of wires, reaching around the prickly boughs of the evergreen, and a bit of frustrated muttering from Dad.

When it was at last completed, we were free to decorate the tree with any and all of the ornaments. Joe and I had certain Christmas balls that were our favorites, and we named them "Jupiter" and "Saturn." Jupiter was a large silver ball with tiny stripes, and Saturn was a smaller ball with rings of iridescent color. Some of the historic Christmas balls were worn, chipped and broken. Then there were the colored glass balls that had no metallic paint on them – just very dated looking pictures of Santa in his sleigh, the reindeer, and other holiday motifs rendered in white paint. My father called these "war balls," because they were made during World War II, when all metals had been appropriated for the war effort, leaving none for such foolishness as Christmas balls. The war balls seemed somewhat pathetic next to the proper, shimmering Christmas balls of the affluent 1950s. Joe, Herm, and I were born *after* the war and could not appreciate such a patriotic spirit. We used a funny little voice to mockingly chant "war balls."

When the tree was completely decorated with the glistening balls, miniature cardboard houses, wax figures of snowmen and Santa, it was time to add the tinsel and the star. And then came the best part. We'd turn off the lights, sit down, and simply *gaze* at the tree. There was usually a fire in the fireplace, and so not only was there something magnificent to *look* at, but there was also the smell of the wood fire and best of all, the anticipation of Christmas Day.

Like all children who celebrate this holiday, we'd awaken early in the morning and the first thought would be *It's Christmas!* I would go downstairs with Herm and Joe while our parents were still asleep, and we'd see what was in the stockings and under the tree. We always got everything we wanted – train sets, a toy piano, Civil War soldiers, ballet shoes, a chemistry set, ice skates, a gold baton, a microscope, a jewelry box with a little spinning ballerina in it, miniature china tea sets, a doll house, rocking horse, a gold pencil case. I remember one gift that I got as a four-year-old: a tiny nursery, which was a box about twelve inches long with ten miniature beds that had little plastic babies lying in them, each with a blanket and holding a baby bottle. I still have many of these toys, including one of those baby bottles.

Then in the ensuing week when there was no school, we went ice skating at Goose Pond, played with our new toys, and went out with friends. In the afternoon we watched *Christmas Carol* on TV every day, thanks to *Million Dollar Movie*, which showed the same movie over and over all week. (By the time we reached adulthood, we knew *all* the words as well as the haunting, evocative sound track.)

But I also remember the first Christmas without presents under the tree. That was the year I was nine, when Dad's paper box business went under and money was suddenly scarce. I wondered why that year my father took us to Masters, a large toy store, and let each of us choose something. I thought this was rather odd, but I did not mind. I chose a Shirley Temple doll with a beautiful blue dress and blond curls.

After that year, Christmas was never quite the same. It was always a great holiday but the *way* in which we used to prepare for it started to dissolve. My father was always worried about money and used to compensate for his anxiety by spending unwisely, using his credit card to buy presents and wrestling with the bills in January. In time, he got turned off to the whole idea of buying presents; his enthusiasm for Christmas waned and we all felt it. My sister helped to breathe life into the holiday; she was already married, and she and her husband Larry would come over in the early evening and Larry would play Santa, distributing gifts. We were the first set of children to sit on his knee. Then he and Eleanore had their own children and brought in another generation. So did Steve, and so did Herm, and so there was more to the celebration — more food, more noise, more presents. Then the grandchildren got married and had *their* children, and there was a *larger* celebration, and even until my mother's last Christmas at age ninety-four, Larry was still playing Santa with us fifty-somethings sitting on his knee! As long as there was a celebration in my mother's house, there was Santa.

Since we could all sing, our Christmases had the feel of a kind of mini-talent show. A few of us played the piano and some of us liked to perform. Dad, for some unknown reason, was partial to Christian hymns, among them "In the Garden," and "The Holy City," which allowed him to belt out the chorus, *Jeroooosalem! Jeroooosalem*! He sang these not only at Christmas, but during the year too. I never associated these songs with religion, especially since it was my father who sang them, and I actually thought that "In the Garden" was one of those sentimental pieces like "Just a Song at Twilight." The chorus, *and he walks with me, and he talks with me, and he tells me I am his own*, always conjured up for me a picture of two lovers courting. Never at any time did I think it was Jesus who was doing the walking and talking. After all, why would my father be singing about *that*?

The family got bigger, but the space did not, and so at the last Christmas celebration of this type, we were mighty cozy – many people in what seemed to be an ever-shrinking space. The Christmas right after my mother died, when we cleared out the house, we saw how large the living room really was. Without all those people in it and without the furniture, the piano, and every other thing Mom collected, the living room had a bare and elegant dignity. We appreciated even more the varnished banister flanking the staircase from which Santa had descended for so many years, pooling at the bottom in a graceful swirl. The large mirror over the fireplace reflected the unadorned walls, now free of paintings, photos, and other distractions. No, the house was not a cozy little cottage; it had just seemed that way because there were so many of us in it at one time.

* * *

I have only a vague recollection of what life was like at our house when all seven of us were living there, that is, before anyone was married or out of the house. Eleanore was studying to be a kindergarten teacher. She had the room upstairs and I loved spending time there with her. Then one day, she got engaged to Larry, a strikingly handsome young policeman, and started to make plans for their wedding. Her beautiful white dress hung from a hook in the slanted ceiling of her room in preparation for the big day.

It was great news to me that I would be a flower girl, but a bitter disappointment when I learned that I would not have a long dress. My mother had spoken to me about what a flower girl was, how you got to wear a long dress and toss flower petals down the aisle. Perhaps Mom should not have told me this, for it was *not* what the bride had in mind.

Eleanore insisted upon my wearing a short dress. I hated it. It was pink and had two roses embroidered on the bodice. I wore little white gloves and white T-strap shoes (which I also hated) and white socks edged with lace. Instead of the basket of flower petals, I carried a bouquet.

This was not at all what I had been picturing and I did NOT like it. I remember being a bit cranky and sullen when I first learned the news. But the disappointment of the flower girl experience was probably good for me, since much of life is not what we want or what we expect. Not a bad lesson at an early age.

Eleanore and Larry moved into a cute apartment in Fresh Meadows, just a short distance from beautiful Bloomingdale's. In less than a year they had a baby girl. The first grandchild in the family, she was showered with attention and praise, but she would be the first of many.

As Eleanore and Larry awaited the arrival of their second child, they moved to Long Island to a new community where everything was young – the people, their kids, the trees so small and spindly, the houses so simple and fresh. They would go on to raise four children in their house and then delight in their seven grandchildren. I have enough memories of that house to fill a whole other book. There were summer days when I went to visit Eleanore and Larry with my parents and two brothers. How nice it was (and still is) to sit in the backyard with music floating out the window from the hi-fi, a very modern record player then. A favorite record featured the mellow voice of Nat King Cole singing "Those Lazy, Hazy, Crazy Days of Summer," which always got people in the jolly mood of a barbecue.

Sometimes during the summer I would stay with Eleanore when Larry went away to do military service. Those days have their own fragrances and flavors – the scent of the morning air enlivened with sunshine, and the fresh paint of this new house. I would keep Eleanore company and have some special time with her and the kids. This went on for many years, even when I was in college. And so although Eleanore and Larry have been living on Long Island for a long, long time, their house always seems new to me. It still feels like life there is about to begin. It will always feel like a beginning, because in my youthful days there, it always was.

* * *

The year after Eleanore got married, Steve got married. That's when I got my long dress, a rose colored taffeta gown, and tiny "high heels" to wear with it. What ten-year-old girl would not have dreamed of wearing that?

But before he got married, Steve had to go to the army. No one in our family had ever gone away before, so it was very exciting. He was not going too far – just to Fort Dix in New Jersey. What made it *seem* far away was that when he came home for a visit, he looked quite different. His head of beautiful, dark hair was shaved down to a crew cut, and he wore army fatigues. Since my father had not been in the military, it was new, strange, and exhilarating for Steve to be the first family member to serve in the army.

This is when I began my long and rich career as a letter writer. I had heard of other people writing letters, but I never had anyone to write to, since everyone I knew was close by. But now someone I knew and loved was far away, and I could write to him. Of course, I had no idea then that letter writing was to have a great impact on me an artist and author.

There were probably no more than a few letters I wrote to Steve, since he was only gone for six months. But even in my childish pencil printing, I was beginning something new. I loved letter writing so much that I began to look for other opportunities to write. But who was there to write to?

Some classmates of mine had pen pals in other countries. When one of them brought a letter to school, the crisp blue paper and airmail markings on the envelope looked so grown up. And the pen pal's handwriting was lacy, as the rules of penmanship are different from ours in America. I decided then that I would find a way to make friends in foreign places so that I could write and receive letters.

Brother Steve never did write me back – I suppose a soldier doesn't have much time for that. But when he came back home, I got a special surprise. One morning Herm, Joe, and I awoke to find that Steve had come home in the middle of the night. In the style of a kind of midyear Santa Claus, he had left a gift for each of us on the piano. Mine was a little ring with a ruffle of gold lace and a pearl. This lovely memory and that ring are emblematic of the beginning of my writing career.

* * *

We three youngest kids had our own theatrical troupe called "Judy,

Joe, and Monk." I was Judy the Dancing Girl and Joe, in his usual no-nonsense way, insisted on using his own name. That leaves Herm, who was Monk the Monkey, among other characters that he created and interpreted for the stage. My specialty was ballet, but Joe and I had an acrobatic act for which we were the Tumblesault and Trickery Twins, a name that must have come out of Herm's head. Herm was actually the genius behind all of this, writing plays and staging epic poems for holidays. I have a memory of an excellent poem he wrote for the Fourth of July, which included an appearance by the Statue of Liberty, whom I impersonated, wearing my mother's all-satin wedding gown which draped so nicely in folds, just as the real Miss Liberty's robes do. I held an exquisitely rendered torch made of tin foil.

This activity was unsupervised by any grown-up. Herm, about nine years old, was capable of composing, directing, and mounting an entire production. He wrote a play based on a Sherlock Holmes-type mystery, in which a woman, home alone at night, is frightened by a noise she hears on the roof. Terrified that an intruder is lurking about, she calls for help. As a six-year-old playing that woman, I had to lift the receiver of the phone – some prop that Herm made from a household object, and say, "Operator! Operator! Give me the police!" The inspector, played by Herm in a smartly buttoned trench coat, came to the house, pipe in hand, and discovered, "Madame," that it was only the aerial (for which we used a coat hanger) flapping in the wind on a blustery London night.

Our theatre troupe became so well developed that we decided to sell seats for the shows. This coincided nicely with Joie getting a miniature printing press, upon which he could print up the tickets. He sold Seats One and Two to Larry, but just as it was time to present the scheduled and paid-for show, we outgrew the activity entirely. Over the next several decades, Larry would occasionally take out his wallet and present us with the faded and dissolving tickets, whose purple ink still promised that Judy, Joe, and Monk would be performing. He would say, "I'm still waiting."

* * *

Television commercials of the 1950s gave us with new pieces of language. The three of us loved to make fun of a coffee commercial in which the very distinguished actor, Edward G. Robinson, used to speak from his well-appointed study. He'd be wearing a velvet smoking jacket, holding a cigar in one hand and a book in the other. Standing in front of a blazing fire in his hearth, he'd look up suddenly, as though he did not know we were there, smile and say, "I've always liked the good things in life…good art (and he'd indicate the large painting above the fireplace), good book (he'd pat the book gently)…good coffee." Then we'd be repeating his words in *his* voice, punctuating them with the words "good, good, good." This little phrase came to mean for us something hearty, something sturdy, something to eat that was filling and in rich supply. Then we condensed the phrase to "3G," which stood for the three times we said *good*. From then on, the term "3G" meant satisfyingly and abundantly good. It has never left us.

Then there was the commercial for Gimbel's Custom Reupholstery, in which a craftsman would be working on the underside of an armchair that needed repair. In a very 3G kind of way, he pushed a curved upholstery needle through the many layers of fabric while the voiceover assured the listener that he was using "imported twine from Italy," another phrase we loved.

Late at night there was an ad for Chop-o-Matic, a gadget that could slice, cube, and peel any fruit or vegetable. This commercial seemed endless. Joe and Herm used to do a parody of it as they lay in bed with the lights out. They called it "The Long Commercial," and Herm, ever the inventor, even had a tune in which both boys said these words as if they were television announcers.

The commercial that so appealed to my father was for Pennsylvania Dutch Egg Noodles. It featured a full-screen face of an Amish elder, white beard and all, who smiled reassuringly and told you to "Get to know what *good* is." This was very 3G. Dad, ever identifying with the most American of Americans, liked this character and liked to quote him. But he always quoted him incorrectly, saying, "Get to know what's *good*," which doesn't have the same punch at all. This phrase was something Dad employed at a specific time, when he felt that we kids didn't know or appreciate the value of something. If, for example, we didn't want the black jelly beans in a mixture, he'd shake his head as if to say, *You can't do a thing with these kids,* and walk away muttering, "Get to know what's *good.*" And I am certain that at that moment, Dad felt a deep kinship with that Amish fellow. His own kids might not understand what's good, but he and the Amish guy did.

In this vein, I am drawn to my thoughts about one of Dad's favorite poets, James Whitcomb Riley, also known as "The Hoosier Poet" because of his love of his native Indiana. We had a richly illustrated book of Riley's poetry that was literally falling to pieces, and we loved to hear Dad read the poems in the dialect that Riley used, which mimicked farm folks of rural Indiana. Dad's favorite was "When the Frost is on the Punkin," once again reflecting that country life he always longed for. These were Riley's hallmarks and he etched them with words. As a librarian, I discovered a poem that was not included in that legendary book. "Lockerbie Street," an ode to Riley's own neighborhood, makes such beautiful use of evocative language.

LOCKERBIE STREET

Such a dear little street it is,
Nestled away
From the noise of the city and heat of the day,
In the cool shady coverts of whispering trees,
With their leaves lifted up to shake
hands with the breeze
Which in all its wide wanderings never
may meet with a resting place fairer that
Lockerbie Street!

There is such a relief, from the clangor
and din
Of the heart of the town, to go
Loitering in
Through the dim, narrow walks, with
The sheltering shade
Of the trees waving over the
Long promenade,
And littering lightly the ways of our feet
With the gold of the sunshine of
Lockerbie Street.

And the nights that come down the dark
Pathways of dusk,
With the stars in their tresses, and
Odors of musk
In their moon-woven raiments,
Bespangled with dews,
And looped up with the lilies for lovers
To use
In the songs that they sing to the tinkle and beat
Of their sweet serenadings through
Lockerbie Street.

O my Lockerbie Street! You are fair
To be seen –
Be it noon of the day, or the rare and serene
Afternoon of the night – you are one to
My heart,
And I love above all the phrases of art,
For no language could frame and no
Lips could repeat
My rhyme-haunted raptures and
Lockerbie Street.

We had other well-worn books on the shelf. There was a pair of fairy tale collections – a red clothbound book of stories by the Brothers Grimm and a green one with stories by Hans Christian Andersen. All three of us kids were highly influenced by the fanciful illustrations and etchings. The language also had a very strong impact.

In the cautionary tale "The Fisherman and his Wife," a poor fisherman accidentally catches an enchanted flounder. The flounder implores the fisherman to throw him back and offers in exchange to fulfill one wish. The fisherman turns down this offer. When he returns home to his "hovel" and tells his wife what happened, she gets angry and demands that he return to the sea to find that flounder again and wish for a better house.

Against his true heart, the fisherman does as his wife asks. Upon returning to the seashore, he finds the water a tad murkier than when he was there an hour ago. Humbly, he stands at the edge of the shore and says:

Flounder, Flounder by the Sea,
Prithee, hearken unto me.
My wife, Isibil, shall have her own will,
And sends me to beg a boon of Thee.

Such lovely language. We were particularly fond of the line "Prithee, hearken unto me," which is loaded with supplication. And how could we not *love* the phrase "beg a boon of Thee," so delightfully archaic? We used it among ourselves as part of our private vocabulary.

But I like this passage the best:

The man went home and found his wife no longer in the old hut, but a pretty little cottage stood in its place, and his wife was sitting on a bench by the door. She took him by the hand and said, "Come and look here. Isn't this much better?" They went inside and found a pretty sitting room, a bedroom with a bed in it, a kitchen and a larder furnished with everything of the best in tin and brass. Outside there was a little yard with chickens and ducks, and a little garden full of vegetables and fruit.

Everything about this description is pleasing to me. The wife sitting on the little bench outside the house is especially inviting. The tidiness of the rest of the house offers us a sense of peace and balance, especially when we are taken out the back door into a little yard. The whole passage conveys rustic simplicity and harmony. But during the course of the story, the wife wishes for more and more and the sea gets darker and rougher. Her every wish is granted, but she is never satisfied for very long. At first she wants a cottage, then a mansion, then a palace, and so on until she wants to be God. The flounder, disgusted with the wife's greed, sends the couple back to their hovel.

* * *

I often wonder how much words and pictures are linked in our minds and memories. If I bring back the feelings of Easter when growing up, my senses wake up. Easter in our home was almost as important as Christmas, and again, it was a completely secular holiday. My father used to go out and buy hyacinths in the softest colors: blush pink, periwinkle, and sky blue. There were no cut flowers, such as Easter lilies, since my mother loathed them, saying they reminded her of funerals. This harkens back to the childhood trauma she suffered when her Aunt Theresa died. It left her feeling ill at ease around cut flowers. A plant in a nice pot covered with colored foil was OK, but there were no bouquets in our living room, ever.

The Saturday night before Easter we colored the eggs with my father. The scent of white vinegar kicked off this activity. My mother would spoon a bit of liquid into each cup to dissolve the pellet of dye. We liked to watch the neat little tablet fizzle away and fill the cup with brilliant orange and dazzling yellow, rich royal purple, and liquid turquoise.

Then out of the box came the little wire holder, a hexagon with a handle for submerging the egg into the dye. We never quite got the hang of the other items that came in the package – the cold, white, wax crayon and the decals with silly 1940s-ish pictures of bunnies with wheelbarrows and lambs with bonnets. We just ignored those and went straight for the coloring of two dozen eggs. When we got down to the twenty-fourth egg, we mixed all the dyes into one cup, creating a dismal grey solution. I am surprised, considering all the private language and made-up words in our family, that we did not have a name for this color.

My parents kept the Easter baskets up in the cedar closet, that wonderful catchall of a hiding place. The baskets, like those Christmas stockings, were old and somewhat crumpled, but we used them year after year. I really stand in wonder at my father's and mother's continued enthusiasm for putting together the Easter baskets, even as we grew into our teen years when we should have thought the whole holiday very uncool. We loved it, though, and looked forward to all the incredibly unwholesome things we would eat *before* breakfast. How they catered to our individual desires and tastes! There was always a solid chocolate bunny for Herm, a hollow chocolate bunny for Joe, a stuffed toy bunny for me, cream eggs that oozed pastel-colored goo when you bit into them, jelly beans, small chocolate eggs wrapped in celestial shades of green, pink, and violet, and Peeps -- those marshmallow chicks coated in grainy sugar. All of it would be nestled into that indestructible fake green grass.

Then came the Easter breakfast, the pancakes into which my mother had planted a strip of crisp bacon during the cooking stage, topped with butter and maple syrup. And one of the truly perverse pleasures of childhood: dousing our syrup-coated taste buds with orange juice, which clashed so dramatically, the sweet and the tart colliding in our mouths, making us wince.

Really, nothing about any of this has the slightest connection to Jesus ascending, and in fact, we were never told about that. So ignorant was I of this bit of history that at age seventeen, I sent an Easter card to a boy I liked who was Jewish.

The balance of Easter Sunday was spent at home, and some guests usually appeared. To be ready for the "company," I always got an Easter dress and hat, new black patent leather shoes, and a matching pocketbook. As Eleanore and Larry's little girls grew up, they also had Easter outfits, but theirs had the additional feature of paper rabbit ears that Eleanore made for them. My mother, in her usual way, prepared a whole Easter dinner, never really knowing how many people she would be feeding. She did this for such a long time and until she died we carried on this tradition, creating an Easter dinner in her house and receiving unforeseen guests.

* * *

Then suddenly, quite suddenly, after these very happy years, I was not a child anymore.

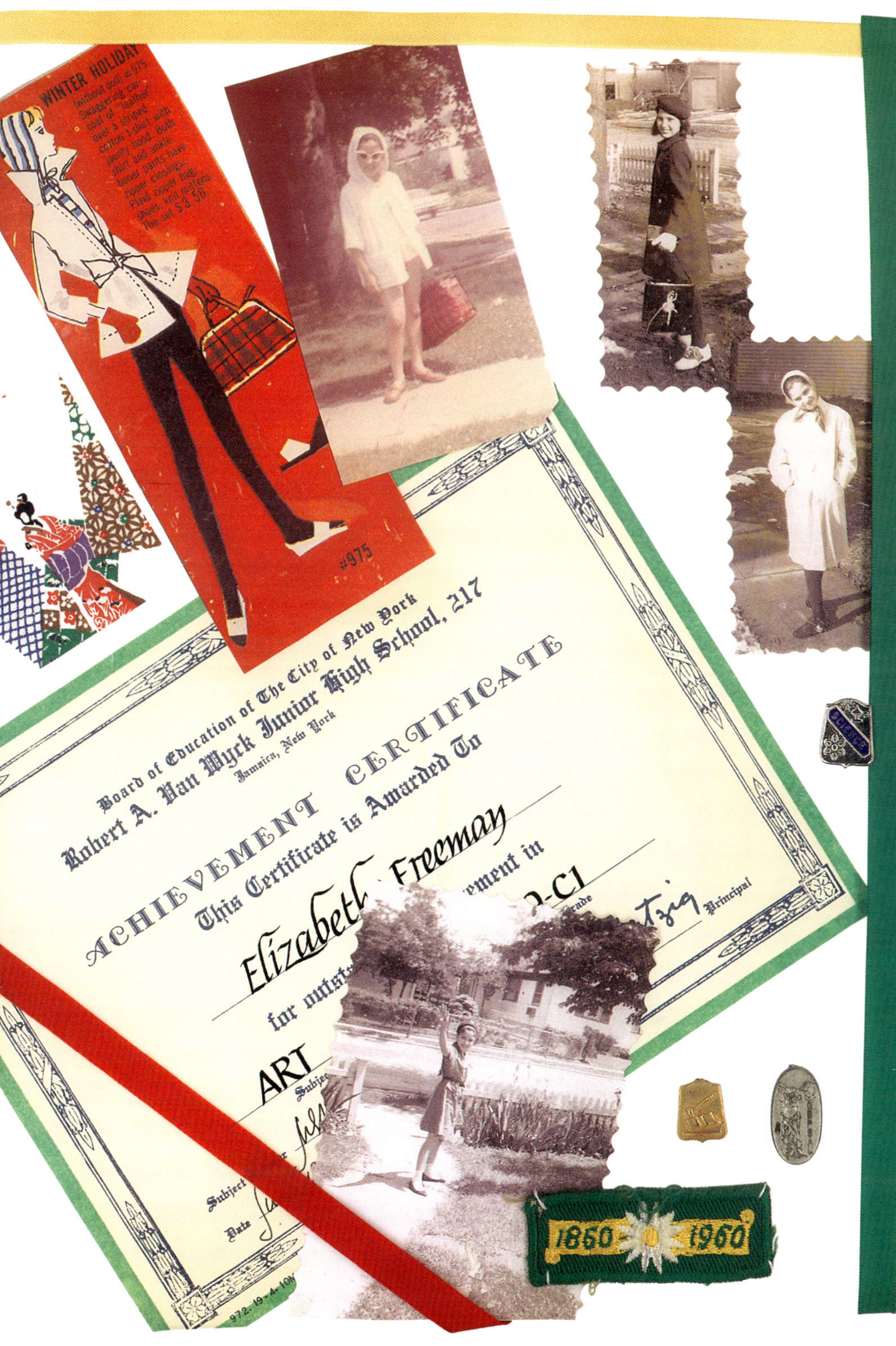
WINTER HOLIDAY
(without doll) #975
Swaggering car coat of "leather" over a striped cotton t-shirt with jaunty hood. Both shirt and ankle-boner pants have zipper closings. Plaid zipper bag, shoes, knit mittens. The set $3.50
#975
Board of Education of The City of New York
Robert A. Van Wyck Junior High School, 217
Jamaica, New York
ACHIEVEMENT CERTIFICATE
This Certificate is Awarded To
Elizabeth Freeman
ART
Subject
Date
Principal
1860 1960

Part Two: Girlhood

It's a good thing that we get to change the scene in adolescence, because that is when we start to need more. Elementary school had been a good but stodgy experience in a traditional, old-fashioned building. Junior high, on the other hand, was new, fresh, open, and exciting. Like Herm and Joe before me, I went to JHS 217, also called Van Wyck. The brand new building was constructed from blond brick and the windows were large and admitted lots of light. Instead of feeling nailed to the floor all day in our seats with the one teacher of the year, we changed classes every forty-five minutes. There was French class, orchestra, art class, gym, with gym clothes and a locker with a combination lock. There was a cafeteria that served a wonderful lunch for forty-four cents, and there were lots of cute boys who were just getting interested in girls.

Of course, as a teenage girl, clothes are of paramount importance, especially clothes that my family could not afford. I remedied this by learning to sew. Back in the 1960s, there was no such thing for teens as "designer clothes" and people did not walk around wearing other people's initials on their handbags. But there were other must-have items. This is what motivated me to make my own clothes.

We had a sewing machine in the house, and one day I asked my mother to teach me how to thread it and run it. She did, and away I went on a lifetime hobby of sewing. I saw how easy it was to visualize a garment, find a pattern, and choose a suitable fabric.

By the time I entered the seventh grade, almost every piece of clothing was my own unique creation. Girls used to ask where I got my clothes and I was only too happy to admit that I made them.

Sewing opened up a vast world for me – one of patterns, fabrics, buttons, threads, trimmings, design, and style. I suddenly had the power to create anything I could visualize, and indeed I did. I went from making simple dresses to blouses, to slacks, suits, even men's pants, a wedding dress, dolls' clothes, vests, robes, and raincoats.

Of course, I would have liked it much better if I could have walked into Lord & Taylor and purchased whatever I wanted, but that was just not possible, so I found another way. I still sew, but now it is by choice and not by necessity. I will always love going into a fabric store to look at the yard goods and imagine what I can do with them. I am grateful that I had to learn this craft, and there is no doubt that the *need* to do so teased the creativity out of me. If I had not been coveting what all teenage girls want, there would never have been any reason to develop this skill.

* * *

Just as I was graduating from PS131, I was selected for the "Special Progress" (SP) program in junior high. There was a choice of two-year or three-year SP. My brothers, who had also qualified when they graduated, had turned it down completely, but when it came to me, my father said *why not*? And so I entered the program, electing the three-year course because it had extra art and music in it. All my other classmates, without exception, chose the two-year program, which meant that we lost touch with each other, for they would be skipping a grade. Later on in high school, they would appear to be a year older than I because they had chosen to take the accelerated path. By choosing the three-year program, I met an entirely new group of kids, some of whom I am still friends with today.

I loved the variety of the new school day, the possibilities of the subjects we could study, the plays we could be in, the people we could meet. I loved that teachers in general seemed more like real people – some were married, had children, drove cars. They were younger and seemed more reachable, as opposed to the schoolmarms of 131, who appeared to have come out of an old black-and-white movie.

In gym class we had to wear funny little blue cotton rompers that were unflattering even to the best figure. The upper part looked like a car mechanic's uniform, especially since your name had to go above the pocket. The lower part was short pants that ballooned out and just looked downright silly. You had to embroider your first name above the front pocket and your last name, in much larger letters, across your back, so that the gym teacher could identify you from a distance as you were playing volleyball.

My mother took a shortcut because she was not about to sit around embroidering "Elizabeth." She bought some white iron-on tape and shortened my name to "Beth," which she spelled out by molding the tape into letters and ironing it down. Since there were students who had not known me before junior high, they assumed this was my name. It stuck all the way through high school. I loved this.

In one class, I used to sit next to a boy named Freddy Popper, which sounds a little like a cartoon character, maybe a man made out of popcorn. Freddy and I both liked to draw, and we used to use our cartridge pens to collaborate in drawing small rows of houses along the bottom of the loose leaf paper. A cartridge pen is very nice to draw with because the nib allows you to feel the paper underneath. Freddy and I constructed many an imaginary neighborhood in our notebooks during homeroom. Interestingly, Freddy and I met up many years later, when we were in our late thirties, only to find out that we had both become professional artists.

Of course, junior high years are also fraught with frustration because you are growing so fast and want so much. You want friends, you want clothes, you want to be liked, to be popular, to have good skin, good hair, to do well in school, and to be your best self, whoever *that* is. When you enter junior high you are still a child, and when you come out the other end, you are a young adult. I learned so much about myself in those three years. I learned how gifted I was with languages and art, and resolved to study these two subjects in greater depth in high school. I learned how NOT gifted I was with the violin that the orchestra teacher had stuck in my hand and made me play. I don't even know how I got selected for the orchestra. But amazingly, I played the violin at graduation – I cannot imagine HOW I did this or what it sounded like, but I do know this – I never picked up a violin again once that graduation was over. I knew what I liked and where I was going to spend my time. And just about then, it was time to go to high school.

* * *

Girlfriends have such an influence on us, especially when we are growing up. There was a girl I met back in kindergarten, with whom I stayed friends until we went separate ways in college.

Arlene, who lived around the corner from me, always had the best clothes and best opportunities, and seemed to always have boys interested in her. She came from a religious Jewish family that left Hungary during the Second World War. This was a totally foreign idea to me, since both my parents had been born here and my father had not fought in the war. In fact, none of the tragedy of the war touched us, and it was only later that I would appreciate the full value of what Arlene's parents had gone through.

Arlene was very pretty and well spoken. Her home was filled with paintings and fine art objects that came from Europe, and everything about her said that she was well-loved, but not spoiled, which is a very nice combination indeed. I think we were just friends because she lived near me, for we really did not have that much in common. Arlene's family owned a jewelry company and was able afford nice vacations in resorts in the Catskills. Later on, Arlene would go to camp, become a counselor, and go to Europe with her parents.

When we were in junior high, Arlene and her family moved to Jamaica Estates. Their home was not grand and elaborate, but modern, with clean lines. It was marvelous to be invited to Arlene's new house for any kind of teenage girl activity. Arlene had a beautiful room, something I longed for, with matching furniture. In the middle of the ceiling was a graceful chandelier made of painted tin designed to look like blue porcelain. If I had not liked Arlene so much, I would have had terrible pangs of jealousy.

As we grew up, Arlene and I grew apart because our high school was enormous and there were so many activities, so we didn't cross paths too often. Still, we had known each other such a long time, and there was a kind of comfortable familiarity when we saw one another in the hall.

When we graduated from high school, we both went off to college, but I later heard Arlene got married before she finished. This did not surprise me, since she always had a guy interested in her, but it did seem rather early to get married. I was just beginning to feel my way through the world when I was in college, having little idea what shape my life would take.

Twenty years later, when our high school graduating class was having a reunion, I contacted Arlene. She was happy to hear from me but said she was not attending the reunion. She was busy with law school and had three children! How different her life was (and had always been) from mine. So I did not see her again.

And then fifteen years after that there was another reunion, and that's when I learned that Arlene had died. She had been killed on September 11 while working at the World Trade Center. I learned then that she had gone on to become a lawyer, got herself a very good job, and in her usual way, was successful.

Learning of her death had a profound effect on me. It was difficult to grasp, of course. How could Arlene not be here?

Apart from experiencing the tragedy, I suddenly realized all the good influence Arlene had had upon me. She had spurred my interest in clothes, in travel, and in just living a better life. Because she always seemed to be several steps ahead of me, I had somewhere to go, someone to emulate. She was not my only role model, but surely one of the more important ones.

I called up her husband. Having never met him, I had to explain who I was. With the World Trade Center tragedy already four years behind us, I asked if he could help me fill in some of the gaps. I wanted to know what happened to Arlene during the years in which I had not seen her. He seemed fine with this, and graciously invited me to the house where he and Arlene had raised their three girls.

The lovely house was very much Arlene's style, with tasteful furniture and draperies, valuable paintings and antiques. We chatted for about an hour and her husband showed me photos; he seemed to have plenty of time for me, and I appreciated it. I needed this to help with my grieving.

A short time after my visit, I got a call from Arlene's brother, notifying me that their father had died. The brother, who remembered me from days gone by, asked me to come and join the family for their Shiva, the Jewish ritual of receiving guests during the time of mourning. And so for the first time in many years, I went to that house in Jamaica Estates where I had spent all those pleasant afternoons.

Seemingly reading my mind, the young man asked me if I'd like to walk through the rest of the house, through the rooms I had not been in so long. He took me to what used to be Arlene's room, and there it was – the pale blue lamp that I had so coveted as a young girl, faded, dusty, but still suspended there as a remnant of a life now lost. I explained what a deep effect his sister had had upon me in those formative years of our girlhood. But he didn't really need to hear it because he knew. There would be many other friends like me, who remembered Arlene with tenderness and appreciation.

What has all this to do with becoming an artist? Maybe only that when you have a friend you admire so, it stimulates you to be more of yourself. So among the many people I have to thank, there is Arlene, my childhood friend who left us too early.

* * *

In 1964, when I was still in junior high, the film *Mary Poppins* was released, and I could not wait to see it. I don't know why; I had not read the book. I could never have had any idea as a twelve-year-old that this film was going to have a deep and lasting influence on my life.

For me, the story's great appeal was Mary's situation: she arrives at the home of Jane and Michael Banks, two unhappy children growing up in Edwardian England. Her task is to be their governess, but she arrives with so much magic up her sleeve that neither the children nor their parents can imagine the vitality she is about to add to their lives. I loved this idea, and put in my head that I wanted to one day be a governess, a teacher, or a mother of many children.

If you view the film today, it still retains its original appeal but appears charmingly unsophisticated. Now, more than forty years later, we have become accustomed to computer-generated special effects, and the old-fashioned effects in *Mary Poppins* seem to be no more sophisticated than those of a school play! Everything, from the set of Cherry Tree Lane to the parks, shops, and gardens of 1905 London, appears to be made of cardboard and plywood. I think perhaps this is the beauty of it – to think that we were once so mesmerized by something so simple and candid.

Just two years after the film came out, when I was fourteen, I had a chance to fulfill my fantasy of being Mary Poppins. My brother Joe was sixteen, and that summer he got working papers and found a job. This left me quite alone for the two months of summer that were yawning in front of me. Too young to get working papers, I answered an ad in the newspaper for a "Mother's Helper," the old-fashioned term for a nanny.

The couple that had run the ad had one little girl and needed someone to watch her while her mother played cards at the country club. They really wanted a fifteen-year-old, but were convinced when they met me that I would be capable and responsible. I was hired for a salary of $20 a week. This, in 1966, was a lot of money for a junior high school student.

The child was adorable, with shiny, coffee-colored hair and a sweet disposition. She was really just a baby and was very receptive to love and cuddling. We spent many pleasant days by the pool and seashore and did all those things that children like – tell stories, sing songs, go for walks, snuggle with a bottle and blanket. I became attached to her and wondered how we would leave one another at summer's end.

Summer did end and I went back to school. A few weeks into September, I went to visit my little charge and was amazed that she didn't remember me! Her mother was embarrassed and felt bad, knowing I had gotten so close to the child. But it was a good lesson in how things sometimes are not what they seem. I was learning about the fleeting nature of life's experiences. We have to glean what we can while we can, because sometimes a chapter of life is very brief.

This idea of being a nanny would play itself out again when the film *The Sound of Music* came out, following right on the heels of *Mary Poppins*. In this film, a young woman marries an older man with seven children and becomes their beloved stepmother. This idea imprinted itself deeply into my self-image and would rise up later, when, in my twenties, I met my first husband. He came ready-made with three little daughters. This was one of the main attractions in the relationship, for I apparently had not yet had enough of this role. But I had a lot of living to do between fourteen and twenty-two.

* * *

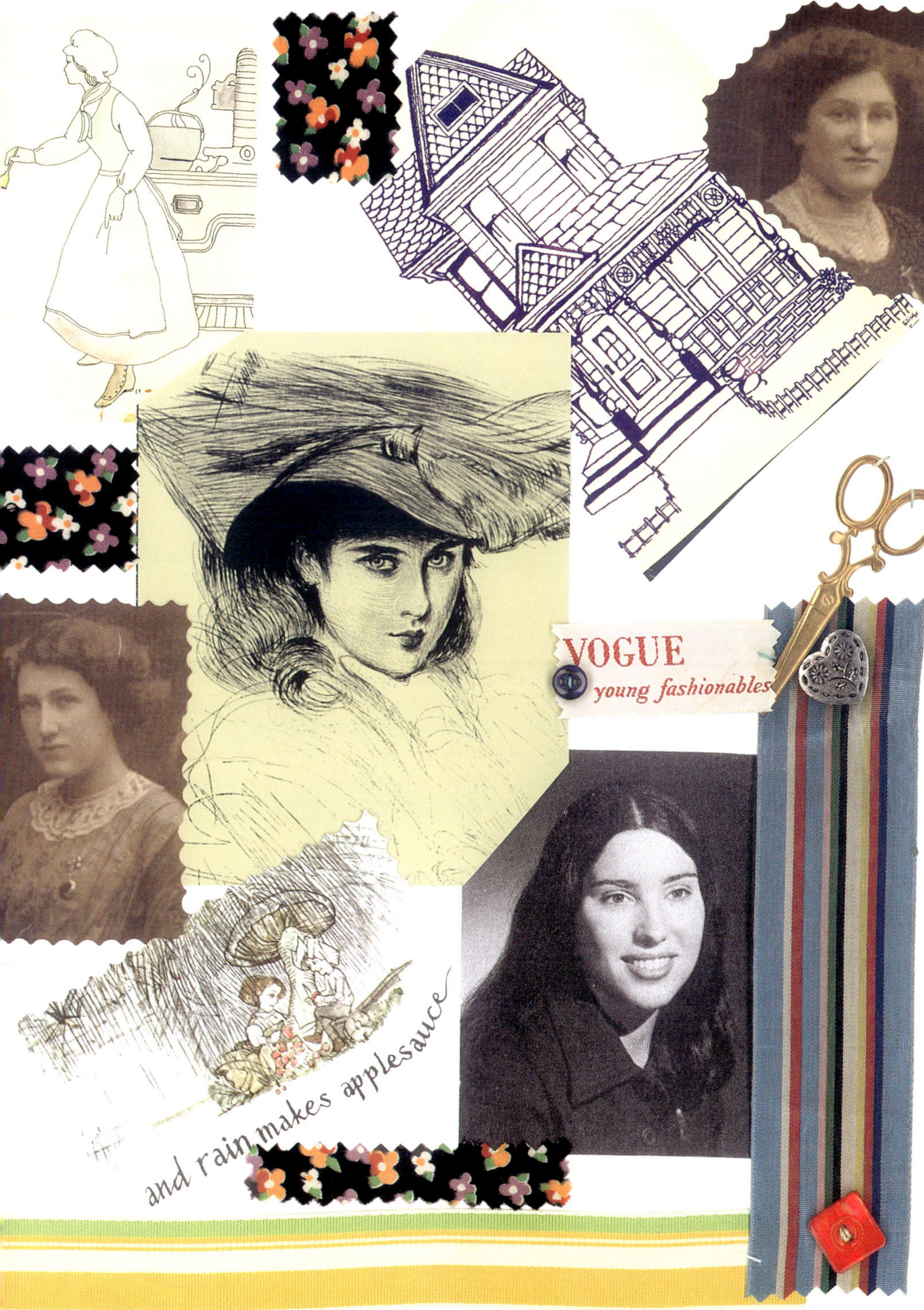
VOGUE
young fashionables
and rain makes applesauce

Part Three: High School

As a ninth grader at Van Wyck, I had heard about the High School of Art & Design from my artist friend, Andrea, and that was where I wanted to go. When I told my father I wanted to apply to Art & Design, he simply could not see the sense of my going to school in Manhattan. Jamaica High sat at the crest of 168th Street, just three blocks up the hill. He would not have prevented me going, but his practical side was strong and he talked me out of it. I have never been sorry about this because going to Jamaica High was one of the truly high points of growing up. So Andrea went off to Art & Design and did, in fact, become a professional commercial artist. I took another path, going to the neighborhood school.

Jamaica High is steeped in history, and it was especially so for me because my four siblings had gone there. It is still a thrill to look at the building, which sits atop a hill and looks down on Tilly Park, that legendary place where my father taught all of us to ice skate. The school's classical architecture nobly nods at all those who pass by, and its beautiful landscaping provides an ideal vantage point, no matter where you are standing.

The inside of the school is equally impressive, for was built from the best materials available in 1925, when it was constructed. Everything is very high quality, from the old panes of glass to the shining, deep brown wood, to the auditorium's tiled floors and magnificent chandeliers. Even when I went back to visit after thirty-five years, everything was in the same remarkable condition, as though all those passing through had treated the school with the respect it deserved.

Perhaps the most mysterious feature is a glass case in the first floor hallway that contains photos going back to Jamaica's earliest days.

Many of us who went to Jamaica High have later admitted to one another that we were fascinated by those photos, as though they had some kind of hold over us. It was true – once you started to look in the glass cases, it was hard to stop. The faces in the photos stared out at you from a time you could never reach – a time of football games, cheerleading, group picnics, clubs with virtuous goals. My own sister, being so much older than I and in a different generation, is in one of those pictures.

In the very first week, while going to school with some new-found walking buddies, I was introduced to girls who would become lifelong, cherished friends – Jeannie, Wendy, and Monica. I think of the three of us in our "school clothes" with our long, brown hair pulled back and held with striped ribbon, walking up that hill that is 168th Street. Everything lay before us – the choices of classes, friends, boyfriends, and later college, jobs, homes, husbands, children. How could we have ever known we would still be friends today?

At Jamaica High, everything I knew how to do was of value. It seemed there was an opportunity to utilize all my talents and interests. This phenomenon would occur later in life, when I became a librarian, but in the meantime, it was great to be sixteen years old and have a chance to express myself in art, dance, literature, and languages.

I knew I was going to add Spanish to my program. I had done so well in French in junior high, and was certain that this next language would be fun. I was right, not just because languages came easily to me, but because Spanish is much easier than French. By the end of my first semester, I felt at home with Spanish and made a mental note that the accumulation of languages was going to be a lifelong effort.

There were many of us at Jamaica who were talented and we found each other. There were the students who excelled in science and math, drama, sports, or journalism. The school was so big and so well developed that everyone had the opportunity to explore his or her own areas of interest. The teachers were top notch and passionate about what they taught.

Woven into my high school experience was my refusal to get

involved in volleyball, basketball, or swimming. I loathed sports so much that on the third day of school I tried out for the modern dance club, which exempted me from physical education class. In order to get into this club, you had to know that it existed, for it was not publicized anywhere. I only knew about it because Herm's girlfriend Phyllis had told me.

The dance class was held in a small room above the gym, which you got to through an unmarked door. Ironically, the door is in the gym, in plain view, but unless you knew where it led, you never asked about it. And so the dancers just blithely walked from the locker room through the gym in leotards and tights and went through that door to the dance studio. I wonder why no one ever asked us where we were going.

Some of the students in the class were aspiring dancers but for most of us, this was just for fun. The class was nothing special, but it was better than being downstairs on the volleyball court. At least it gave us a chance perform in school plays and stay involved in the dance world.

I have taken ballet lessons pretty much my whole life, but never in a serious way. It was always just to enjoy the beauty of it. I started when I was about five, when my mother bought me a pink tutu and ballet slippers. Like a lot of other little girls, I pranced around the living room. It would be many years before I would go to a "real" ballet school, in which girls strived to be as skinny as possible and bend themselves out of all reasonable shape to accomplish remarkable positions. I was not that kind of student anyway, but in time I would come up against that kind of class. Not until much later, though.

As a little girl, I attended a neighborhood school that had only two teachers, Miss Joyce and Miss Anne, who taught ballet, tap, and jazz. Imagine my disappointment when my mother took me to observe a class and I learned that you don't wear a tutu, but rather a leotard and tights. The classes were very low level and did not resemble the true world of ballet, but they gave me a good start. I learned to appreciate classical music and the nature of dance.

Miss Joyce had one record, a 78 rpm, in that notable *medium* size that 78s had, and she used to play it at the beginning of every class. I loved the piece that we always used for the *barre* exercises. The record had a round, hot pink label on it and was called "Music for the Ballet Class." I told my mother I wanted that record, and hummed the tune. In her usual way, Mom went to the music store and found something *like* it, but when she brought it home, I could see it was not the right record because it was the large size 33 rpm.

We put it on the Victrola and out came a completely different melody, as I was sure would happen. After we listened to it I said, "But can I still get that other record, the one I wanted?"

Mom got very angry. "How ungrateful they are!" she shouted, using the word *they* to catch in her net of discontent *all* of us children, us ever-wanting, ever-needing-new-stuff children, who always desired the next thing to cater to our constantly growing appetites for the creative, artistic, and expressive.

I did not get the record because it probably did not exist anywhere but in Miss Joyce's dance studio. But some time later, I heard that melody again, and learned it was Mozart's "Little Night Music." So as a little child, I had heard the genius of Mozart and knew I was near something worth pursuing, worth obtaining.

The story illustrates an ongoing challenge I had with my parents to gain exposure to classical music. They really had little interest in it and favored instead country western music and Elvis's or Ed Ames's popular songs. I would have to forge my own path into this world of music for the ballet, as well as opera, which could send my parents running from the room.

* * *

At the age of ten, I got a white tutu for Christmas. It was trimmed with gold sequins and had lavish gold straps. Magnificent. So magnificent, in fact, that I put a photo of myself wearing it on the back of my book *Anna Pavlova, Jewel of the Ballet*, a memoir of a famous ballerina.

When I went to junior high, I attended another ballet school with my friend Arlene. Ballet Arts was a bit more rigorous, but also not too serious. Still, it was fun to take the classes, wear the ballet clothes, the pink leather slippers or silken toe shoes, and move to lovely music.

But when I reached high school and met my lifelong friend, Monica, I learned that there were girls who gave up their Saturdays to go to ballet class. While the rest of us teenagers were shopping, ice skating, or visiting each other, the ambitious and competitive ballerinas were slogging away in Manhattan, hoping that this would lead to a lifetime career as a dancer.

Not only did I not have the training and strength for this, but I really didn't want to sacrifice my personal time to dance. It also was not possible for me to be a dancer because when I was twelve years old, just before I started junior high, I had an accident with a bicycle. I was taking a ride with my brother Joe when I carelessly turned my head for a moment and crashed into a parked car. I was not aware until I went to get up that I had a very deep and ugly cut in my thigh. Amazingly, this accident happened just across the street from a hospital. Some noble onlooker jumped off his porch and carried me, all bloody, into the lobby. It was quite dramatic, a true emergency. I had surgery that night, and the leg was stitched up tight. The doctor promised that I would be able to walk again by the time school began.

And that was just what happened. When we are young, we heal so fast. But my right leg has never been quite the same; it is just not as strong as the left. I have often thought that this weakness may have stood in the way of my considering dance as a career, and so I must link this event to my having become an artist instead. Desire, talent, and drive are what separate earnest dancers from the rest of us. I certainly endorse anyone following their vision to become a dancer, but it seemed that there was so much heartbreak in store for the girls who did this. In New York City, what would be the chances that a ballet student would blossom into a real-life professional dancer? This was what Monica wanted, and had always wanted, even before I knew her. She had cultivated an image of herself as a professional dancer, and despite the lack of support she got from her parents, she maintained her vision and kept on studying. She wanted to be a dancer *more* than she wanted to go shopping, have a boyfriend, or go out with her friends.

Once, as a high school student, I attended one of Monica's classes and saw the huge gap between the kinds of lessons I had been taking and those she was taking. The teachers were strict and unsmiling, the students looked as though they were being persecuted, and it was just downright hard work. I was more fascinated with the Russian and Hungarian pianists who did the musical accompaniment for these classes. They were old world musicians who could play the piano with no sheet music. The ballet teacher would take only a few seconds to demonstrate the steps she wanted the students to do for the next exercise and the pianist knew exactly the kind of music to play to match the rhythm of those steps. It was awe-inspiring.

Seeing these pianists play made me wonder what their pasts must have been back in Europe. Where and for whom had they played? In some beautiful, sunlit conservatory? When had they started? How long does one have to practice the piano before being able to play like that? Why did they apparently have no knowledge of English? Did they live in a cocoon of the world of ballet school, never venturing out beyond its borders? They were mysterious people to me, and I was intrigued by them. I still am.

And so I had tried to take these "real" ballet classes, but I could never have kept up with them and I didn't want to. Not only did I not have the necessary background, I also lacked the drive. I did go on to take all kinds of dance classes and to teach dance in various venues. But my love of ballet would really come to fruition when I would write and illustrate that memoir of Anna Pavlova. Long after I stopped taking lessons, long after I stopped expressing myself through dance, I poured into this book all my knowledge, love, and interest in ballet. What might have happened if I had never gotten that first pink tutu?

* * *

Despite my revulsion of sports, I was dying make the cheerleading squad. This is rather comical, since I did not even know how athletic games were played and had no idea what we would be cheering about. I think this goal was rooted in the coziness surrounding the Thanksgiving Game, the basketball game played on the eve of Thanksgiving. Because this event took place in the deep autumn, it had the glow of the oncoming holidays, reminding us of family get-togethers, friends, cider, and all that a sniff of autumn air evokes. The Thanksgiving Game was the event to which those who had recently graduated would return to the school, so some boy that I may have had a crush on the year before might show up. The whole gymnasium vibrated with the excitement of who *might* be there. Of course for me, none of this had anything to do with basketball.

I thought that the best way to experience this feeling was to be out in the middle of the court as a cheerleader. Cheerleaders got to wear a little red corduroy dress with a flare skirt lined in dark blue satin. When you twirled around, it spun out like a pancake, and when you did a cartwheel, it flowed right over you to the other side. Across the front of the bodice was a huge felt **J** (for Jamaica) that sat atop a two-dimensional felt megaphone. Then there were the saddle shoes and white socks, and you got to wear the uniform *all day* in school if there was a game that afternoon. I wanted it so badly.

I got it. I remember when the phone call came in after tryouts. It was as though I had won the lottery. It was the best thing that had ever happened to me until then. It meant that the Thanksgiving Game would be mine to experience as I had dreamed of it.

Like many things in life, the actual experience was not nearly as good as the dreamed-of one. After Thanksgiving, cheerleading became a somewhat isolating activity. You were no longer a *part* of the crowd, but were instead someone separate, some kind of performer. I remember that toward the end of the school year, I wished I did not have to go to the games at all.

This lesson has followed me through life so far. We cannot know something until we are doing it. We cannot know it from the outside, because the outside image is distorted. We have to *do* a thing to know what it is. Many times, the doing is even better than the imagining. But sometimes it turns out to be so different from how we imagined it that we cannot fathom why we ever wanted to do it in the first place.

This should not stop us from wanting to try something, because many things turn out to be better than we thought. I am in favor of trying all healthy activities that do not endanger our lives – jobs, friendships, travel, or education. We should not say to ourselves, "I really want to try that but I am not going to because I probably won't like it." Whether or not you will like it or profit from it cannot be predicted. You have to try and see. You can always do something else.

* * *

At Jamaica, I wanted to join everything that had to do with art, and found my way into the various clubs that painted scenery for plays and prepared students for an art career. I had a vague idea I wanted to be a children's book illustrator, although I had no idea how to make that happen. Looking back, I realize I just should have asked some grown-ups how one prepares for such a career, but it never occurred to me. Hence, when the time came to apply to an art college, I did not have a portfolio ready.

There was a club at school called Publicity Council, whose mission was to create all the posters and banners for the school events, elections, and plays. Publicity met in the art room at lunch time. I joined the minute I got to school, so never in three years did I even set foot in the cafeteria. Being in this club meant you spent your lunch hour with other artists, and that all of you were involved in the behind-the-scenes artistic work of the school. In joining PC, as it was called, I felt I had made contact with like-minded people, artists who had an outlet for their creative talent and who could make their art visible to their peers.

But if it had not been for Eleanore and Herm, I would not have known about PC because there was no central source for this kind of information. Like so many things in life, you had to be "in the know," or have heard about it from someone else. All through my life I have repeated this experience, so often finding myself on one side or the other – totally out of the loop about what is going on, or in with the in-crowd. To this day, I maintain there is no way to really get the information we need without asking, asking, and asking.

There were some art students who had a clear idea about what they would do with their talent, but most of us just wanted to make pictures and enjoy that process. Our art teacher, Mrs. Lipitz, said that if you wanted to be an artist, you had to carry a sketchbook at all times and *draw from life*. Those were her instructions, and so draw we did. We all carried notebooks, sketchbooks, and journals and we filled them with whatever was in front of us. Many students thought of being fashion designers and had pages and pages filled with drawings of long-legged models. Others wanted to be set designers, and some just wanted to paint.

In the front of the art room was a real human skeleton. It you were in the figure drawing class, you had to commit to drawing this skeleton, and that meant every last bone you could see. The reward for this tedious task was that once you had the structure of the skeleton in your brain, you would be able to draw a human figure in any position, even without a model. It took about two weeks to complete the assignment. Every day for two weeks, you took out your enormous sketch pad and picked up where you left off, making a fine pencil drawing of the skeleton. Boring, very boring. The teacher told us we should not be whining and complaining, and that one day we would thank her. She was right, for there is no better training for drawing people than to know what is under their skin. To this day, I always put in the basic bones before drawing a figure.

* * *

In the summer between my junior and senior year of high school, I got a job at the Queensboro Public Library in Jamaica. I was not looking for a job at all, but was just walking by the library one day when my eyes fell upon a glass showcase that looked out on the sidewalk. There in the window was a charming display made up of small paper figures. These little figures were so appealing to me that I knew I wanted to work in whatever department made those displays. I boldly walked into the library and asked the first important looking person I saw, a woman behind the desk.

"How can I get a job in the display department?" I inquired.

The woman looked at me tenderly – a seventeen-year-old girl asking to be hired for the library's publicity department.

"Those displays are made by our Public Relations Department," she said, "but I do need someone here at the circulation desk."

I filled out some papers and was hired as a circulation clerk, a very pleasant and amazingly prestigious job for a high school student. It meant checking out books, working at the return desk, and also doing some alphabetizing and organizing. Back in the 1960s, libraries were not run by computers and there was a lot of work that required busy fingers. There were piles of cards and papers – in fact, everything was done with paper.

I loved it. I worked all day Saturday and on Wednesday evenings. My paycheck was $60 a week, which was great money. I enjoyed working with the public and being visible in the community. On Saturdays I used to see many of my classmates, and also became familiar with older people in the neighborhood. I worked at Queensboro that entire summer, all through my senior year at Jamaica, and through that last summer until it was time to go away to college. But not one moment of this work had anything to do with my later becoming a librarian. The most powerful image I had was that glass case in which I had seen those paper figures; I wanted to one day do some kind of work that would involve paper and scissors and my imagination. But that would come later, much later.

* * *

Solitary activities like drawing and writing help us to evolve. In our backyard, we had a small patio that was made up of large square pieces of cement. Sometimes it served as a makeshift court for basketball, handball, or hopscotch. But at other times, it served as a giant drawing block for me. I used to work with colored chalk, making my first primitive children's book illustrations. Because the patio was a series of squares, it was almost like a storyboard on which I could draw pictures in succession. Old photos that my mother saved show crude chalk drawings I made of scenes from *The Wizard of Oz*, complete with the cornfields of Kansas, Emerald City, and the Yellow Brick Road.

I picture myself as a teenager, alone, down on my hands and knees, drawing on cement. Why was I doing this? I had a very early inkling that I wanted to be an illustrator, but of course, I had no idea how I could ever get there. This has been a theme running through my life: how can we get to where we want to go? It is rarely a straight path, but if we have a picture in mind, even a vague one, we may find our way. I could not have known then that so many children would one day see my pictures in a bigger way, reproduced in thousands of copies of books.

As I poke around my bookshelf, I see some reference books that have been with me for a long, long time, One of them was given to me when I was just sixteen: *Costumes Through the Ages*, which has detailed drawings of clothing going all the way back to ancient times. I got this book as a gift from Herm's girlfriend, Phyllis, who has now been my sister-in-law for almost forty years. She recognized my love of clothing and how I studied it, made it, wore it, and drew it, and chose this book for me. I have used it over and over and over, and it shows the signs of wear – spots of ink, torn pages, worn-out corners. A short time later, Phyllis gave me another lifetime companion of a book: *The Gibson Girl and Her America*, which shows the work of a favorite artist, Charles Dana Gibson. Gibson was keen to record the life around him as he lived in an America of about one hundred years ago. His pen and ink drawings show the many faces of womanhood, the clothing, the surroundings, old New York, the rich and the poor. Since so many of the illustrations I have made reflect that time period, Gibson and I are good friends.

These two books sit on my shelf and have traveled with me wherever I have lived. I think of the drawings in them as silent teachers whose wisdom I can count on when I need help with an illustration. I am happy to think I have never outgrown my need for them.

I shared my love of drawing with several high school classmates, among them my dear friend Wendy. We are still close today, although we no longer live near one another. The friendship was not just with Wendy; it was also with her grandmother. I guess it was a combination of not having a relationship with my own grandmother and loving to speak French that allowed me to be enchanted by Wendy's grandmother, Adele.

When Wendy and I were teenagers, I liked to imagine that Adele was my own grandmother, for this is the kind of grandmother I thought I *should* have had. She was French and had an interesting past. She had a sister living in Queens, whose name was Suzanne, but everyone called her "Auntie." Adele and Auntie came from a family of four sisters; two came to America and two remained in

Europe. One of them survived the Second World War by hiding in the south of France. The other sister did not survive.

Wendy had an album with very old photos of all these and other family members, dating back to the 1890s. It was great to sit up in her room and look at that album, to see the women in long dresses with enormous hats, men with three-piece suits with pocket watches and serious expressions, and other unidentified people. These photos were like Gibson's drawings, except that the people were real characters in my friend's life and they were haunting, since Adele was still living and I could actually talk to someone who had lived during this distant time period. The images in the photos stayed with me all my life, influencing my artwork and my love of French life and literature.

Adele died at the age of ninety. She was about the closest thing to the grandmother in *Gigi*. As we grow up and lose one friend after the next, we come to realize the role that people have played in our lives. Sometimes we are too young to fully understand their influence, but as time goes on, we come to appreciate it. The impact of this friendship is still with me.

* * *

As a teenager, I was as fond of drawing old houses. I used to take my sketchbook and go out on my bike to draw the loveliest old homes in the neighborhood. As I was sketching, I was thinking that these rough drawings were going to be re-done someday into formal, finished pictures. But that never happened because I cannot recreate the relaxed and unself-conscious style of the original sketch. But these pieces have served as inspiration and reference material for later illustrations.

In the summer before my senior year, I took a trip with my family through the Midwest. It was good to collect images so unlike those in my daily life – a lone tree stump standing where a grand oak might have been; a classic American farmhouse rising up from the flat landscape; a sign reading *Hay for Sale*; a clapboard barn with diamond-shaped windows, and snowball bushes, heavy with white globes of flowers. This was magnificent corn country, with mingled smells of grass being cut and flowers blooming. As we drove through Pennsylvania to Ohio, Illinois, Indiana, and Missouri, we saw splendid old American homes with turrets, porches, bay windows, garden gates, and attic windows. I did not know that they would find their way into books one day.

When I returned to school in the fall, I had an expanded view of what to paint and draw. My artwork improved greatly that year. All seniors were given a space on the large bulletin board outside the art room where we displayed our best artwork at the end of the year. I started a project that was a children's book, mimicking the drawing styles in old-fashioned books (I was, as always, *way* out of step with modern times) and using some of what I had seen during the summertime trip.

One of the contemporary books I admired was *Rain Makes Applesauce*, published in 1967. We were *all* trying to draw the way the illustrator, Marvin Bileck, did. *Rain Makes Applesauce* is a book of nonsense poetry with extraordinarily detailed pictures of more nonsense. There is so much going on in the pictures that no matter how many times you look, you always see more. This book set us amateur artists free to create in a relaxed and happy way. We all tried our hands at imitating Marvin Bileck. In time, though, we each found our own style.

To my amazement, when I graduated from Jamaica I was awarded the Alexander Medal, which Herm had also received when he graduated four years earlier. It was one of the highest honors for art, since only one medal is given out per high school. With the receipt of the Alexander Medal, I have never felt the need for any other award. When children ask me if I would like to win a prize for a book, I think immediately of the Alexander Medal, which satisfied the need for that kind of recognition a long time ago.

What if I had not gone to Jamaica High? How much I would have missed. Regardless of what I might have experienced at Art & Design, I would not trade what I have from my days at Jamaica, for what I learned, and for the person it helped me become. No, I would not trade it.

* * *

My mother's mother, Lucy, whom we called "Nonie" (rhymes with *Shawnee*) had fourteen children. We Freeman kids were just a few of her many, many grandchildren, and from my perspective, not among those closest to her. I was her forty-first grandchild, so I did not get any special attention nor did I have much of a relationship with her.

Nonie was large and soft-spoken. She had been a young woman in the 1920s and retained something of a "flapper" image of herself. She always wore a fancy dress, replete with beading and fringe, even in midday, sitting in the tiny kitchen of her railroad apartment. She was poor, poor, poor, but was always dressed as though she were about to go somewhere and do the Charleston.

Nonie's second husband Alfred, who was called "Papa," had been the great love of her life, and although he died in the late 1950s, his bathrobe, and no doubt the memory of his warm spirit, were always present in Nonie's bedroom. It was as though Papa had just stepped out for a minute and would soon be back.

The mixture of upbringings among Nonie's children (my mother's sisters and brothers) created some variations in identities. Because my mother married a Jewish man and moved out of the Italian neighborhood, we kids were physically separated from the extended family. All of Nonie's other daughters (there were eight of them) lived right near her – literally around the corner, up the street, or even upstairs in the same building. They married Italian, Polish, or Irish men from the community. My Aunt Rosie, who lived in the house with Nonie, never married at all. When I used to go and visit with my mother, all it took was Aunt Rosie making a phone call to one of the sisters and within a minute the door would fly open and in would walk any number of aunts, uncles, and cousins. It was impossible to keep track of who went with whom – in fact, we are still trying to make sense of it.

We kids probably seemed like oddballs to our cousins; we were Jewish, lived way out in Queens, had a private house with a yard and two cars. Unlike the rest of the kids in this huge family, we did not go to Catholic school or to church. But this did not prevent us from having some nice relationships with some of the cousins, all of whom were and still are warm and affectionate.

Mom's sisters had been raised in Brooklyn and lived the life of Italian Americans with Nonie and Papa. But Mom had grown up in

Connecticut, and despite her Italian heritage, she identified more with New England and the Founding Fathers. On Thanksgiving she produced an authentic American holiday meal, complete with homemade mince pie. She was *completely* repulsed by the idea of mixing Italian food with the traditional Thanksgiving menu. Her sisters did that, and she considered it a total travesty; you just did not combine these two cuisines.

It was on Sunday that we always had the true Italian Sunday dinner: macaroni and tomato sauce, meatballs, pork chops swimming in the sauce, salad, Italian bread, and artichokes or eggplant *parmigiana*. Sometimes the meal varied and we had macaroni and garlic, which was heaped in a large baking pan and topped with small, gleaming brown pork chops. We never grew tired of this.

My mother made all the food every Sunday and didn't need to know who was coming, but someone always showed up. We did not know how she did it. She would be in the kitchen for about a half a day, stirring the sauce, singing along with the radio and drinking wine. She started early in the morning, producing food whose aromas conflicted with the smell of bacon and eggs frying in the pan, the Sunday breakfast that my father prepared.

We used to like to sleep late, but Dad would have made the food and wanted us to eat it while it was hot. He had a little poem he used to recite to get us downstairs:

Canteloupe for breakfast,
Honey in a bun!
Get your shoes and stockins on
And run, run, run!

The clash between the smell of these breakfast foods and the other smells and tastes – garlic, tomatoes, meat – was somewhat unsettling. But there was no other way to do it, because in those days, all Italian sauce was made over a period of many hours. So you had to start early.

No one really knew Mom's recipes, because there weren't any. This cooking was done strictly by feel. I remember when Steve's first wife, Bobbie, a nice Jewish girl from the neighborhood, stood next to Mom at the stove and said, "Teach me how to make your food."

"Well, you put some olive oil in a pan, like this," Mom said, pouring the oil around the frying pan in a large circle.

"How much oil is that?" Bobbie asked.

"*This* much," Mom replied, now making the arm movement *without* the oil can in her hand. "Then you add the tomato paste," she continued, scooping the paste out of the little Contadina can, "and you add boiling hot water." For this you had to pour the steaming water into the can and add it to the mixture three times. The can got very, very hot, so you had to pour and dump and pour and dump and pour and dump very fast or you'd burn your fingers. I don't know how Mom did this.

But Bobbie did learn to be an authentic Italian cook. She made better lasagna and meatballs and sauce than my mother made. And a generation later, her son Michael became a better cook than *she* was.

Cooking on Sunday was one of the few areas of life in which Mom thought of herself as Italian. She sometimes used her Italian-ness as an excuse to lose her temper, flirt with men, or act impulsively. I think she felt more at home in her "Yankee" persona. Dad did, too. On Thanksgiving, which he enjoyed because of its thoroughly American theme, he took on a faux-Quaker persona as he made a blessing over the food, bringing forth a language reserved only for that occasion: *Lord, we thank Thee for Thy bounty, and all this food we shall partake in*...and he might go on and on with this until my mother, standing there in her apron, would explode with, "All RIGHT!!"

Unlike his prosperous extended family, Dad shied away from anything that may have been mistaken for bragging or social climbing. He was not impressed by fancy hotels or cruise ships, frequently using the phrase, "I wouldn't give you two cents for the whole thing." He hated false elegance and pretense, and this included restaurants with tablecloths made of *cloth*, or going anywhere that did not include the kids – except for family weddings, which he also hated.

I have a late night memory of my parents coming home from those weddings, of which there were many because I had so many cousins. I can see my mother, still with her coat on, bending over my bed in the dark to kiss me. Dad was probably already getting out of his starched shirt and shiny shoes.

No, Dad did not like to go out on the town. He had no ambitions other than to read books, cultivate his mind, and enjoy his home and family. We thought he was as good as a husband and father could be. He knew nothing of looking for outside pleasure. He did not care about friends and did not play cards with other men. He didn't go to the races or drink alcohol, apart from a beer in the summer. He much preferred to eat at little homespun places by the beach or a lake, where you could order fried clams and French fries that came in paper containers and eat them standing up while gazing at the shore.

Dad came from a good, solid family of six siblings, had a mother who was a devoted homebody and a father who worked hard. As adults, Dad's brothers and sisters had better houses and seemed to be more connected to worldly things, but Dad *was* not and *could* not be like that. This brought about some problems between him and my mother. A couple of decades into the marriage, when Herm, Joe, and I were teenagers and Eleanore and Steve were already married, some little part of Mom felt there was a life somewhere that she was missing. It was a world that she had perhaps read about in ladies' magazines, a place in which people were drinking cocktails and women were wearing brocade dresses. She had focused for a long time on being a wife and mother, and now that we were older, she wanted something more.

Mom had fallen in love with Dad because of a certain wholesome quality he had. She was seventeen when she saw him loading a truck outside his father's factory, which was across the street from her family's house. Being Italian, she had grown up around men in two-toned shoes with snazzy pencil moustaches, who had impure thoughts about women and spent time in bars. She did not want any part of this and had no plans to marry at all.

But then one day she saw Henry. He was wearing a clean white shirt, sleeves rolled up to reveal strong arms, a lock of dark hair falling onto his forehead. *A father for my children*, she thought. He seemed to belong to a world apart from hers, and she was right.

When they met, he told her he was Jewish. "Jewish?" she asked, incredulously. She had never met a Jewish person before. "You mean like Jesus? Like the people in the Bible?"

"Something like that," he said.

As she got to know Henry, Mom learned that there were homes in which the mother made a different meal every night, not just for the family, but for each son. In her own family of fourteen children, everyone got a plate of spaghetti with one meatball sitting on it. In Henry's family, each son got his favorite dish—for *you*, pot roast, for *you*, chicken, for *you*, stuffed cabbage. Like a restaurant.

There was a day when, after they had met one another, Mom was home on a break from nursing school because Nonie had just had a baby. Mom was scrubbing the front hallway when she heard a strange sound coming up the walk. It was kind of rhythmic, repetitious *bumpety-bump*, *bumpety-bump*. She turned to see young Henry rolling, if you can call it that, a very large plywood crate up her front walk. It must have been a box in which a large piece of factory equipment had been delivered, and he was now bringing it to her house. *Why*?

She opened the screen door and saw him standing there, one hand on the wooden crate. "Hello," she said.

"I thought the kids, that is, your little brothers and sisters, might like to use crate this as a playhouse."

"Thank you," she replied. She was not sure how to make the most of this moment but was not going to let him leave just like that. "Would you like to see the new baby?" she asked. And with that, he came into the house and into her life.

When they were courting, Mom was a student at St. Vincent's Nursing School on Staten Island. Dad used to take the trolley, the ferry, and a bus from Brooklyn to go out and see her for a half an hour. That was *all the time* one was allowed, and you had to stay in the chaperoned lobby of the school. On their first date, Dad brought Mom a bouquet of irises, thinking they were orchids (a far more costly flower). *She* knew the difference but did not say anything because she found such sweetness and innocence in the gesture.

Many of their dates consisted of riding the Staten Island Ferry back and forth, just to be together. Mom did not think Dad was contemplating marriage; she thought they were just good friends. After five years, friendship suddenly blossomed into romance. They got married in the autumn at City Hall, and then walked through Prospect Park. Mom was wearing a creamy satin gown with a white velvet braid on her dark hair. As she walked, her long, long veil floated behind her. I like to imagine them as they took their first promenade as husband and wife. They did not know what a very long road it was going to be.

The fall would always be their favorite time, when the chrysanthemums would bring the promise of winter and snow. Old home movies show my parents with their first two children, Steve and Eleanore, striding through Highland Park, everyone with Pilgrim props that Mom had made – the girls in crepe paper collars and white aprons; Steve and Dad with tall, black, buckled hats and carrying cardboard hatchets. Mom walks up to the camera, her wavy hair bouncing over the collar of her beaver coat. Eleanore, dressed as a miniature Priscilla Alden, is holding Mom's hand as they descend one of the many steep hills, now awash in wet leaves in the decaying autumn.

In another film, they are all on sleds, gliding downhill through the silent whiteness of the woods. Mom and Eleanore on one sled brush past the other two, a cold sparkle on their girlish cheeks. And on what must have been a splendid, cold night, all four of them are marching in the snow around a Christmas tree that has served its purpose, is stripped of its ornaments, and is now going back to nature. This appears to have been a happy time that lasted all the way through the life in Brooklyn and into the next part of life, in Queens.

It was all good fun, but as the years went on, my mother longed for more romance. When we were grown, Mom suddenly decided it was time to be out in the world of candlelit restaurants with soft music. My father could not see this coming. They had just spent the last few decades being so very wholesome and now she wanted him to be what she termed "a sport." This meant wearing a nice dinner jacket and maybe surprising her with a spontaneous present. She used to compare Dad to our neighbor, Henry Pick, who liked to spoil his wife with little romantic baubles – a sapphire-studded ring, a bottle of champagne, a spur of the moment getaway.

My father found all of this most distasteful, since it had nothing to do with family life, and until a certain moment, my mother did too. But then she wanted it. She wanted *her* Henry (the two ladies used to refer to their husbands as "my Henry" and "your Henry") to make all those romantic gestures, which *Dad* considered to be "buzhwah," his word for something shallow, worthless, and time-wasting. He would have no part of it. Sometimes he made a feeble attempt to please her, forcing himself to have a glass of wine to let Mom feel they were living a more sophisticated life, but it was never authentic. Dad really just wanted to sit and watch baseball on TV, eating a bag of peanuts.

Sometime during the 1960s, Mom heard about a restaurant in Queens called the Broadcaster's Inn, and got a bee in her bonnet about going there with Dad. She imagined herself wearing some chic little black dress; Dad would be sitting across from her in a finely cut jacket, and the two of them would be sipping the drink of the day, the daiquiri. We heard a lot about this fantasy, until one day, Mom got Dad to agree to go there. I had my doubts about this; I just could not picture my father following through with it. But they did actually get dressed and go out that night.

Herm, Joe, and I stayed at home, watching television. A short time later – way too short to include dinner – my parents came back. Mom had obviously been crying and Dad just looked defeated. What had happened?

Mom stood, still with her evening bag in hand, and as if addressing a jury, angrily and sobbingly told the three of us how Dad had indeed taken her to the restaurant and had even ordered the drinks. But he would not eat.

"He ordered *one* dinner!" she shouted. "What kind of a sport is that?"

"I don't want to eat in a place like that!" he said in his own defense. "It's all *buzhwah*."

"How come it's not *buzhwah* for Henry Pick?" she shouted, now very angry and hurt.

"I'm not Henry Pick!" Dad answered. "I'll never be Henry Pick and I don't want to be."

But it got worse, for in an effort to boost her own case, Mom described how, when Dad had refused to eat anything, she too, did not want to eat – after all, she had not fantasized about sitting at the Broadcaster's Inn in a smart little dress, eating *alone.* She had said, "Let's leave," and Dad, only too happy to get out of there, stood up and the two of them marched out. As they walked across the parking lot to their car, they passed many a happy couple on their way *in*, no doubt to enjoy the kind of evening Mom had been dreaming of. Mom stopped one of the women walking past her.

"I just want to know," she said, her voice quavering, "What do you think about a man who won't even sit and eat dinner with his wife in a restaurant, just once in thirty years? Do you think that's right?"

The woman, a stranger taken by surprise, turned and looked at her own husband and shrugged. No satisfaction for my mother and probably a moment in which my father wished the very asphalt of the parking lot would swallow him up.

Yes, they did have their rocky times. They loved each other, but were so different in their approaches to life. They had each had their own experiences and contexts from which they had come, and sometimes the paths they were taking through life did not merge.

My mother's own history with her family was a bit strange, since Nonie did not raise her. In the book *Grandmother Mary*, the reader learns how Nonie (or Mama, as she is called in the story) gave her little daughter Mary away to live with Nonie's well-to-do sister, Theresa. Let me say right now that that name "Grandmother Mary" is an invented one. No one ever called my mother this except for a family member who came into our midst through a marriage. Being a southerner, this relative referred to my mother in this quaint way. When I heard the name, I liked the sound of it and decided to give it to my mother in my book. Once the book came out and became well known, many people started to refer to Mom that way, either as a joke or because the name had come to suit her.

Actually, my mother was not even called *Mary* by her family. She was always referred to as *Mannie*, a name that had dubious origins. This is what anyone related to her by blood or marriage called her, and it carried over to my father addressing her as Mannie. Later, the first grandchild in the family, hearing this name, called my mother *Grandma Mannie*, and it stuck.

Where did this name come from? I heard various explanations, but the only one that pleased me was this: the wealthy Aunt Theresa was pretentious and social climbing. She was Italian, but in order to be accepted by society, hid this fact. My mother's name was Mary Simeti, but Aunt Theresa knew that Mary would never be accepted at the snooty Catholic school if she were Italian, so she enrolled the child as Mary *Smith*. But at home, Aunt Theresa had yet another name for her – Emmanuelle, because Mom had been born around Christmas. So like Jesus, my mother was thought of as *God With Us,* which is the meaning of *Emmanuel*.

Aunt Theresa suddenly died in a car crash, and twelve-year-old Mary went to live with Nonie again. Nonie had since remarried and had more children, and when Mary arrived, they may have poked fun at her, mockingly calling her "Emmanuelle," which deteriorated into Mannie.

I was always amazed at my mother's devotion to Nonie, considering that Nonie was not too much of a mother to her. I only learned as an adult that my mother used to visit Nonie almost every day. This meant driving to Brooklyn while we were in school, paying a short visit, probably giving her mother money, and driving home again. This was a part of my mother's private and secret life she did not reveal to us – a sort of undying loyalty that she had to a mother she really did not know.

But all those cousins living in Brooklyn had immense appreciation for Nonie; their lives practically revolved around her. Nonie's home, wherever she was at the time (she moved around a lot) was a central meeting place for all her locally living children. On

Christmas and New Year's they all congregated in her railroad flat and made lots of noise, drank festive drinks, and ate platters of Italian cookies. This was a ritual in which we Freeman children did not participate, but I learned about it when I was seventeen, on the New Year's Eve just before Nonie died.

We had already celebrated New Year's at our house, for which we had our own traditions. Our celebration at home was rather tame, and it ended around 12:30 a.m., after all the cocktail franks had been eaten, the glittering silver ball had dropped, and the TV had been turned off. We had watched the old home movies, that is, once we got the ancient projector to work. The projector and the old screen would be brought down from the cedar closet upstairs, along with the green linen bag that held the sixteen-millimeter films. Then, with much struggle to keep these old films from slipping and sliding and breaking, Joe would thread the delicate strips onto the projector wheel and we'd turn out the lights and watch. There they were – Mom, Dad, Eleanore, and Steve walking through the parks and playgrounds of Brooklyn, Steve in his little sailor outfit and Eleanore in her prim dress. All the neighborhood mothers in the playground are fully dressed in suits and have with stylish hats perched on their bobbed hair. All the men are wearing fedoras.

Some of the films were shot backwards, and we loved seeing the horse and carriage of Tally-Ho Farms as it carried a stagecoach-full of children backwards through the landscape of Long Island. In the later films, when the family left Brooklyn and moved "out to the country" (Queens) to have their own home, we saw a ten-year-old Eleanore and a four-year-old Steve romping through the grounds of what would become the very house and yard in which we were growing up.

From one New Year's Eve to the next, the movies seemed more and more mystifying – there was Dad, swimming in an ice-cold river in Upstate New York, and Mom, looking the very picture of 1940s elegance in a chic bathing suit and sunglasses, waving the camera away as she sat on her striped beach towel. We saw my parents with their Airedales and nine pups, and in one touching sequence, Mom, in wide-legged pants, snug blouse, and plaid snood holding her hair, is in the backyard dancing and singing, "I'll be down to get you in a taxi, Honey." Of course there was no sound, only the *tick-tick-tick* of the projector as we watched Mom wink into the camera at the end of her song. Many years later, we had the films put onto video tape. They are still great to watch, but without the *tick-tick* in the background, something of their soul has vanished.

When Herm became old enough to spend New Year's Eve outside the house with friends, Joe and I used to spend the early evening upstairs in the large bedroom playing cards or Monopoly as we waited for Mom to tell us that the "party" was beginning. We knew that at about 11:30, we would come downstairs for eggnog and punch, Times Square on TV, streamers, noisemakers, and miniature franks and beans.

Joe and I suffered a rude awakening as we got older – quite a bit *too* old for this stuff – and learned that our parents had gotten older too. We were in the middle of a card game when we glanced at the clock. Eleven-thirty! We must get going for the celebration. We opened the door to the bedroom and went to the landing. Looking downstairs, we saw...darkness. Nothing. There was nothing going on downstairs. We looked at each other and burst out laughing! Mom and Dad had gone to bed! There was no New Year's Eve that year. And henceforth, we added this phrase to our personal lexicon: *Eleven-thirty at the top of the stairs*, which would mean those times when we have great expectations and find that nothing has been done to meet them.

But the New Year's Eve that I was linking with Nonie was different. We had had the usual festivities at home. Dad went to bed, Herm was out, and Joe was probably up in his room reading. But I was still wearing my black velvet dress, so my mother proposed that we take "a hop to Brooklyn." Unbeknownst to my snoring father, we got into the car and drove straight to Myrtle and Grove, to my grandmother's house.

I could not believe the crowd inside, the festivities that were taking place, while our own household slept quietly in Queens. The house was full, and all of my Italian relatives were celebrating. People were squeezed into that place and were spilling out into the hallway.

We were not the last to arrive. At 1:00 a.m., more and more cousins kept coming in the door. And there was more to drink, more sweets, more platters being passed around. There was noise, music, laughing, and kissing. I learned that night that they had always been celebrating this way. This had been going on the whole time I was growing up in Queens, but I did not know it. And I never would have known it if we had not gone there that night, for Nonie died the following spring.

* * *

Mom had other little madcap adventures that we learned about *after* they occurred. She had a cousin named Genevieve, who was flamboyant, ill-behaved, and entertaining, and considered by my father to be a "bad influence."

"Keep her away from my kids!" he warned, as if she could corrupt us. Really, Cousin Genevieve was harmless, but was always aching for a new thrill. She was savvy and crafty and knew how to get in and out of sticky situations. She and my mother, though close emotionally, were living completely different lives, but once in awhile, those lives, like comets colliding in the sky, touched one another.

Mom, a stay-at-home wife and mother, was a foil for Genevieve's wandering ways. But somewhere deep inside, Mom longed for a bit of that caprice that Genevieve had. Every now and then, we would hear at dinner some bizarre experience that Mom had had that afternoon. Like readers of *The Cat in the Hat*, we could not believe that everything that had taken place had been so thoroughly cleaned up by the time we got home from school that not a bit of it showed.

Mom always loved the idea of a job for which you wear a uniform. She had a fantasy about having a job at the airport, where she could wear a navy blue dress with matching shoes and preferably a small gold airplane tacked on her pocket. One day Genevieve showed up and spirited my mother off to the airport where the two of them were going to get jobs as counter girls at what was then quaintly called The Milk Bar. And they *did*! They worked there for three hours, collected their pay, and drove away. By the time we three kids got home from school, Mom was back in her housedress, standing at the ironing board. The Hostess cupcakes were laid out for us, *The Edge of Night* was on TV, and we heard the sweet *prink, prink, prink* — sound of water coming through the perforated stopper stuck in an old vinegar bottle – as Mom sprinkled a white shirt before ironing it.

At dinner Mom told the story, laughing all the way, about how she and Genevieve showed up for "work," donned their aprons, stuck the fluffy waitress hanky in the pocket, and served coffee and sandwiches to travelers for three hours. She had even made a few dollars! But at 3:00 p.m. when they had to leave, the boss asked, "Where are you going?" and Mom replied that her *kidsies* were coming home from school and she had to run.

My father thought Mom was nuts. "HOW do you get yourself INTO these situations?" he asked, disgusted.

"Henry!" she protested, "It's funny! I thought you would get a *kick* out of it."

"I don't get any KICK out of it," he said. "It's NOT funny. And keep that woman away from my kids." Mom was disappointed at his reaction.

But no one could deny that Cousin Genevieve had some qualities we would all want. Despite her unstable nature, Genevieve had a buoyant spirit. In 1969, when I was a teenager, she was diagnosed with cancer and was lying in bed in Mary Immaculate Hospital. My mother was on the phone with one sister and another. The byword was, *They opened her up and they closed her up. There is nothing they can do. She has a week to ten days left*. For every sister Mom spoke to, this was repeated.

It was then said that Genevieve, upon hearing the news from the doctors, got herself out of bed and stumbled down the hall to the chapel, where she threw herself at the feet of the statue of the Virgin Mary and said, "Please, Blessed Mother, don't let it end just now."

Mom made Genevieve a nice pot of chicken soup, poured it, still warm, into a clean mayonnaise jar, and sent Phyllis and me down to the hospital to deliver it. We did not stay long, and the next thing we heard was that Genevieve, feeling rejuvenated by her visit to the

Virgin Mary, and maybe the chicken soup, threw back the blanket and said to the doctor, "If I only have ten days to live, I am not living them *here*." She got dressed and left the hospital that day.

Cousin Genevieve lived for another thirty years, got married at least two more times, sometimes to the same man and sometimes to men decades younger than herself. For her ninetieth birthday, her six devoted children, several of whom she had totally neglected in their childhood, gave her a fabulous party and she received gifts perfectly matched to her personality – a feather boa and dozens of American Beauty roses, among others. Just before she died at age ninety-three, she was still playing the accordion at a nursing home where, she said, she liked to entertain "the old people." No, you could not take away from her what she had been. There was no one else like her.

* * *

Just shortly after my seventeenth birthday, my Great Aunt Lenny died and left money to everyone in the family. This was quite remarkable, since I really had no relationship with Aunt Lenny, and I suddenly found myself $10,000 richer. So did my brothers and sister, as well as my father, who inherited $100,000.

Lenny was my paternal grandfather's sister, and since I did not know this grandfather, Lenny's relationship to us was even more abstract. We just knew that she was very, very rich. She had so much money, there was no way she could *not* have given everyone some of it.

The whole thing was unbelievably confusing, because Lenny Freeman had married a gentleman named Harold Herman, who was quite lucky in the stock market. We called him Uncle Herman, but he was neither our uncle nor was he named Herman. We should have been calling him *Great Uncle Harold*. To add to the confusion, Lenny's brother (the grandfather I did not know) was named Herman, or Grandpa Herman, but since he was already gone by the time I was born, I didn't call him anything. Don't try to figure this out.

Anyway, Harold and Lenny Herman, my father's uncle and aunt, lived on the Upper West Side across the street from the Hayden

Planetarium and The American Museum of Natural History. Their apartment was huge, with rooms that went on and on, but there was an elegant, sad emptiness to those rooms because they had no children or grandchildren. They had one daughter, Eileen, who died at age twenty-six. She was adopted and cherished by her parents, but a sudden illness took her and it was said that she "keeled over" one day while sitting on the sofa.

Eileen had a *lady's maid* — a young-ish woman who lived in the apartment with the family, and whose job was to comb Eileen's hair, care for her clothes, and help her dress. One day my father took us three kids to the museum and afterwards, we stopped in to see Lenny and Herman. They were so taken with my long, dark hair that they insisted the lady's maid "do something" with it. I was ushered into Eileen's gorgeous bedroom and asked to sit at a vanity table with a three-way mirror. The maid took out a rather old-fashioned hairbrush, undid my ponytail and brushed out my hair. Then she curled it and coaxed it into beautiful waves until I had a magnificent, lustrous, long corkscrew hanging down over my shoulder. I suppose many wealthy ladies had such maids at that time, but what a contrast to my life, in which my mother or sister would have to chase me around the house with the brush to get me to sit to have my hair worked on.

Not long after Eileen's untimely death, Uncle Herman died too. He left Aunt Lenny with millions of dollars and tons of stocks worth more millions of dollars. And a few years later, when Lenny died, those millions were distributed. Most of the money went to charity. A large chunk of it went to Lenny's sister, my Great Aunt Estelle, who had never known wealth before. The rest was distributed among the nephews, nieces, grandnephews, and grandnieces, all the way down to us kids, some of the youngest members of the family.

It's a good thing my father inherited that money, for that was what pulled him out of the valley of struggle he had been in for ten years. After he lost his paper box business he was floundering in debt and did not know how we'd get through the future. With his newfound wealth, he paid off all the bills and was able to breathe more easily. Then all he had to do was play around with the stocks he had inherited and feel like a rich guy. Eventually, though, he would lose everything, lock, stock, and barrel, and leave my mother with nothing.

For us, though, new possibilities opened up. We had each received an inheritance and could do as we pleased. Herm and Joe both were going to tuition-free colleges, so their money was gravy. I was able to have more of a choice because I could actually pay tuition. But more important was that I could now look forward to going to Europe, a dream I had had since I was in the fourth grade. First, though, I had to think about college.

While I had my mind on what was happening in my little life at Jamaica High, I got a jolt that I could not see coming. One night at dinner, Herm announced that he had applied for an art teaching fellowship at Indiana University and would soon be going to live there. I felt something rip itself out of me. There was no preparation for anyone going away, so far away, to *live* somewhere else. When Eleanore got married, she only moved ten minutes away and was always back at our house with her husband and the babies. This was different. Herm was going away for what seemed like a long period of time, and to make it worse, Phyllis, whom I adored, was going with him. The two of them had been planning this, applying for it, visualizing it, but no one knew it. It was exciting for them and heartbreaking for me.

I am reminded of a scene from the classic *Little Women*, in which the main character, Jo March, has trouble coping with the news that her sister is going to get married. In the beginning of the book, the four March sisters are struggling through the Civil War and waiting in joyful anticipation for their father to come home. And he does come home, but shortly thereafter, the oldest sister, Meg, gets engaged. Although this should be happy news for everyone, Jo is deeply grieved because she was hoping that the family would be whole again, with everyone under the same roof. And now she has learned that her sister will soon be leaving, making the household, once again, incomplete.

We had a copy of *Little Women* at home. Its frontispiece had a color plate showing this very scene from the story: a despondent Jo is sitting on the floor in her bouffant crinoline, with her head on her mother's lap. The mother is looking down at her tenderly and the caption reads, "What is it, Jo?" This picture so illustrated my own pain, which emanated from the same source – the loss of someone from the household. This sentiment was to plague me my whole life, even as I was the one to leave, to go away to school, and even to move to another country.

In time, Herm and Phyllis did come back east and in fact got married, moved to Connecticut, and there they stayed for a long time. Herm went on to become a master art teacher and Phyllis became a social worker, assisting mentally challenged people in finding their way back into community life. In the scheme of things, their stay in Indiana was very brief, a short chapter. It seemed so final when it happened, but was merely a step in the continuum of our life as a family.

* * *

There was one summer of my high school years when Phyllis and I took modern dance lessons at a very hip school called The New Dance Group Studio. It was the usual hot, grimy New York summer, for the city was dirtier, more dangerous, and in a way, darker back then.

The school was a respectable place, and many good dancers had come out of it. It has been described as having been "… a major hub of activity in the vibrant New York City dance scene…." I wish I had written those words, for that is such a good description. It did have a hub-ish feeling. Located on West 47th Street, up a dim and dingy flight of stairs, the studio was totally no-frills. Sooty windows looked out on dismal 47th Street and the street noises were audible.

All the students were very skinny, but not the way ballet students were. There were no neat little chignons, no pink tights, no painful stretching and pointing. This type of dance was all about free-flowing and freely-curling hair, mismatched, torn tights, leotards in odd colors like briny green and washed-out maroon. Bare feet, no pink leather ballet shoes. This was something different, something natural, with spontaneous, melody-free piano music, and open movements. It was the beginning of the new freedom we would feel in the 1970s, as the '60s broke everything apart and made room for new ways of thinking.

I remember how Phyllis and I used to come home on the hot subway, then the bus, having worked our bodies in this relaxed and easy way, swirling around the studio. *Contract, release, brush! Contract, release, spin! Step, step, step, glide, step, step, step, turn*. No teachers with canes angrily tapping on the floor, no sneering looks of disapproval. Those steps, those positions, and that style of dance have never left me. Those muscles have a memory.

* * *

Soon after Herm and Phyllis left for Indiana, I got ready to go to college. I had been involved in so many activities in high school that when it came time to apply to college, I was not too prepared and did not have any feeling, desire, or idea about where I wanted to go. In those days, students used to consult an enormous college catalogue that listed all the schools, what they offered, and the cost. I remember sitting up in my room with the book, flipping through it very casually and spotting *McGill University, Montreal, Canada*. There was something about this idea that appealed to me. I had never even been to Montreal and knew nothing about it except that it was a French-speaking city. The idea of going to school in Canada was enormously attractive and suddenly this idea of *college*, which had had no previous importance to me, became paramount. I applied with great gusto and assumed I would get in.

But I didn't get in. My SAT scores were not high enough. I was quite disappointed, but fortunately, I had also applied to a local school, C.W. Post, and was accepted there with a scholarship. The advantage of Post was that it was "away" from home, but no too far, just out on Long Island. It had a beautiful country campus and a good foreign language program. My father offered to buy me a car if I wanted to commute, but I had no interest in driving and opted instead for life in the dorm. I also secretly resolved that in two years I would apply to McGill again and transfer there.

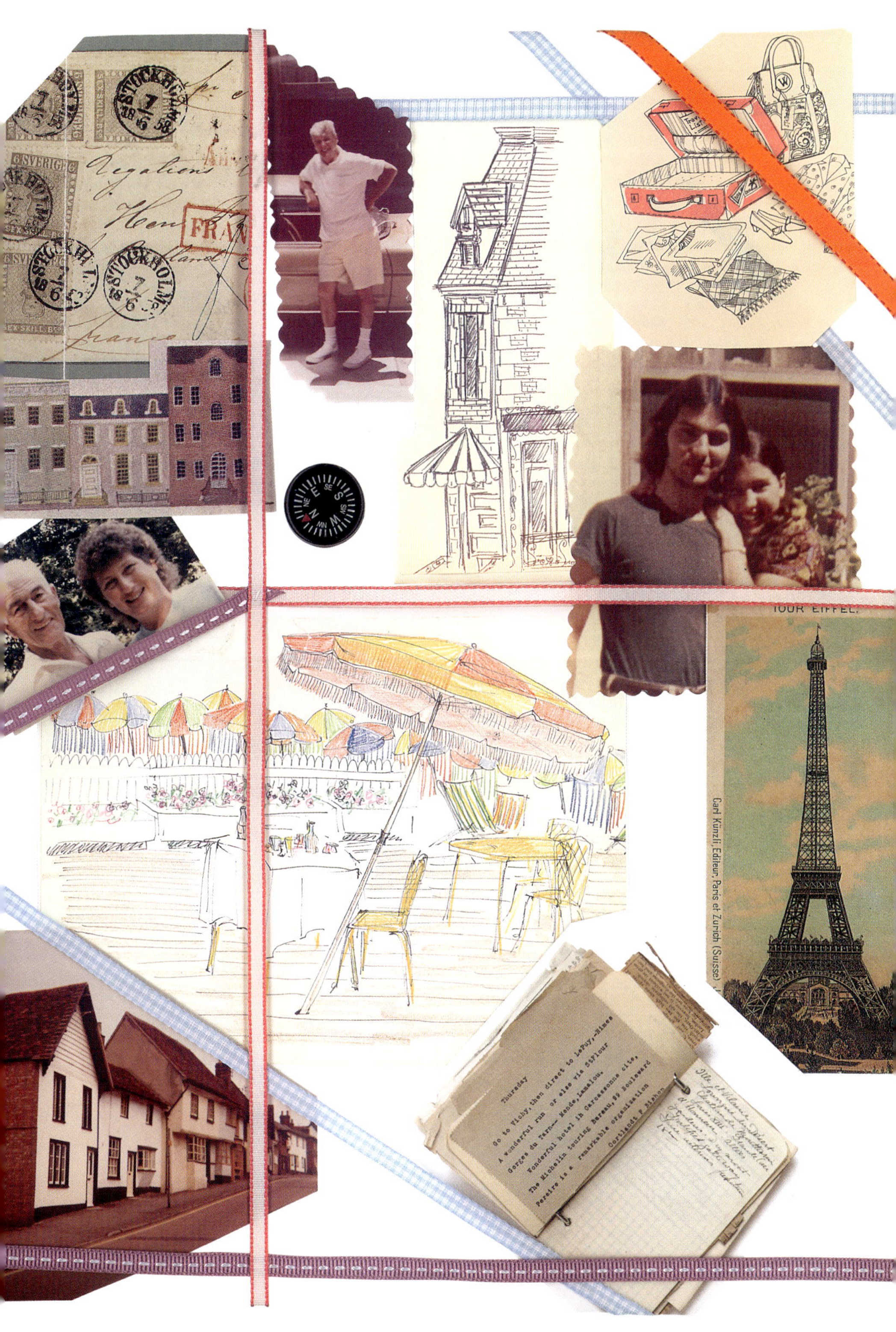
STOCKHOLM
FRA
TOUR EIFFEL.
Carl Künzli Editeur, Paris et Zurich (Suisse)
Thursday
Go to Vichy, then direct to LePuy,-Nimes
A wonderful run or else via StFlour
Gorges du Tarn-- Mende, Lamalou,
Wonderful hotel in Carcassonne cite,
The Michelin touring Bureau, 99 Boulevard
Pereire is a remarkable organization
Cortlandt F Bishop

Part Four: College

When I arrived at Post, I had no idea who I would get for a roommate. Neither did anyone else. Some roommates were grossly mismatched and needed to be changed – they had clashing values, habits, and personalities. But I was so lucky. Fate dealt me a friend for a lifetime.

I checked into my room to find it empty. It was obvious that my roommate had already been there, for on the floor was a pair of riding boots, and on her desk a very large dictionary. Not too much else. I started to put my things away. I had never lived anywhere but at home with my family, so this was very exciting.

Then the door opened and Kim walked in. I had never seen anyone like her before. She was very tall, with a large build, clear blue eyes, and curly, curly hair the color of lemon ice. She smiled in a genuinely friendly way and introduced herself.

In the whole world of people I have met, I have never again met anyone like Kim. She has to be the most unique person with qualities one rarely finds lumped all together in one individual. Kim had come to Post from New Jersey, and brought her horse with her. Her first passion was horseback riding, and there was no way she was going to go off somewhere and leave Impy back home. C.W. Post College was built on what once was a wealthy family's estate, so it was all fitted up with stables, pastures, and corrals. Kim was a very serious equestrienne and in fact, did not want to go to college, but rather, had hoped to train for the Olympics. Her mother would have none of that, so they struck a compromise – Kim would go to school if Impy came with her.

For the first hour, we sat on our beds and talked. I thought Kim was just tops and knew I was very lucky. But although she might have liked me, too, she really didn't want to be there, and told me so. She had made a deal with herself.

"I'll give it until Thanksgiving," she said, "and if I am not happy, I'm leaving." *Thanksgiving*, I thought. *That'll be here before we know it*. It was quite disappointing to me. I had been looking forward to college and had no thought of leaving, especially not the first day.

As we unpacked our bags and filled the drawers and closets, I noticed that Kim and I both owned very little. An interesting coincidence. We both traveled very light, had few clothes, no boyfriends (not by choice), a love of art, literature, and music, and no interest in drugs. At the time that I started college, drugs were already a mainstream activity for students. None of this held the remotest interest for me. I never nodded in the direction of either drugs or alcohol, and looked in bewilderment at the young people who did. I was so in love with what I was studying that I had a kind of immunity to what was going on around me. Now, as a grown-up, when I speak to other people my age, I learn that most of them did experiment with marijuana or something stronger. I don't know what price they paid for this, if they now regret the hours lost in the oblivion of a drug-induced stupor or the money they threw out on drinking. I still feel this way: there will never be enough time in one life to draw all the pictures I want to draw, write all the stories I have in my head, learn all the languages, and see all the places I want to see. How would there ever be time to waste with something as self-destructive as drugs or drinking?

But Kim and I were also very different, which amazingly, did not create one bit of conflict. She was a nature girl who loved the great outdoors, horses, and dogs. She drove a car, and thought nothing of driving home to New Jersey every weekend. She'd skedaddle out of there on Friday afternoon, jump into her tiny green convertible and whiz away from Long Island as fast as she could.

I was more of an indoor girl. Kim had admiration for everything that interested me, knew quite a bit about all the arts, and had been to Europe. She treated me with great respect and I had nothing but awe for her.

But what was more significant was meeting her family. The

Eckerson family had come to North America in the 1600s and had settled on land in what is now New Jersey. Kim's family lived on the original land that the Eckersons had purchased when they came to the New World from the Netherlands and Germany. Although they lived in a modern house that Kim's father built, the property was full of history.

In back of the house was a family cemetery with graves going back centuries, and at the foot of the hill was a diminutive white house in which Kim's great-grandmother had lived. Down the street was a tiny, white Dutch Reform Church built by Kim's great-grandfather that had served the whole town for several generations.

The Eckersons had stories and stories about their ancestors, sweet stories that would make wonderful children's books. I remember hearing about how, more than one hundred years ago, Kim's grandmother, then a young and beautiful girl, was sitting on her front porch when a fellow went by in a horse and buggy. As the story was told in the family, he saw the beautiful girl, pulled on the reins to stop the horse, and said to himself, *That's the girl I am going to marry.* And he did.

I loved hearing these tales and seeing the family photos. Where I had grown up in Queens, there was no one who had come here before the United States was an independent country! This was like meeting people from books. But it was not only the family history that was so engaging, it was the Eckersons themselves. They were a clan of amazing people, doing, going, and being everything that they wanted. Kim had a little sister who was an accomplished ballerina, and a brother who would later go on to be a professional football player. It was inspiring to meet people who knew exactly what they wanted and had the confidence to go after it. After college, as we grew up, Kim would continue to make more deliberate choices and mold her life as she pleased, becoming a horse doctor with her own farm and clinic in North Carolina. But the road was not easy for her – she had to make the same twists and turns the rest of us make to get where she is now.

Not only did the Eckersons have a simply beautiful home with all their heirlooms in it – the Oriental rugs, baby grand piano, antique glass and porcelain, art objects from their travels – but they had a real log cabin on a lake in New Jersey. Kim took me with her one autumn weekend and we spent two cool, crisp days up at the lake. How I remember the smell in the air of log fires, disintegrating leaves, and scent of the forest. We spent the weekend talking and reading books, walking her dog in the woods, and rowing a boat on the lake. Kim's mother had added her touch to everything in the house, making it a warm and inviting, with quilts, rugs, and soft cushions.

I was so impressed with this family, their values, and lifestyle that I had to share it with my parents. One weekend I had them drive out to meet the Eckersons and asked Kim's father, Wilbur to show my parents the property. As we walked through the woods and cemetery, I knew just what Dad was feeling – he had finally met a modern-day person who was just like Thoreau or Emerson. For him, the Eckersons became the icon of "real" Americans, the kind he fancied himself to be. In the future, my father would hold Kim up as the epitome of American womanhood, for she stood tall and straight and knew just where she was going.

My father was later to be disillusioned when Kim fell off her pedestal – and why shouldn't she? We all need to. She fell in love at age twenty and ran off with an exciting, mysterious man, leaving her horse behind! This was the most mystifying part for everyone who thought that the horse came first. But Kim was a young woman like anyone else and had to experience life the same way we all do, doing some things "right" and some things because you have to, even if your parents don't think it's right. By the way, she and her mysterious man have been happily married for more than thirty-five years.

But I will jump back to the two young girls in the dorm room, who were looking toward the future. Kim did keep her word. After Thanksgiving she was still unhappy, and although she liked me and I liked her, she just was not cut out for dormitory life. After the first semester, she went to live nearby with an aunt and uncle. I would occasionally run into her on campus, but she was a commuter now, and the whole experience is different for them. Students who live on campus have a bond that comes from eating meals together in the cafeteria, walking to and from class, and socializing in the dorm at night. Kim did not want to be part of this and so she made her choice. But we stayed friends.

She left Post altogether at the end of the first year and went to a school closer to home. Bored and frustrated with life in New Jersey and longing to do and be more, she found her way out of the family circle and left to join her boyfriend in Florida. I carried on with college, and despite our paths being totally different, we always stayed in touch. Kim was a champion letter writer and kept me apprised of the ever-changing events of her life. She always lived with courage and made independent choices.

Some years later, Kim's mother died. Wilbur fared quite well, being a strong and cultivated person. For many years he lived in that house and carried on with activities, including building a log cabin with his son-in-law on Kim's horse farm in North Carolina. Many years afterward, when Kim and her siblings were all married and living far from New Jersey, old age got the better of Wilbur. In true Eckerson style, Kim and her husband brought him to live in that log cabin that had been built years before. And there Wilbur ended his days, close to the land, close to his daughter.

The Eckerson children were then faced with the task of sorting through their family home and getting it ready for sale. This would be the end of the Eckerson family on that property, a phenomenon that had been intact for hundreds of years. Kim called me to say she would be coming up from North Carolina to sift through generations of property and asked if we could get together. Thinking that this task was going to leave her in a puddle of tears and grief, I offered to help.

Was *that* a surprise! As Kim, her sister, and I went through the boxes, bags, and drawers full of incredibly beautiful "things" stored in the basement (not to mention the magnificent items on the ground floor) the girls were laughing and joking, remembering the stories attached to each item – the year Mom wore *that*, their Girl Scout memorabilia, which they did NOT want, the dishes and glasses and tablecloths that they could never use. I could not believe these girls did not want any of this gorgeous stuff! No, they didn't need it. They had their own homes and their own stuff, and if I wanted it, well, I could take it. I also don't want stuff, but I wanted the Eckersonian quality of their lives. I wanted to have and remember what they had been to me, what *knowing* them had done for me. If a small porcelain object from that house could remind me of those times, I wanted it. The Eckersons. They left a creative and courageous spirit in me that I am still cultivating.

* * *

When I finished my first year of college, my father booked a two-week trip for us to Europe. He knew that I had always wanted to see Europe, the world that I did not live in, the time that I did not live in. I had longed for this distant dream and had no idea how I would ever get to it. I could not have foreseen that I was going to go to Europe many, many times.

It had started with seeing the haunting illustrations in those two books of fairytales by Andersen and Grimm. Since these authors were Northern Europeans, the world of their tales was that of Denmark, Germany, and the many mountainous, wooded regions around those countries, the Europe of castles, cobbled streets, and church steeples. This was the Europe I wanted to see.

For this first trip, Dad chose a sort of introductory tour that included a few days each in London, Amsterdam, Geneva, and Paris. I cherish the memory of having gone with my parents. They were so innocent and wide-eyed, as most Americans are the first time they go abroad. My father really had little interest in Europe – it would have been more interesting for him to go to Wyoming or Montana, but for the two weeks that we traveled, he adopted an optimistic "Let's see what all the fuss is about" attitude and was open to enjoying himself.

In each city, Dad suggested we take a day to explore on our own, since each of us had such individual desires. At around 6:00 p.m., we would all reconvene at the hotel and compare what we had seen. I wanted to walk around and draw pictures; and Mom wanted to shop. Like a true American tourist, Dad would take all the pre-planned excursions, sitting in a double-decker bus and learning the layout of the city, acquainting himself with the famous landmarks. So when we came back to our hotel in the evening, our experiences were completely different. In a way, we were like three friends traveling together.

I commend my father on getting into the swing of things no matter where we went. He ate whatever the locals were eating, did not worry that he did not speak any of the languages, and did not question any of the cultural adjustments he was forced to make.

There was a day when we took a long, long train ride through England to see my mother's pen pal, with whom Mom had been corresponding for years. The trains back then had a sort of trolley that came around with some rather unappetizing offerings. A uniformed steward would come through the cars ringing a little bell to announce that the tea trolley was approaching, and the passengers would choose from the assortment. I remember not wanting *anything* from that trolley, it all looked so dreadful. But my father ventured out and bought a packaged "pork pie" which looked so terrible – a pasty, greasy piecrust filled with some overcooked meat. He opened the cellophane, bit into it and chewed for a moment, and then gave an approving nod and said, "Not bad." It sure looked bad to me.

I had my own lens through which everything was filtered. This was the lens of the artist, always looking for potential illustration material – children, castles, cottages, small winding streets, fields of flowers, and farm animals. Everything I saw became a possible picture in a book that I would someday illustrate. And indeed, that is exactly what happened. The children, windows, chimneys, and country lanes that are on the pages of my books all come out of the images I collected on this and other trips. They started as small pencil sketches made while standing in the street, then became more formal drawings, and ultimately evolved into colored pictures destined for the eyes of young readers.

Apart from my sketchbook, I had a small camera for recording images of children playing in the park, or cats sitting in lace-curtained windows. And some of the images had to be written – written in the form of diary entries, letters or postcards. I did not know then, as I traveled through Europe with my parents, that I would return again and again to amass more of these ideas and pictures; I did not know *how* or *when* I would actually use them. I just kept collecting.

We enjoyed all of the cities on the tour, some on our own and some of the time together. My mother and I were particularly enchanted by the old hotel in Paris, in which we had rooms whose windows faced a courtyard and looked out at each other. For a few days it was as though we were neighbors in Paris. And in Geneva, my parents watched as I fell in love, the way a nineteen-year-old girl falls in love, with a wholesome, young Swiss soldier who strolled past me in a park.

And so, with these experiences and memories, we headed home. On the plane, my father, greatly satisfied that he had fulfilled his promise to me, smiled and said in a contented way, “Well, I’ve seen Europe,” which makes me chuckle to this day because in my forty-two trips to Europe, I still feel I have hardly made a dent. But it did not take that much to satisfy my father. He had seen enough and was happy. He did not need to go back. Later, he and my mother would travel out West to see what he had really wanted to see – the vast expanses of America, the big sky country, and the Native Americans on their reservations. No, he had only done this for me. He was happy and so was I.

* * *

After my first year of college, my brother Joe surprised us all by announcing that he was going to graduate school in California. I just did not know what to do with my feelings about this, since Joe and I were so close. Even though I had gone away to school, I was not really more than forty minutes from home, so it wasn’t a *real* move. But now, after graduating with honors in physics from the prestigious Cooper Union, Joe was going to live on the west coast, totally unexplored territory.

I wondered where I had been while Joe had been making this plan. Sometimes in a large family, people have to create their own private “space” because most of the time one’s space is shared with so many other people. I guess Joe had been thinking about graduate school for a long time and had finally made his choice. It was early one morning at the end of summer that he came into my room to say goodbye. I was still in bed and I sat up. He gave me a hug and kiss, and that was it. He was off to his new life.

But although Joe was euphoric, my father suffered quite a shock and went into a deep depression. He used to sit in the backyard on a lawn chair and just think. He did not read or talk. He just sat there quietly and felt the emptiness. In time, though, he came out of his slump. It would not be the last.

Joe and I used to write letters to each other. We were good letter writers, always enclosing clippings and pictures. Every once in awhile we would call on the phone, which was a rather extravagant thing to do then, since long distance phone service used to be very expensive. I can still remember the preciousness of every minute and how we sometimes waited until Sunday after 9:00 p.m., when the rates went down.

As the years went by, Joe would come home (we always called it *home*) to visit regularly. We used to make the most of the time together by running all around New York, seeing friends, going to our favorite places, to the movies, out to eat, and talking, talking, talking. I hoped that would never change. It did, though, years later when our mother died and the house was sold, leaving an emptiness that cannot be filled.

* * *

After two years at C.W. Post, where I learned Italian and German and added to my knowledge of French and Spanish, I achieved straight **A**s. Now I would be able to transfer to the school I had really wanted to go to, McGill University. In the summer between the two colleges, though, I went to school in Paris. This was the fulfillment of another long-term dream, to be in a French-speaking environment, to be *living* in Europe rather than just visiting.

As a college student studying the works of my favorite French author, Colette, I learned that Gigi, the character whom I had loved so much, was a creation of this very author's youthful memories. I had no idea all those years ago that this story was actually the work of a writer I so admired.

Much of my desire to go to school in Paris came from *Gigi*, and to this end, I arrived in Paris, twenty years old, wearing a large hat with ribbons down the back. Deeply in love with a notion of Paris and the French language, I found everything just as I had imagined. I filled my letters home with pictures of buildings, windows, doorways, children, and shop windows. I kept a diary of what I was seeing, not knowing if I would ever return.

One weekend I took a train out to the coastal town of Deauville. As I stepped out of the station, I was filled with delight at the beauty of the large wooden hotels, one hundred years old or more, the boardwalk with its multicolored umbrellas, tables, and chairs, the ornate and stately houses, their gardens of pink hydrangeas that poked out their heads from behind tiny white wooden fences.

I found a small hotel and put my things away. Then I rented a bicycle so that I could see all of Deauville. I did not care that it was raining – I just rode and rode, stopping to sketch, to take notes. This would be one of many times I would travel alone. There would be many letters and journal entries, and there would also be return trips to many places.

No one could ever have warned me about how homesick I would be that summer. In my mind was the constant presence of family life back home. Sundays were particularly hard, for Paris is so quiet then. People go to church and then are at home with their families. Walking through the streets on a Parisian afternoon and hearing the tinkling of silverware in other people's dining rooms brought on a tide of wistfulness. Maybe I was just too young to be so far from home.

One of the objectives of this stay in Paris was to be near my boyfriend, Paul, who lived in Switzerland. Like a lot of youthful experiences, this did not go exactly as planned. Paul and I had met in Geneva the year before, when I was with my parents. We had corresponded for the whole year and made a plan to see each other again. I guess I had been imagining spending time with him the way I did when we met – walking along a lakefront on a summer evening, speaking German, drinking lemonade, and talking. This was quite different. First of all, I was not staying in a luxury hotel in Geneva, but in a downtrodden student dorm in the south of Paris. My room was very small, quite Spartan and devoid of charm. But that was OK, because Paul never got to see it. He stayed in a hotel in the north of Paris.

By the time I got to France, Paul and I had not seen each other for a long time. One would have to imagine a world with no email and no cheap telephone rates – a world in which the next best thing to a real visit was a letter. The suspense, tension, and excitement of seeing someone after a long time was much greater than it is today. Add to that the thrill of being twenty years old and in love for the first time, and you may imagine my anticipation.

We spent a rainy, very innocent weekend seeing Paris together. It was cold and gray most of the time, but those are the best conditions in which to see Paris. Then Paul went back to his hometown, Basel, Switzerland. The next time I saw him was a month later, when we met up in a tiny Swiss lakefront town. We were in a supremely picturesque spot, but despite the beauty of the setting, something about that weekend was tinged with sadness. It foreshadowed the end of a relationship that would not work, not because we did not love each other, but because neither one of us was going to leave our home countries and live somewhere else.

I did see Paul one more time, at his family's home in Basel. But then he had to leave to go to the army. I left and went to Rome. As my train pulled out of Basel and crossed through the green countryside, I looked out the window and saw a small horse jumping in a poppy field. And I thought to myself, *I am going to be all right*.

I returned to the States and sure enough, a month later, a letter arrived from Paul, explaining that because we were from two different cultures, our lives were headed in different directions. Anyway, we were way too young to be thinking so seriously. But true to my romantic nature, I took it very badly and left in September for McGill University with a thoroughly broken heart.

* * *

I had not thought about where I was going to live before I got to Montreal. I assumed there would be a room for me in the dormitory, as there had been at Post. So when my parents and I drove up to Canada and arrived at the school, we were a bit surprised to learn that nothing was available. Of course, this was typical of the way we did things in my family – a kind of a seat-of-the-pants, "It'll all work out" attitude was the usual style.

At the school housing office we were told that although the dorms were full, many of the local residents in the little Victorian row houses had rooms for students. They recommended one house in particular, that of a Mr. and Mrs. Hibbert at 3483 Hutchison Street, just three blocks away.

We walked over and did not find either of the Hibberts at home, and were told to come back in a few hours. I was so impatient that I did not want to wait and urged my father to just help me find *anything*. He was reluctant to do that because he had a "feeling" about the Hibberts. But we did go to a few other houses in the neighborhood while we waited for them to return.

Each room we looked at was dismal – that is the only word. The houses themselves were old, dating from 1840, and we could see that they once been charming. They had graceful outdoor stairways, balconies, large windows, and shingled roofs. But in the 1970s, they all needed a good dose of love. Inside, the wallpaper was faded and stained, the hallways dark and narrow. The rooms were sparsely furnished, usually with just a bed and a chest of drawers. Worse than the rooms were the landladies, who were utterly joyless. The whole thing was so depressing, but I was so hasty that I was willing to take one of these places, and were it not for my father, that is where I would have ended up.

Fortunately, Dad insisted that we hold off deciding until we saw the Hibberts, so we went to find a place to eat and wait out the time. My mother was quite silent during the entire episode. Over lunch my father asked her what the problem was, but she could not articulate it. It was just one more big mystery about my mother that would be unraveled later.

My mom had lived some brief part of her life in Montreal. Her dreary childhood was all coming back to her as we walked around the city, bringing back only bad feelings. I think her memories were all mixed up as she recalled those days of being shunted around, after the death of Aunt Theresa, from one relative to the next, maybe living in – horror of horrors – *a furnished room*. It's too bad she could not tell us about it because it put such a pall over the day, not just for her, but for my father and me. How different things would have been if she could have located the memory and talked about it with us, maybe even cried about it. Certainly, we might have helped.

Fortunately, my father was in a buoyant state of mind and stayed on course. In time, we did go back to 3483 Hutchison Street, and it's a wonderful thing that we did, because no one would ever have known, judging from the grey exterior of this house, what waited inside.

When Juana Hibbert opened the door, a whoosh of tropically scented air greeted us. We introduced ourselves and she led us through the house, showing us the choice of rooms. The Hibberts were from South Africa and had made their Montreal home into a clean, bright, and welcoming haven. The walls were white and the rooms were spacious and sunlit. Juana herself was a rather timeless looking woman with gorgeous, prematurely silver hair. When she smiled, the largest, whitest teeth glistened and her grey eyes shone. And to add even more charm, she had a crisp South African accent. We soon learned the source of the tropical scent – all the floors were covered in woven squares of sea grass, a kind of dried yellow hay, which Juana kept watered.

I wanted all the rooms! One was large and open, another was cozy and small with a great view, and still another was at the top of the house looking out on the city. But the ideal room was the one with the balcony. It reminded me of Gigi's room, and I knew it was mine.

The beauty of this house was that the Hibberts lived in it too. Juana's husband, Ambrose, was a delightful man whose charm matched that of his wife. His accent, more Dutch that English (his first language was Afrikaans), was difficult to understand, but that only added to his appeal. We knew it would be a good place to live and took the room.

My parents left for home, happy that I was safely installed in such a nice environment. Over the next few days the other students arrived, and in time, we had a group that felt remarkably like a family with parents. At the start, no one knew anyone, but we soon became quite close and felt very bonded to Juana and Ambrose. We shared meals in the kitchen, exchanged news about our lives "back home," celebrated holidays together, and sometimes went out as a group. Having come from a large family, I loved this. While we were all individuals with our private lives, we were also a small community. We were interested in each other, in the letters that came from home, in what happened to each of us during the day at school. We missed each other when we went home for seasonal breaks and were glad to see one another when we returned.

It felt so much like a family that I used to sometimes bring a classmate "home" from school. My friend Maria lived out in the suburbs ofMontreal, so for her, a trip to school meant taking a train. While she was in town for classes we used to have coffee together or go back to my house to mingle with friends. Maria was three years younger than I, and at that time that seemed like a large gap. But we are still friends today, and the gap has closed. When I left Montreal in 1974, we wrote to each other, and the correspondence and friendship were rich and full. Thirteen years later, Maria came to New York to audition for a part in an opera. When she walked into my New York apartment, I was surprised to see a grown woman instead of a teenager! There she was, quite sophisticated in a long, glamorous coat. We had been students together struggling with schoolwork, boyfriends, and our hair, and now we were both were grown-ups.

In 1972, when I first moved to Montreal, almost all the beauty of the city was being demolished. Each week, some quaint little street would disappear, leaving a pile of grey rubble. And by the next week, some modern, sterile structure would appear. I took it all very personally and could not find a way for it to not hurt me. But there were two streets in Montreal that somehow escaped the wrecker's ball – Mountain Street and Crescent Street. They sloped down from the main road, Sherbrooke Street, and managed to remain intact with their original architecture, antique shops and cafés. My mother had stumbled upon these two well-preserved streets, which were around the corner from the hotel. She made me aware of both of them, knowing how I loved everything old. That neighborhood would come to have special meaning for me.

A bit into the fall semester, I felt a certain emptiness in my college experience. The classes were somewhat dry, and much more difficult than those at Post. I realized that college was not enough for me and I needed to go to ballet school as well. After looking in the phone book, I found a listing for a school with a Mountain Street address, which I found rather inviting.

The school was in one of the small prewar buildings, on the third floor, up a narrow, lengthy staircase. On the door was a sign: *Charlotte Susta School of Ballet.* I rang the bell and Madame Susta answered the door with a somewhat frosty but not unfriendly smile. She asked me in.

In her tiny little apartment, this remarkable woman had created her own school. The living room had been sacrificed to make a studio, and Susta confined herself to living in a front parlor and a back kitchen. The space that would have been her living room was fitted up with wooden floors, mirrors, and ballet *barres*. On a small table there was an old-fashioned record player and a stack of very old records for our musical accompaniment.

Madame must have been about sixty-eight years old when I met her, but still retained a self-image from her younger days when she had been a great beauty and a famous dancer in Europe. She was slim and blonde and spoke with a thick German accent. Like a lot of ballet teachers, she did not mince words and told you exactly what she thought – "You're too fat," or "You come down from a jump like an elephant," (which she pronounced **AY**-LAY-FONT). "You have too little energy for a girl your age," she would tell me with disdain.

When I started taking classes, Madame immediately noticed that my adolescent heart had been broken by a failed romance. When I asked her how she could possibly know this, she said she could see by how high I kicked during the *barre* exercises. Susta could read all the students' emotions through the ballet movements.

She was also very vain, proud of her good figure and her once-beautiful face. She enjoyed the company of glamorous people, too. She took me to a party with her and I was amazed to see her "doing" the room, flitting about flirtatiously with her champagne glass and cigarette in its foot-long holder, saying things like, "Yoo hoo! Hans Martin! Haven't seen you in *hundert* years!"

At first I used to go to ballet school twice a week, but after a while I decided that was not enough and signed on for lessons every day. I bought myself a white bicycle for getting back and forth. I used to carry that bike up and down two flights of steep stairs every time I used it. This is amazing to me when I think about it. I cannot imagine how, with daily lessons at Susta's studio, I had time to do my homework or concentrate on my classes. I loved what I was studying (French, Spanish, Italian, and German) and I was doing well, but this alone would not have satisfied me. I also loved the world of dance, this tiny little world in this ballet school.

After some time, Susta confided in me that she had, as she put it, "No more patience for *ze little shildren*," and asked if I would like to teach them. In exchange for my services, I could have my own lessons for free. Most of the children were French-speaking, so this was a great deal: I loved children, French, and ballet, and in this I had the combination. This role of dance teacher would be revisited later in life.

The community of the school was intimate. It was not a serious ballet studio, but a place in which one could take lessons and just enjoy the practice. We were a somewhat odd group of women. There was a very talented young German girl named Ilona, who had only started to study ballet at age seventeen, which is *very* late, but she had made rapid progress. Ilona was a true snob with a snooty German accent and personality. Madame Susta had such faith in Ilona that she gave her a letter of introduction to a ballet school in Paris, where she had some connections. And so Ilona left for Paris, saying a theatrical goodbye to the rest of us, whom she fancied she was leaving behind. She was off for better things, for a career in ballet in Europe. The only problem was that a few months later, Ilona came back to Montreal, quite humbled, for she had frittered away her opportunity in Paris, squandering all her money and energy, staying out late, not showing up to class. She was soon back at the *barre* in Madame's little studio.

Then there was Hildegarde, a vibrant, attractive flight attendant for Swissair. She was leading a very glamorous life, flying back and forth to Europe in the 1970s, a time when flying was still glamorous, both for the passenger and the crew. Hildegarde had beautiful dark hair and fabulous clothes, but very little talent as a dancer. She would breeze into school on a frigid night in a white fur coat lined in ivory satin, throw off her clothes and change into her leotard. Her mass of thick, black hair was impossible to tame into a bun, so she'd just tie it back. She was clearly just dropping in.

There was also an ice-blonde German beauty named Evelyn, who was really more of an athlete than a ballerina. Susta used to call her "sportster," which is pronounced *shportster* in German, making it even more masculine. There was nothing about her that was balletic, but she had a kind nature.

And what of small Maria, a teenager of some Middle Eastern extraction – perhaps Egyptian – who had a most flexible back and beautiful, dainty feet? She was like a little butterfly, darting across the room. And Lina, poor Lina, who was not suited at all for ballet, and whom Madame really persecuted, saying things like, "Lina, stretch!! Zat's right! Over ze cutlets!!" referring to Lina's chubby midriff.

And then there was me, whom Susta also persecuted. She was always telling me I was too fat, too tired, too serious for a young girl. She thought I should be enjoying life, living with fearlessness, making the most of my youth and not pining for some lost boyfriend in Switzerland. Of course she was right, but we don't listen to adults when we are that age.

I don't know what I would have done without Susta during my two years in Montreal. Although she was not motherly, I felt close to her. She was my connection to a world that I loved, to a prewar Europe in which I had never lived, to the German language that I was trying to learn. I loved her, and when I graduated from McGill and went back to New York, I wrote to her. Eventually, Madame Susta closed her little school and moved far away to Vancouver on the west coast of Canada. One day I stopped hearing from her, so I can only assume that that is where her life ended.

Many years later I was back in Montreal and went to Mountain Street to see what had become of the dancing school. I walked up the three flights of stairs and stood right in front of the door that I had entered so many times as a college student. There was not a trace of Susta anywhere, except in my memory.

* * *

By the time I went to college, I still did not know how to cook. Unlike my sister-in-law Bobbie, I had not stood at the stove and asked my mother about her recipes and methods. I only began to get interested in cooking when I went to Canada. In Montreal, the Henri Bernard Cooking School offered a ten-week course in basic cooking techniques. It was all in French and was done theatre-style. Women sat in terraced rows and watched Mr. Bernard prepare various dishes. These were visible via a mirror that was hung on the oblique over his head. If you looked into the mirror, you could see right into the bowl or right onto the chopping board. You could see him frosting the cake or whipping the cream.

In the space of an hour and a half, Mr. Bernard prepared a four-course meal consisting of a salad, a main dish, a side dish, and a dessert. At the end of the preparation, each student received a small plate with a tiny sampling of each of the elements of the meal. It was absolutely ingenious. We did not have to do any work, and just by watching, we learned to cook.

I felt very accomplished after completing the course. I knew how to chop and slice correctly, how to mix a perfect salad dressing, and how to make a good sauce for meat. I had learned how to make a soup from scratch and how to create puff pastry.

When I graduated from college and returned home to New York, I announced gleefully that I was going to do all the cooking. My father was a good sport about it, tasting a bit of this and a bit of that, but in the end, he really wanted nothing to do with this food. He just wanted scrambled eggs. It would be a few years before I would have the chance to cook to my heart's content. I would have my real "customers" later on — my first husband and his three children, who were *always* hungry.

* * *

When I think back on my McGill days, I always remember that they were tinged with loneliness. From my little balcony I used to sit and look over the rooftops of Montreal, write letters, and draw. My sister and I used to write to each other every day. I looked forward to her letters on pink paper. The mail was delivered twice a day (heaven!) and I used to stand at the top of the steep stairway and look down, always hoping to see a pink envelope come through the slot. If it hadn't come in the morning, it surely came in the afternoon.

Eleanore and I used to write about everything that was happening in my life of college, ballet, and friends, and she in her life as a young wife and mother. Getting her letters helped me get through the tremendous sense of homesickness that I had the entire two years in Montreal. Although I loved my Canadian "family" and the other friends in my circle – my ballet teacher, my classmates – I always had a space inside me that was filled with longing for my own family, especially for my parents. And so this daily letter writing helped.

I learned later that my sister saved all my letters, not only from my Montreal days, but from all the trips I took, all the places I had ever been. In the letters were not just words, but also drawings around the margin of whatever was in front of me – a lively street, an interesting looking person. My sister put them in a book, and some years later, when I reread them, I saw a girl who was in love with life, but always tied to home.

I used to go back to New York frequently – too frequently, I think. But my father had plenty of money in those years and it was nothing for him to buy me a ticket to fly back home for a weekend. Traveling was so much less complicated then. In New York, I would eat Sunday dinner with my family and then Dad would drive me to Kennedy Airport. We would walk up to the Air Canada counter and purchase a ticket as if we were buying a loaf of bread. Dad could actually get *on the plane* with me until it was time for takeoff. Can you imagine such a thing in this world of multiple security checks?

After I came back to New York for good, I heard that the city of Montreal underwent gigantic changes. The city was pulling down all the row houses that had so characterized Montreal, and it made me sad. But when I went back many years later and looked for my house, there it was, unchanged. Somehow it had survived the rapid and sweeping renovation of the city. I looked up and saw the tiny balcony from which I had generated so much writing. I wondered who was using it now.

* * *

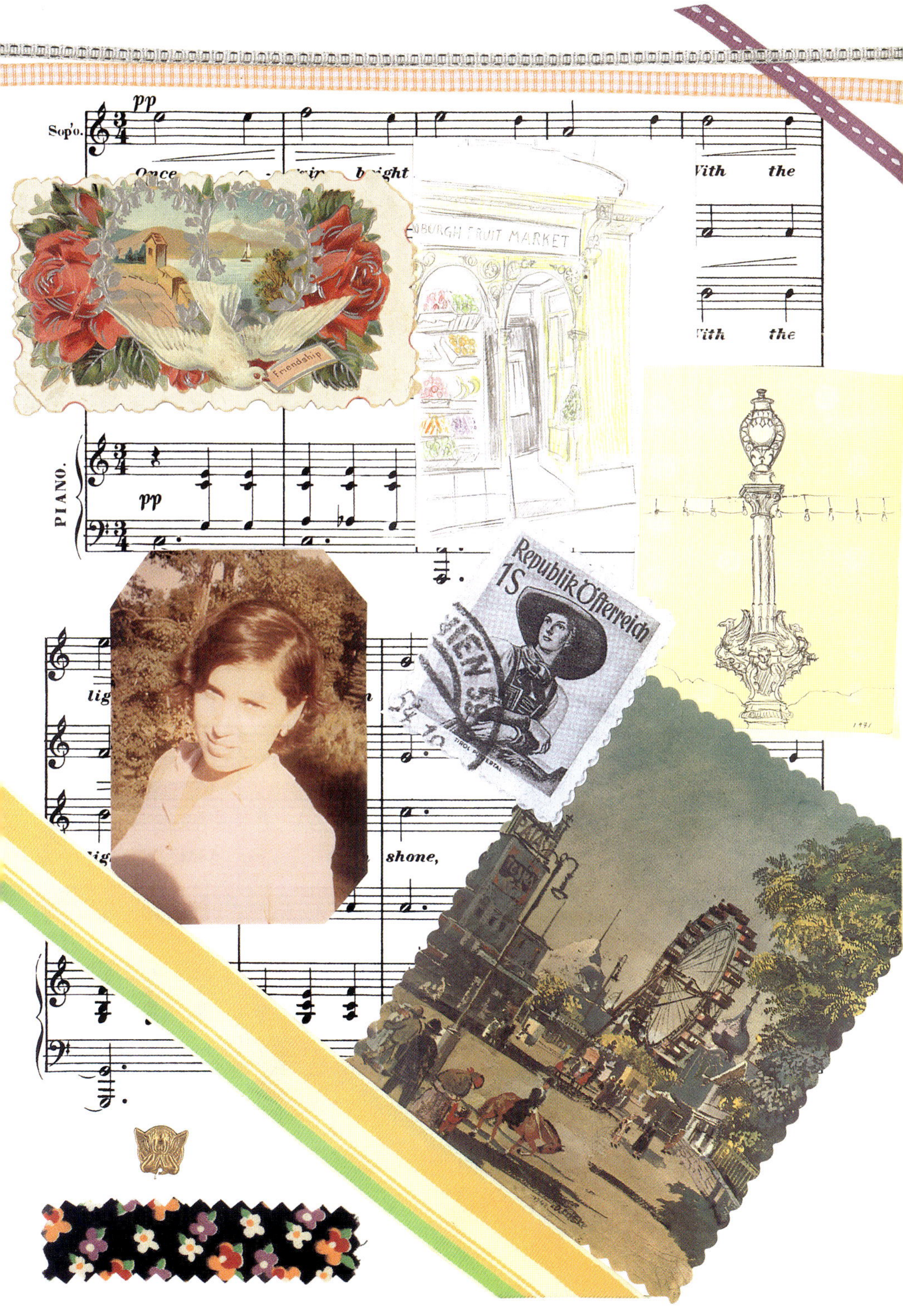
pp
Sop'o.
Once
bright
With the
PIANO.
pp
shone,
BURGH FRUIT MARKET
Friendship
Republik Österreich
1S

Part Five: Young Womanhood

After graduation, Eleanore and Larry came up to Montreal, ready to take me back to New York. I was a little surprised by this, for I had been expecting my father. But we had fun packing the car and bidding farewell to everyone and the city. I left the white bicycle with Juana.

When I got home I found my father in a depression. He was making a habit of sitting in the backyard, just staring into space, as he had done when Joe first moved away. He did not have the usual vigor for planting flowers and puttering around the garden. He didn't read or sing, and he wasn't talking too much either. And while he was glad to see me again, his enthusiasm soon waned and he retreated to a kind of dim world.

"What's the matter with Dad?" I asked my mother.

"He lost all his money," she said. "He lost about $40,000 in the stock market, so he's depressed. That's why he couldn't come up to Montreal and get you." *He had $40,000?* I thought. *Who knew?* "He's been like this for a while," Mom continued.

"How did he lose it?"

"He trusted someone with it; they invested it and lost it, and now he has nothing."

Funny that she was telling me this dreadful news and was not at all upset. It was as if she were saying, "Well, he fell off his bicycle and scraped his knee. He'll get over it."

"Mom, are you worried?" I asked.

"I never worry about money," she said. "There are fat years and lean years. You can always make money if you need to."

But my father didn't get over it. He went into a funk and could not come out. He had always been prone to melancholia, but this put him over the edge. My mother made various attempts to breathe energy into their lives. She started collecting antique dolls, took up quilting, and suggested they visit venues of historic interest in hopes of Dad finding a new focus. All of this had little effect on him but it brought *her* great joy. She made a new circle of friends and became a master quilter, producing praiseworthy works of art over the next twenty years.

No, the answer for Dad was to go back to work, which he did, and it proved to be a miracle. At first he took a small, local job, night supervisor at the St. John's University Library, for he had always loved libraries. But then he found that he didn't want to leave Mom home alone at night, so he got a day job. This was a great, adventurous job delivering cars to people who had purchased them in New York but lived outside of the city – sometimes out of the state.

This opened up a new world for Dad. Just as Mom's new-found activities had expanded her world, the driving job did the same for Dad. The money was minimal, but the freedom was terrific. He loved getting up every day and not knowing where he was going to deliver a car. Even better, once he'd delivered the car, he had to figure out how he was going to get home. He, who had spent forty years working in the same place, now welcomed something much less structured.

Dad would report to work in Manhattan and then find out where he had to drive that day. Sometimes he'd call Mom and say, "Mannie! I have to drive to Washington today! You wanna come?" And she'd frequently call one of us to say that she and Dad were "taking a jaunt." This arrangement appealed to both of their spontaneous natures and in a way, brought them closer.

I was happy for my parents, but I still had to figure out what was going to happen with *my* life. I had graduated from school and was trained for nothing. At a time when other parents were advising their children to go into professions that made sense or held out the promise of security, my parents had always told us to do what we *wanted*, what would make us happy. Their blessing on this kind of choice didn't make it any easier for us, but it certainly allowed our individual talents and passions to emerge.

It wouldn't have been such a bad thing to have gotten some advice about a career, but both of my parents had arrived at the same philosophy from two opposing and then converging paths. My father used to say, "I am not going to tell you what to do because my father made me go into the family business." My mother used to say, "I am not going to tell you what to do because my mother let me do what I wanted." As a result, they both reached the same conclusion. I am not sorry that they did. I rather like the idea that each of us found our paths on our own. There were no family connections, no friends in high places, no wise recommendations. We had to figure it out for ourselves.

It was the same way with God, since my parents came from two different religious backgrounds. Dad was Jewish, but for him it was only an ethnicity. We considered ourselves Jewish, perhaps because we lived in a predominantly Jewish neighborhood. But when it came to religion, all we had was God. And God could be whatever you wanted. Somehow, as with our careers, each of us found our own way to God. We found our spiritual directions with no help, prodding, education, or convincing from our parents.

My mother was a "closet Catholic," who communed with her God quietly and privately. She'd light a few candles and say some prayers. A small prayer book called *My Daily Life* and several strands of rosary beads were in the drawer of her night table. But not one of us had any idea what you did with rosary beads or what secrets were in that little book.

Mom did reveal to me when I was older that she had had me baptized, "just in case." She had wanted to raise the children Jewish, but my father's mother would have none of it, saying that it's hard to be a Jew. My father would have none of it because it was, as he said, "all nonsense." So I guess when child number five came along, Mom thought that at least one of us should be christened.

She took me, a tiny baby, to a church in a neighborhood where she had once lived. But she was unprepared, as she had no witness, and the priest turned her away. As she exited the church holding me in her arms, she dropped the baby bottle. Struggling to pick up the broken glass and hold a baby at the same time, she did not notice the handsome young man who sprang to her side from his sports car.

"Lady, let me help you!" the youth offered. It was her brother Primo, the thirteenth child of the family, who had only seen a pretty young woman – not his sister – in distress.

Primo spent most of his life in and out of prison for small crimes. My mother would exonerate him by always saying, "He's not a *thief*, he's a *crook*." Primo, the unpopular and unwanted brother who never found his way in life, was usually in the wrong place at the wrong time. But on this day, he was suddenly *exactly* where he needed to be.

"I need a witness for the baptism," my mother cried, grabbing her little brother by the wrist and pulling him into the church. "Wait, wait!" she called to the priest. "Don't go away! I have a godfather for my child!"

* * *

About three months before I graduated from McGill, suddenly it hit me that I had no plan for my professional life. I was so steeped in my own interests that I never really thought about what to *do* with them. It was a bit terrifying to face this question, so I just let it sit there.

When I came home, I didn't wait two minutes before I went out and looked for a job. At that time, if you had a Bachelor's degree, you could probably get hired somewhere. Since my degree was in French, I thought about working for the airlines, and there was an airline agency in Queens that was looking for young, employable people. When I walked into that agency and told the recruiter I was a new graduate with many foreign languages, she instantly told me there was a job opening at Air France. That was about the best thing I could have heard, and it was only a matter of a day or two before I went on the interview and was hired.

For a first job out of college, this was a good one: a reservations agent in a fancy Fifth Avenue building. The salary wasn't bad and I would get to use my languages, especially French. In time, if I could perform well, there would be travel benefits, a prospect that was very attractive, as it was a goal for me to see as much of the world as I could. I went home overjoyed and so excited that I had to walk all around the neighborhood telling everyone that I had just gotten a job at Air France. This was a truly prestigious achievement.

Air France had a one-week training program for the five of us who were hired for the summer season. We were told that at the end of summer, we would either be selected to stay on with the company or be laid off. The compensation for being laid off was a free round-trip airline ticket to anywhere in the world. But I was sure that I was going to succeed, so this didn't seem too important.

In the training program, we learned to use the computer, make reservations, connections, and handle different kinds of requests. A supervisor in the front of the room might listen in on our calls at any time, and would also be there to help if we got stuck.

Of course, the job was NOT AT ALL glamorous, because being behind the scenes at the airlines is just plain hard work. It's only elegant when you are a passenger. The job was nine to five in a large room on the eighth floor of the Air France building, far above the beauty of Fifth Avenue. If I had known how terrifying this job really was, I probably never would have taken it, but I was innocent, as I am sure the airline was aware.

Air France wanted us to understand that our job was to get people to fly to wherever they were going *through Paris*. When an Air France plane leaves the U.S., it MUST go to Paris first, so regardless of where the passenger said he or she *wanted* to go, our job was to sell space on Air France. *Sell, sell, sell*, that's what they told us.

After the one week of training, I got my own desk and they "plugged me in." All agents were literally plugged into the computer and phone line, and you just waited for the next call, the next potential sale. When my first call came in, the passenger said he wanted to know the quickest way to get to London. *Hmm*, I thought, *this is really not the right airline for him.*

"Well, Sir," I said, "you could take one of our daily flights to Paris and catch a connection there to London." I knew this was stupid, but I had to say it. So he did not surprise me when he responded, "Paris?!? I told you I want to get to London!"

I really didn't blame him, and I couldn't help but say, "Right. You ought to call British Airways."

It's a wonder I wasn't fired right then and there. My supervisor came running over and plugged herself into my phone line. "Sir, Sir," she said, "we have some wonderful flights through Paris, and the stopover is *free*."

What difference does that make? I thought. *He said he wanted the quickest way to London.* Unable to salvage the sale, the supervisor must have then decided that Air France had made a mistake when they hired me. And because of this, she was on my back the entire summer, watching me from her desk, monitoring my calls. If there had been any chance of getting the hang of this job, it was gone because I was frozen with fear. And I stayed frozen.

I hated to go to work. My mother felt bad for me. She knew I was suffering and found a way to ease the pain. She created a little routine of coming to Manhattan every day to meet me for lunch. She would stand outside the Air France building on Fifth Avenue, lunches in hand. We would sit in Paley Park, a small green space in midtown Manhattan, eat our lunch, and talk. Then we would walk along Fifth Avenue and look in the windows of the fancy shops, admiring pretty things that were out of our reach. Nearing 1:00, I would go back to my office, my stomach turning.

One day as we strolled along, my mother saw a pair of shoes in the window of Gucci. This is when Gucci was a truly exclusive brand and the people who shopped in the store were wealthy and privileged. The people who worked in the store were snooty and cold, but that was part of the mystique. The shoes Mom spotted were pumpkin-colored suede pumps. They had a delicate gold chain at the throat, and just looked like heaven. Because Dad had just lost a significant amount of money, Mom debated with herself whether she should even try on the shoes.

It took her many visits on the Air France lunch hour to decide about this. Since merchandise used to stay in shop windows for a longer time than it does today, Mom had many chances to stare at these magnificent shoes and imagine herself in them. And one day, she finally went in and tried them on. Some time after that, she bought them. It was such a monumental event in her life. I don't remember her ever wearing those shoes. I think they were so special that she rarely had an occasion to wear them. I don't think it mattered, because she really just wanted to own them.

About thirty years later, long after my mother had given up fancy shoes and could only wear practical ones, I found the Gucci shoebox in her closet.

"The *shoes*!" I said to her. "I remember when you bought these! It was the summer I worked at Air France." They were still so beautiful and so classic. The style did not look at all dated.

Mom was already senile by then and did not know what I was talking about. In fact, she did not know the shoes were hers, or that we were even in her house. In *fact*, she did not know who I was.

"Mom," I said, "can I have these?" She did not understand what I was asking, and didn't respond. She just smiled.

I took the shoes home and was delighted that they fit me. By the look of the soles, Mom had only worn them a few times. They had been more like a museum piece to her. I was glad they would get some use instead of being buried in a closet.

That fall, I tried to wear them. But although they were my size, they really didn't fit. They weren't my shoes. They were hers. I knew I would never wear them, and I did not want them to be hidden away for another thirty years. So I donated them, along with some of my suits and blouses, to a charity that furnishes women with clothes to go on job interviews. I hoped they would bring someone good luck.

When I walk on that part of Fifth Avenue now, I feel so much tenderness, thinking of my mother taking the bus into Manhattan every day so that she could make my day a little better. I walk past the shop windows we used to look in and the benches where we would sit until one minute to one o'clock, when I reluctantly went back to work. I think of how she did not want me to be unhappy, and how she found a way to take some of that unhappiness from me.

At the end of that summer, I did get laid off from my job at Air France. They told me something to which I should have paid more attention: "You're not sales minded." This shortcoming of mine would resurface in other sales jobs where I put the customer's needs before the needs of the company. But I did get my free ticket, and I used it.

All summer long I had been making reservations for people going to places I had always thought about going, like Budapest, Edinburgh, and Copenhagen. I decided I was going to see those places. We were coming into the fall season, a time of opera, ballet, and music. I decided I would get myself to the heart of Europe and see as much as I wanted of these performances. I still had some money left from my inheritance and I was aching to get out of New York, get away from this job, and go abroad where I would find my true love again – the arts. So when the people at Air France said, "Where to?" I answered, "Vienna."

* * *

Like so many travelers before me, I landed in Europe and felt that everything I saw was made just for me. This is selective observation – we look at what we like and what we can relate to and discard the rest. It is an especially useful technique for an artist, for it allows you to see only what you hope to re-create. And of course, I was looking for the old world again, the world I had never lived in but one for which I felt nostalgic.

There isn't too much in this world that is more evocative of a bygone era than Vienna in the autumn. It is so beautifully melancholic, and the Viennese thrive on wallowing in this melancholia. All day long, I walked, drew, and wrote to my sister. The letters were ornamented with tiny drawings of elderly Viennese couples, balconies of prewar buildings, chandeliers with tinkling pieces of crystal. I wanted Eleanore to see what I was seeing and words were not enough.

After a day of walking, exploring, and learning about where I was, I attended the theatre, as I had planned. I saw all the Viennese operettas I wanted, most of which are never performed in the United States. I spoke with people and got to use the German I had studied in college. I visited churches, shops, and town squares. I felt right in the groove of what I had come to accomplish.

After two weeks in Vienna I crossed the border into Germany and spent time there looking at castles and clock towers, Christmas markets, and winding streets. There were ballets to attend and operas in fantastic opera houses and plays in small, intimate theaters. There were good things to eat, too – grainy, seed-filled breads, all manner of cultured milk, yogurt, and cheese, and steaming coffee with cream. One evening when I returned to my small hotel, I caught sight of my face in a mirror. I looked so healthy. I then understood the meaning of the phrase "rosy cheeks," for my face was glowing with the radiance of lots of fresh air and good food. I was probably also beaming from the absolute satisfaction of living life this way, as a traveling artist, writer, and observer.

My next destination was Denmark, and to get there, I took an overnight train in which I had a private room. Adorable. Tiny bed, miniature sink, narrow closet. We rolled out of Germany and into the night. At about midnight, the train stopped in Hamburg. I opened the window shade in my little compartment and saw in the river the reflections of the wrought iron street lamps on the bridge. It was like a dream. Then I went back to sleep.

In the early morning, the train pulled into Denmark and little towns whizzed by the train window. The flat Danish countryside was dotted with large, half-timbered farmhouses, around which cows were grazing. The country gave way to the city and suddenly we were in Copenhagen, with its tall copper spires and twisting, cobbled streets.

It was late November and the city was starting to show signs of Christmas. I was completely happy, homesickness notwithstanding. I visited the home of Hans Christian Andersen and felt the very beginnings of a life for myself that would include working with children and stories.

From Denmark I crossed by ferry to Sweden, and there I had a memorable moment of self-awareness. Germany and Denmark had been cold and dark, which was to be expected with the oncoming winter. But somehow when I stepped off the ferry and set foot in Sweden, the sun came out. I was in a kind of "pocket" of springtime. I walked through a park where the mossy grass was soft under my feet. Birds were chirping madly, like hundreds of bells ringing at once. Nestled in the park was a tiny white church whose door was open. I walked into the dim and hushed stillness and stepped onto a clean, well-worn tiled floor. For no known reason, I lay down on the floor and pressed my check to the cool tiles. *Thank you, God*, I said softly, *for letting me see all this.* I was not the same as when I had arrived.

* * *

From Scandinavia I flew to Scotland, landing in Glasgow, a dark city in a dark time of year. I loved it for its grimy streets and small-scale theatres. I enjoyed the naive and friendly manner of the people I met while meandering the streets on rainy evenings. And in Edinburgh, with its delicate church steeples, pointed roofs, and sloping streets, I sought out the childhood home of Robert Louis Stevenson, who wrote *A Child's Garden of Verses* and *Treasure Island*. It was a small stone house on a curved street with old-fashioned gas lamps.

As a child, I enjoyed Stevenson's poems in *A Child's Garden of Verses* and the visions they conjured up – a Victorian childhood of large, comfortable houses, walled gardens, and parents close by. Consider the last verse of the poem "Picture Books in Winter:"

How am I to sing your praise,
Happy chimney-corner days,
Sitting safe in nursery nooks,
Reading picture storybooks?

Why, this very poem may have planted a seed in me to be a writer of poetry for children.

It is interesting that Stevenson wrote such cheerful poems because he was a sickly child. He was confined to bed for much of his youth, and had spent long hours peering out the window at the little park outside. In that park there was, and still is, a small pond, which Stevenson imagined to be Treasure Island. His young mind invented the story to while away the lonely hours.

He was at once adventuresome and nostalgic. We can feel this in the last stanza of the final poem in the *Garden of Verses* collection,

"To Any Reader:"

He does not hear; he will not look,
Nor yet be lured out of this book.
For, long ago, the truth to say,
He has grown up and gone away,
And it is but a child of air
That lingers in the garden there.

* * *

Of my travels I could not write fast enough. The letters were flying out of Europe every day, and so were the postcards, which my mother preferred, always filled with enthusiasm that never waned. Occasionally I would get a letter from home, sent to the American Express office. My sister wrote to tell me of a man she had met whom she thought I would like. This seemed too far away to me, the idea that she was back in New York thinking about a boyfriend for me. I put the thought in the very back of my mind. But it would resurface sooner than I could have imagined.

Meanwhile, I continued my journey. From Edinburgh I went straight south, through England, stopping at small cities where I could glean inspiration. And then...London, the very heart of the world for me. I have always felt that London in some way is home, even though I am American, and have not one drop of English blood. Soft snow was falling, and there was just enough of it to make a visitor feel they had walked into a Christmas card. I felt caressed by such beauty.

Then suddenly one day, I wanted to go home. I had seen enough for one trip, had collected enough ideas. Although I loved the preseason excitement of London, I wanted to be in New York with my family. It had only been two months since I left, but I felt as though much more time had gone by. I had a new storehouse of creativity; my mind had been expanded, my inner vision enriched. I felt more alive now, and I would bring this creativity home with me. Also, something told me that a change was about to occur, and I had better head back. I made a reservation and flew home on December 11, 1974.

As always, right before Christmas our house was filled with the anticipation of being together. My brother Joe came home from California, the house was full and happy, sweet-smelling with the holiday preparations. The scent of snow would whoosh in the door each time someone came in or went out. I loved this atmosphere; there has never been anything like it since.

When I saw my sister again, she showed me the scrapbook she made from all the letters I sent her. In a sense, she had taken the trip with me. My mother's bulletin board was full of postcards, and my father's face was full of bewilderment. "I had no idea you were going to make such a pilgrimage!" he said. He just could not understand my fascination with traveling. For him, our two-week trip to Europe back in 1971 had been enough. For me, it was just the beginning.

But a new stage of life was about to start. It was January, and I now faced the same situation I had when I graduated from college back in June. Where to work? What to do? I was no closer to knowing this. As a stopgap measure, I took a job at the luxurious Singer Sewing Center in Rockefeller Plaza, a huge fabric store that occupied two floors. I liked being around fabrics and patterns, and enjoyed working with the public. All day I handled creative materials and talked to customers about the clothes they were making, what pattern to choose, what fabric was suitable. The job paid very little but it was right in the heart of Manhattan and the atmosphere was vibrant. It was certainly more interesting than being attached to a telephone all day making airplane reservations. At least I got to talk to real people and work with tangible materials. I knew it would not be forever; it was just a step on the way to finding the right path. My job was a background kind of activity anyway, because early in January, I met that man that my sister had been writing about, and my focus changed.

When I met Robert, I was twenty-two and he was thirty-six. Despite our large age difference, we had some unusual things in common. We each spoke a few languages, loved classical music, and were familiar with life in other countries. These qualities were not easy to find in the men in my age group.

My sister had been right – this was a good match, at least in the beginning. Robert and I were not destined to have the safe and comfortable friendship I have with my current husband, but this marriage was to be an important experience, one that I would not trade or wish it had not happened.

Robert was born in Brazil, the son of Polish Jews. After his first thirteen years in Rio de Janeiro, his parents put him on a boat and sent him to New York to go to Yeshiva for a serious religious Jewish education. He told me how he had arrived in New York on a cold day in January, 1952.

"I had come from Rio de Janeiro," he said, "the most beautiful city in the world, and got off the boat in New York... grey, dreary, and cold New York." Imagine being thirteen years old and coming by yourself to a strange country. He did not speak any English and did not know anyone. And he was delivered into the hands of a strict boarding school in Brooklyn.

Robert's parents did not intend for him to stay in the U.S. He was just supposed to get through high school and go back home. But by the time he graduated, he was so Americanized and had done so well in school that he applied to college and got in. *Why not stay another four years?* he thought. After college there was the world of work, and then the first girl he married. Then after his first child was born, he heard that his mother, whom he loved dearly, had died back in Brazil, and that dissolved the idea of going home at all.

In the ensuing years, three children – Debbie, Barbara, and Jeannie – came along, and Robert didn't make that long-intended trip to Brazil. He and his wife were busy raising the girls, working, and establishing their life on Long Island, and as a result, he never went home.

When I met Robert, he was just getting divorced. He told me that at age thirty-three, shortly before we met, he had decided to make a number of changes in his life: he wanted to switch careers, get married again, and finally go back to Brazil. He had not been back in twenty years, and longed to see the brothers and sisters he had left behind. He had made the first trip back with his oldest girl, Debbie, who was just seven.

During our courtship and subsequent engagement, we talked about making the second trip and taking the second daughter, Barbara, with us. I wanted to meet the extended family and see a place I had never seen before. I can still remember the fragrance in the air when we got off the plane in Rio, that unique perfume that is a mixture of very ripe tropical fruit, diesel fuel, and the sea.

It was December, when the weather in Brazil is hot, hot, hot. The sidewalks are just *burning* hot, but the *Cariocas*, as the natives of Rio are called, think nothing of walking around barefoot! The people, a mixture of blacks, white Europeans, and native Indian peoples, are jolly, carefree, and fun-loving. Some are very rich, some miserably poor, quite religious, and a bit mystical. There is a strong African influence and surviving traces of voodoo, which they call *Macumba*, which can be a bit eerie to the unknowing visitor.

The language of Brazil is Portuguese, and my despite my knowledge of Spanish, French, and Italian, I did not understand one word. We stayed in Brazil for a full month and it was frustrating not to be able to speak. I resolved that when I went back to New York I would take some lessons. I was sure we would be returning to Brazil some day. It's a good thing I made this resolution because hidden in my future was a time when we would be *living* there.

When we got home in the beginning of 1976, we planned our wedding. My father did not want me to marry Robert, not because he did not like him, but because he thought this was a large "package" for a girl my age. A religious man, much older than I, with three children and a new career. I knew I was taking on a lot, but Robert and I loved each other and I had grown very close to the three girls, and also to their mother.

We were married in my parents' backyard. It was a small outdoor affair that felt like a country wedding. My father rented a large yellow tent and white furniture, and placed lots of flowers around the edges of the yard. I made all the food, which seems so unbelievable to me now. There were seven flower girls – my four nieces and my three stepdaughters; Eleanore was my matron of honor, and Larry was the best man. I wore a heavy, lacy, out-of-date dress that I bought for $9 from a shop window. The whole event was very homey and unpretentious, and we were very happy, at least for a while.

Just before we got married, Robert landed a job as the assistant administrator of a hospital in a very livable part of Manhattan near Greenwich Village. We had a beautiful apartment with a picture window overlooking a park, and the hospital was conveniently located right across the street. I could not believe my good fortune. I could not have planned this better! For the next three years, we lived on East 15th Street, walking distance from everything. My three stepdaughters used to visit us on weekends, a time they now refer to as "dream time," because of the wonderful afternoons we spent together. I grew very close to them and forged a bond that would last into the future when times became less rosy.

But I still had not figured out what to do for work! I spent the next few years *trying* to figure it out while working in Macy's in Herald Square. By a series of unplanned encounters, I found myself working as a manager in the very busy and chaotic cosmetics department.

The main floor of Macy's is always a madhouse, but it was *really* a madhouse back in the 1970s. The store was not air conditioned, and on a crowded Saturday in a New York summer the place was incredibly oppressive. I just don't now how we did it, all of the salespeople and managers, standing on our feet all day, waiting on customers. And in winter, especially at Christmas, it was total bedlam.

The store's cosmetics buyer used to put me on cosmetics lines that attracted foreign customers because I could speak so many languages. I marveled at the elegant women who came in from Venezuela, Brazil, or France, who wore lovely clothes and big silk scarves. They just walked up to the counter, pointed to the biggest, most expensive products, and plunked down plenty of money.

Working in Macy's was hard and paid very little, but it was a valuable experience. I developed a sense of style and fashion being around all that clothing, jewelry, and makeup. Although the work was boring and tedious, some of what I know about life could only have come from those years. Once you work in a department store, you realize how hard some people work and for how little money.

As I was enjoying marriage, being a stepmother, and living in Manhattan, a change occurred. Because of a shift in Robert's job, we moved to Brooklyn, and shortly after that, we were offered a chance to live in Brazil. I was twenty-seven then and it seemed like a great idea to live abroad. When we are young, we think our parents will live forever and that they will be there when we get home.

We planned to live in Brazil for at least three years, and so in a sense, we were going for an "indefinite" period. It was then that some of the differences between Robert and me arose. Life got much harder, making those differences impossible to resolve. I was going through my twenties, a time of great change, and the marriage could not withstand some of those changes. It was to last only five years. Of course, I could not see this coming.

Despite the boiling up of trouble in my marriage, I wanted very much to have this adventure in Brazil. We were not going to live in Rio but were instead destined for São Paulo, which is a much more serious city. When I said goodbye to my family, it was not under the best circumstances, but no one tried to talk me out of it. Anyway, no one could have. We left for Brazil on a murky November night, not knowing whether this project would be a success or failure. To this day, I have not determined the answer to this question, but if I had to choose one, I'd say it was, overall, a success.

* * *

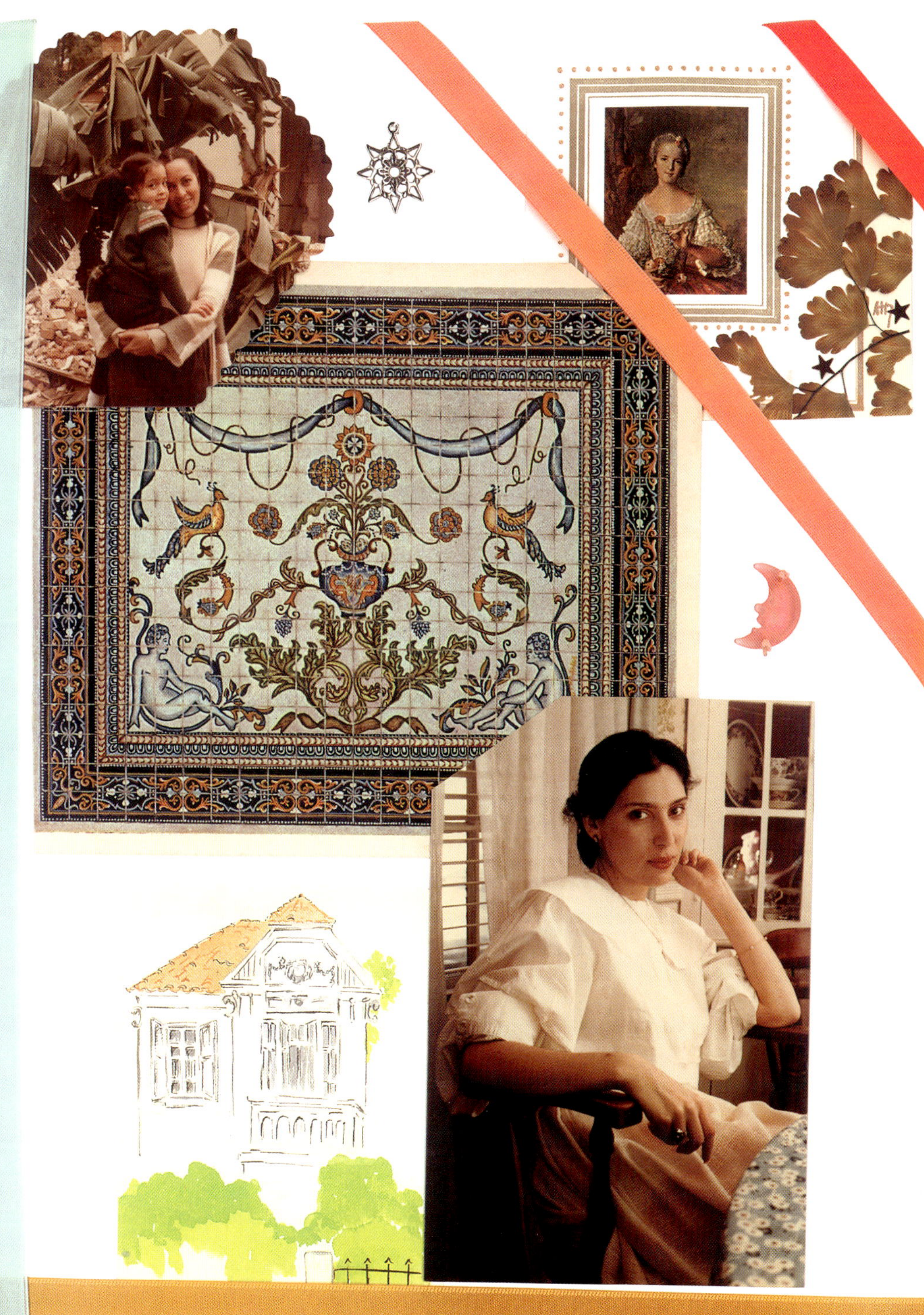

Part Six: In a Far-Off Land

The difficulties between Robert and me had surfaced only months before we left for Brazil, and so the year that we lived abroad was a painful one. I found solace in walking alone in the park, the cool, peaceful haven in the middle of São Paulo. I spent time sketching, painting, and writing letters home. A letter came from my brother Joe, saying that Phyllis and Herm had had a baby boy. I remember wondering when I would get to see this new nephew.

As I was going though this quiet and introspective period, I found a new form of artistic expression — needlepoint. It seemed that every woman I met in São Paulo knew how to do needlepoint. It was a hobby for wealthy women who had lots of time on their hands, but for me it was a form of meditation. It took me out of my ever-present homesickness, a plague that has followed me no matter where in the world I have gone. I loved all the different threads, the nuances of colors, the many shades of peach, coral, apricot, the families of green. I used to go to the craft stores and open the large, shallow drawers filled with threads, and just peer at them. Each color offered another possibility.

Years later, long after I returned home and was living a whole new life, I found among my mother's things a small square I had embroidered and sent home. It was a garland of flowers, in the middle of which are the stitched words *Be of Good Cheer*. I wonder what I was thinking when I made this. Was I telling myself to cheer up, or was I telling my mother to be cheerful, since I knew she missed me?

In order to bridge the ever-present loneliness and separation, I used to buy American editions of magazines like *House & Garden*. Robert and I were hoping to have a house in the countryside of Brazil one day and I liked to imagine it and plan the décor. American magazines were very expensive in Brazil, so it was a treat to get my hands on them. In one particular issue, there was a long article with pictures about the home and lifestyle of the women's fashion designer Oscar de la Renta. Page after page showed his marvelous house in Kent, Connecticut, where Oscar was living with his beautiful wife, Françoise. I found it all so inspiring that I ripped the magazine pages out and mailed them to my mother. *Don't you love this?* I wrote.

A short time later I got a note from her: *We just visited that house in the article, and we met Oscar and his wife.* I did not know what to make of this and when I returned to the States I asked, "How is it that you visited the house?" Mom told me that Dad had delivered a car to Oscar himself! Finding him so gracious and charming, Dad said, "...Hmmm...de la Renta, de la Renta....I think I know that name."

Oscar, who, I am sure, was used to being recognized, said with his delicious and seductive accent, "Perhaps your wife has heard of me. I am a designer of women's clothing."

"Maybe that's it," Dad replied.

"Wait just a moment. I will be right back," Oscar said and disappeared. He returned with a box of soap scented with the famous "Oscar" fragrance. "Give these to your wife with my compliments."

My father thanked him, took the soap home, and told my mother the story. "Mannie, you'll never guess who I met today!" he said. I can imagine how the two of them must have sat in the kitchen, Dad talking and Mom listening.

"That's amazing!" Mom said when he finished. "Mizey just sent me an article from Brazil about those people and their house!" And she showed him the clipping.

"That's it!" he said. "That's the place! I was there and I met the guy."

Well, that was not enough for my mother. She wanted to go there too and see Oscar and see the house. Dad *called* Oscar and said,

"Listen, my wife really wants to meet you," and Oscar agreed to it. Imagine a man who is busy with runways and models and drawing boards, with shows in Paris and guests from high society, saying that it's fine for Mary and Henry Freeman from Queens to drop in!

And they did! And not only that – Mom told me that when they approached the house, the lovely Françoise stood at the threshold, opened her arms and said, "Mary!" and hugged my mother, as if she were some relative who had finally come to see them.

From then on, the "Oscar" fragrance became my mother's trademark. I bought it for her every year for the rest of her life – the cologne, the powder, and the soap. Mom loved the memory of her adventure, the way those people treated her, the coincidence of my having sent the article to her. It was more than a fragrance to her. It was an experience.

* * *

In Brazil I did not just sit around stitching, sketching, and reading. I got a job in a small school teaching English to Brazilians. The school, which had the peculiar name "English Team Course," was a little community of middle-class people who wanted to travel abroad and knew that speaking English would be necessary. They were good students and they cared about me, sensing that my life circumstances were not perfect.

I made a lifetime friend there. Anna-Maria, a student in my class, was nine years older than I, but we became very close very fast. Anna-Maria noticed during the English conversation lessons that I was always talking about my parents' house and all that went on there. One day after class she approached me and said, "I would like to invite you and your husband to my parents' house for Sunday lunch. I think you are very homesick and you will find that my family is a lot like yours – large, close, and affectionate."

That Sunday Robert and I went to the luncheon. Anna-Maria was right. It was a household very much like my own family's, and the afternoon did feel like an afternoon at my parents' house – lots of food, piano playing, singing, some dancing, storytelling, men watching sports on TV while women talked in another room, and children playing outdoors. It was good medicine for me. Later the same year, Debbie, Barbara, and Jeannie came to stay with Robert and me for one month. During that visit, we spent another day at that wonderful, love-filled house. There were people in every room, children in the backyard, and other guests dancing in the driveway. It was so reminiscent of the home I had grown up in, a bittersweet sensation.

Years and years later, long after I had returned to the States and Anna-Maria and I had been corresponding, Anna-Maria sent me a photo of that house where her family had lived. Her parents had passed away and the house was being demolished. In the photo, she is standing in front of the ruins of the once vibrant home, now a pile of rubble. I thought that this had to be one of the saddest moments of her life, for it was a sad moment in *mine*, and I had only been there twice.

As in my Montreal days, I went back and forth from Brazil to the States a few times. On one trip home, I went to Macy's to see my old friends. Now it was I who had come from South America to shop there. I was standing on the other side of the counter, as I had seen so many well-dressed South American women do when I worked there. It was odd to be on the outside looking in, to be the customer instead of the salesgirl. As I asked for the largest size of the product I was buying, I felt as though I were looking into my own past, through some kind of magic mirror, to a piece of life that was now behind me.

And soon, this Brazilian life would be behind me, too.

* * *

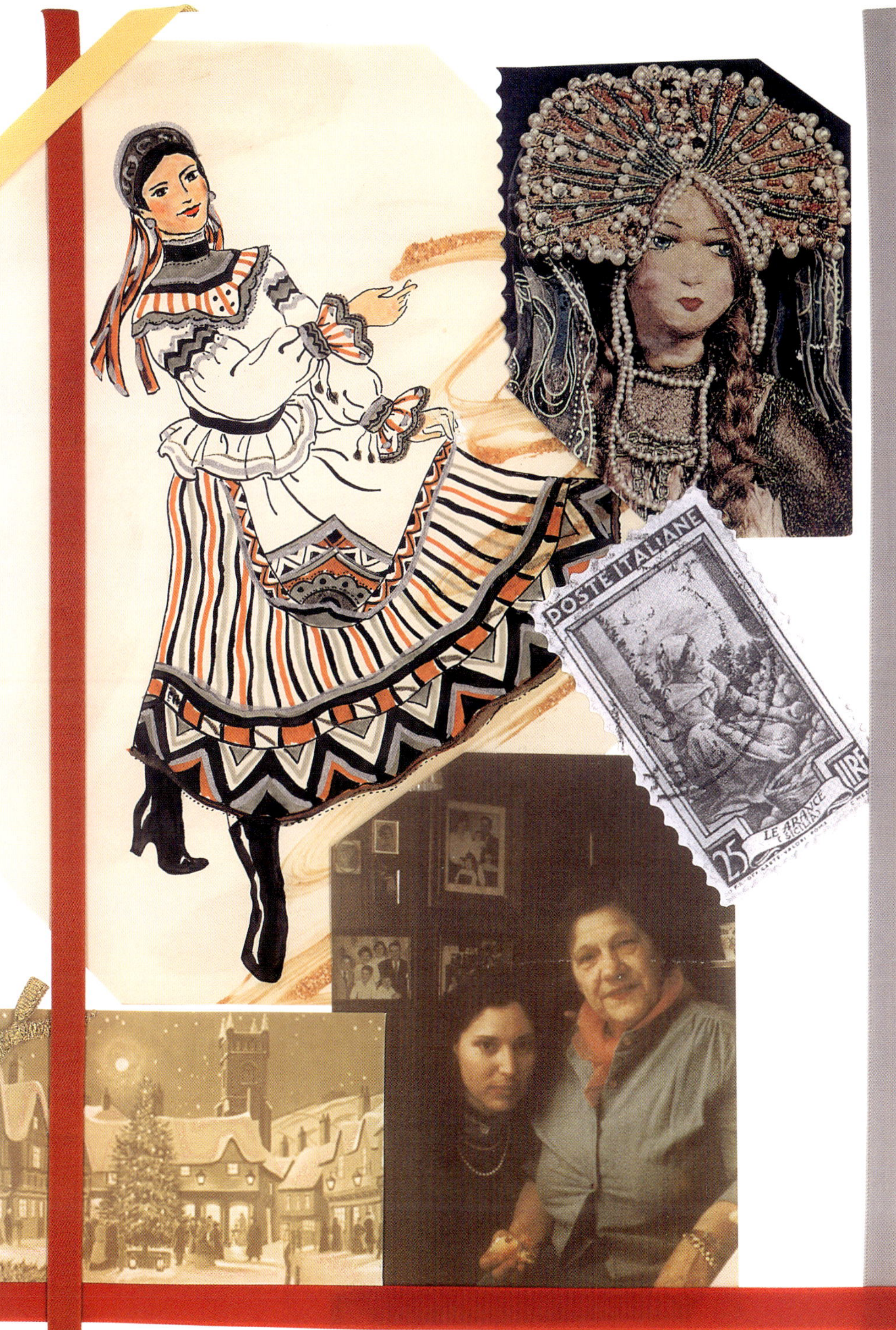
POSTE ITALIANE
25
LE ARANCE
(SICILIA)

Part Seven: Home Again

Ultimately, the job in Brazil did not work out for Robert, and we went back to the States to look for something else. Our personal problems had not disappeared and we were about to file for divorce when the Robert's company placed him in a job in Houston, Texas. I felt bad for him, going to such a strange environment alone. I was going home to New York, but he would be on his own. I offered to go with him, hoping that in a new place we might heal our differences.

I was wrong. Our problems did not go away. The girls were bitterly disappointed and often told me that the years that I was married to their father were the only childhood years that had any semblance of stability for them. I hated to disappoint them, but I could not keep my life from going forward. The bond between the girls and me was not going to change, regardless of the circumstances. We would go on to create our own relationship that would endure through all the years and life changes to come.

Although I was soon going to separate from Robert, I did not see the need to alter everything else in my life. I liked living in Texas. I got a nice job and had made new friends. There was plenty to learn about the people, customs, and culture of the American South. My job as a buyer's assistant in a department store wasn't terribly creative, but I had to do something, and I had experience in retail. The office was small and cramped and had no windows, but the job paid decently and at least I did not have to stand on my feet all day trying to sell something. I could never have foreseen what an important step this would be in my life, for it was there that I met Alexandra, who would later connect me with one of the most pivotal characters in my life story.

Alexandra was a young woman from New York who had married a Texan and was now living far from her family, as I was. When I told her I was planning to return to New York, she insisted I look up her mother, who lived out on Long Island. "I just know you and my mother will like each other," she said.

"Why?" I asked, although I was always ready to make a friend.

"You just will," she said. I believed her and made plans to follow through.

Then in the spring, Robert and I did get divorced. Well, at least the technical part would be final, but the emotional part would take years to right itself. I had to decide then if I should just pick up and go back home or stay in Houston. I could have stayed; I had friends, a job, and I felt at home there. But then I thought about what my story would be twenty years later. Did I want my story to be that I had once landed in Texas by chance and had stayed by default? Or did I want the story about me to be that I had made a deliberate choice to restart and reconstruct my life from scratch? Yes, that sounded like the better story.

When the marriage ended, it was painful for a long time. Robert and I had had some good experiences. I learned to speak Portuguese, lived in Manhattan, Brooklyn, Brazil, and Texas, and had three stepdaughters. The girls are grown now and two of them have children of their own. I have not been married to their father for decades, but their relationship with me has not changed. Their mother's friendship with me has not changed either, except perhaps to become deeper and more valuable. This is one of the surprises of life, I think – we cannot predict who will stay in our lives and who will drop out. People we thought would be lifelong companions sometimes die prematurely, or the friendship breaks apart. And others turn out to be enduring.

* * *

I packed up my things and went back to New York, back to my parents, back to the home and to the room where I had been a single girl. It was frightening and saddening, the thought of starting my life all over again. But I also knew I was lucky to have a warm, safe, and loving environment to come back to. It was good to see everyone again, including the newest child in the family, who had been born in my absence. He was the first grandchild in twelve years. It felt great to be around new life.

When I got home, I was tired and sad. My father had told me to just relax, to rest, to heal. "As long as I am here, you have nothing to worry about," he assured me.

I had some long and short-term goals. The first thing I knew was that I would have to find a job, then get my own place to live, and I hoped to someday get married again. I had to re-root myself in my hometown and see what kind of work I could do. My father wondered why I was in such a rush to go out and work again when I had been through such an enormous change, but I just knew I had to start doing *something*. I was only twenty-nine years old and there was still a lot of life ahead of me. I was curious and interested to see what I was going to do with it.

At the very least, I thought, I could teach English to foreign students. I had experience with this from my days in Brazil and there was a school in Manhattan that was looking for teachers. I presented myself there in hope of landing a job. They hired me immediately and gave me my own class, in which most of the students were Chinese. This was a good move and the class was fun. The students were very responsive and respectful, and wanted so badly to speak English, to live here in New York and become "real Americans." They worked very hard and had a true intention to learn the language.

But my time there was to be shortened, because a better paying job with more of a future came along within a few weeks. I answered an ad for a secretarial job at a public relations firm, one of the biggest and best known in New York City. I had never been a secretary, but I had a feeling that this was something I could do – I knew how to spell and type, communicate with people, and organize material. I made a date to go on the interview, not knowing what to expect. How could I know? I had never done this before. I wondered how I would fare in the world of business, a world in which I had never really worked.

The offices were in what was then one of New York's most posh locations. I took the elevator to the thirty-first floor and went to reception and was buzzed in. This place was like something out of a 1960s movie, except that some of the high-level employees were women. There were offices with windows for the account executives and desks in a long corridor for the secretaries. It all looked very glossy to me, since I had only worked in department stores and schools.

A soft-spoken woman took me to a conference room and told me very briefly about the nature of the job. There were phones to answer, letters to write, and files to organize. I would be working for two women who would "share" my assistance, and both women, she said, were very nice people. Then she gave me a spelling test, and after I scored 100 percent on that, I took the typing test. There were no word processors in this office, so every typing mistake would show. I was so inexperienced that I typed the sample letter with *double* spaces. I should have been disqualified right there, but I guess the office manager wanted to give me an extra push because she quietly slipped the letter back to me and whispered, "Do it again, single-spaced." When I was done, she told me that I could go and meet one of the women for whom I would be working. This was a good sign.

The purpose of this company was to represent notable people in the media. This meant getting their pictures in the paper, scheduling events where they would be visible, and making them feel as important as they thought they were. There were a lot of black-and-white photos of celebrities on the wall, with lavishly scribbled autographs on them. I got the feeling the executives were making big, big money and working very hard to please both the boss and the clients.

One executive to whom I would be reporting was a good-natured woman named Fran. We had a brief interview and she "OK'd" me for hire. The salary was $15,000 per year, which was an absolute fortune for me. It was a tremendous step forward. The second boss was not in that day, and I would meet her when I showed up for work on Monday at noon.

Over the weekend I discussed the good news with my parents. My father was proud of me for going out and getting something so good so fast, and punctuated it with his usual *That's my daughter!*

My mother just thought this was my normal way, and was not surprised. Both forms of support are good.

I felt so lucky to have been hired with no experience. That is really when the great things of life happen – someone gives you the chance to do something you have never done, but they believe that you can do it. But I also had funny little thoughts in my head about being almost thirty years old, a college graduate, and working as a secretary. Part of me said I was doing fine, having just come home from another state, gotten divorced, and having my life turned upside down. But another part of me undermined these thoughts and said I ought to have more to show for my education.

So when I came to work on Monday, I had the whole mixture of thoughts and judgments running through my brain. *Did being a secretary have dignity? Was I making the most of my education and experience? Had I come all this way* (whatever that meant) *to do this?*

And then I got out of the elevator at floor 31. It was exactly twelve o'clock and a large group of secretaries was leaving to go to lunch. They walked toward the elevators like a single cloud moving across the sky. They all looked the same – same age, height, style of dress – except for one. In the middle of the group, rising head and shoulders above the others, was a gorgeous redhead. She stood out from the rest, not just because she was much taller, but because she had a certain *something*. As she walked toward the elevator, she cast a purple shawl around her shoulders, and it caught the ends of her cascading red hair. *That girl*, I thought, *gives dignity to the position of secretary. I want to be like her.*

I went in and reported for work. I was shown to a desk, which was quite large and polished. I had a telephone with a lot of buttons on it, a modern (for that time) typewriter, lots of message pads, and all kinds of paper. Then I was told that all I had to do was sit at this desk and wait for instructions from Fran. The other boss, Katie, would be back later that day.

To me it was astonishing that all I had to do was be there in case someone needed me, and for this was getting a good salary. I had worked so hard in Macy's standing on my feet all day hoping to sell a lipstick, to make $72 per week! And here I was in this plum job in a fancy and important place. I guess it did have some dignity.

Later that day Katie returned to the office. A tall woman with beautiful red hair and a purple shawl. Yes, that was Katie I had seen leaving the office at noon. I had noticed her immediately. In a sense, I had bonded with her at first sight because of her impressive stride, confidence, and air of assurance. I could never have known at the moment I spotted her that she would not only be my boss, but was going to be my friend for life.

And so I began my career in the world of business. Being a secretary is something everyone should do once. It creates such a sense of order in your life because you have to be aware of someone else's correspondence and schedule. Actually, working for these two women was not hard. They really asked very little of me and were quite self-sufficient. Being at this job was really more of an opportunity for me to learn about myself and the way the world works.

Offices were filled with the sound of typewriters tapping and telephones ringing back then. There was no email and no voice mail. If a phone rang and you were not there to get it, you missed the call. This is one of the reasons people had secretaries. These important executives (at least they thought they were important) were always in each other's offices chatting, planning, or gossiping. So when they heard a phone ringing, they'd come dashing into the corridor saying, "Is that my phone?" This went on all day long. They were always hoping for that critical phone call to come in. As a secretary sitting at a desk, it was like watching a vaudeville show. You just sat there as these executives ran from one office to the other and into the corridor yelling, "Is that my phone?"

Everyone dressed very well. This was the 1980s when we still wore silk blouses and high heels to work. It is unreal to me when I think now about how we used to stand on the subway in uncomfortable shoes and much more formal clothing. Women wore lots of silk scarves, makeup, and jewelry. Of course, everyone wore stockings and it was the age of great, huge hair. I didn't have that '80s look because I always wore my hair long (a preference from the world of ballet), but the more contemporary women looked really with-it, especially Katie with her lustrous curls and expensive silk dresses.

Although I had no interest whatsoever in the business of this company, I developed a nice relationship with both my bosses. They were admirable women and decent people. Other secretaries reported to maniacs who worked them very hard. I had lucked out.

There was a wide range of personality types, and I got along with all of them. In my experience in the world of work, I have found that there is always one person in the office (or in the shop, or the school, or wherever you work) who is everybody's favorite. This person rarely has any outstanding traits and there never seems to be any apparent reason why everyone likes them. This has always been a mystery to me.

At this firm, there was a rather nondescript blonde girl named Kathy, who, for some reason, had no enemies. As far as I could see, there was absolutely nothing special about her, and with no effort on her part, she met with everyone's approval. It was customary when someone had a birthday, to acknowledge it with a card or flowers, and everyone in the office got equal treatment in this respect. But not Kathy. When her birthday came, one of the executives took up a collection to buy her an expensive camera. Now, decades later, I still have not figured out why he was inspired to do this, and even more so, why did we all feel that we *wanted* to contribute, too?

Everywhere I have ever worked, Kathy has been there - sometimes she comes in the guise of a woman, sometimes a man. Sometimes she is old, or she can be quite young and inexperienced. But she is always there. I have often wished I were the Kathy of the workplace, but I clearly am not. I am, instead the person who has many enthusiastic admirers and a few really strong enemies. No matter. This is the world with its various personality types - they occur over and over, and we learn to recognize them. I'll never be Kathy, but I'll always like being around her, whoever she is.

* * *

My luck and contentment with this job were not to last. There was an office at the end of the corridor that was the president's suite. The company president, who had built this business from scratch and was now well respected, was known for not being able to keep a secretary. He had one woman — the Number One secretary — whose job was ONLY to answer the phone, and another who did everything else. Supposedly, Number One would supervise the work. That second secretarial position was regularly vacated, almost always by a young lady running out of the office in tears with all her personal effects under her arm. I was to be the next victim, not only of the big boss, but of his Number One secretary. The world is full of people like this, so there is no sense running away from them. We come up against them time and again in different forms. They make going to work a frightening, frustrating experience, but there is no way to get around this. At some time or other, we all have to confront these demons. Now it was my turn.

Number One was a beautiful woman whose insides unfortunately did not match her outsides. If she were in a cartoon she would be a character perhaps made of ice, a shimmering, cold figure with a beautiful face and glass-blue eyes. But inside, the wheels of jealousy and insecurity were always turning. As a result, she was never able to be a leader or mentor to the secretary occupying second place. Instead, she added to their misery by whispering in the boss's ear, making that person look bad. But I did not know *any* of this until I got closer to her.

One day, Number One came sauntering down the hall and spoke to Fran. She said that the big boss had "noticed" me, and for his next secretary he'd like *that girl with the hair*. He did not even know my name! He was offering a salary of $18,500 and the title of Executive Secretary. Of course I was tempted.

"Don't do it," Fran warned me. "You'll be running out of here in a few months the same way all the others did." But I did do it. And I did go running out, but not in a few months. I lasted a year.

I worked in the front office with Number One, which made for a hard and demoralizing day. Of course, I had had other demoralizing jobs, and I knew it was only a matter of time before I found my way out. The boss knew that he was making me miserable with his bad temper, conflicting sets of instructions, and merciless criticism, but he always apologized after he'd see me cry. It was a typical abusive work situation that was making me tense and sick and was undermining any of the confidence I had gained in the months with Fran and Katie.

Then one day in the middle of winter, my father died. His death led me away from the workplace for a full week, and when I returned, my perspective was different.

My dad dropped dead of a heart attack on the kitchen floor one morning. He had not died from a previous heart attack, but was weakened both physically and emotionally. When the doctor told him, "Mr. Freeman, from now on – no more eating eggs, no more shoveling snow, and no more driving," something went out of him. Those may have been his favorite activities, along with raking leaves and taking a walk.

But what really broke his heart was that during his recuperation he was longing for a visit from Joe, his beloved boss at his driving job. For some reason, it was Joe that Dad wanted to see more than anyone. He even said to my mother, as he sat resting in an armchair, "Just wait, Mannie. Joe and all the guys from work are going to do something special, I just know they are. We'll be seeing them here."

But they did not appear. I even went upstairs to my room and made a call to the office.

"Joe," I said, "my father keeps asking for you. Do you think you could come visit?"

"Oh, yes," he said, "I've got to get there and see Henry."

But for whatever reason, Joe did not come. And Dad was aware of it, and he was disappointed. So were we. A month later, Dad had another heart attack and died.

That morning, I was getting dressed for work and heard a thud. I went downstairs and there he was. I remembered that he had told me when I came back from Texas, "As long as I am here, you don't need to worry." Now he was gone. I went into the bedroom and woke my mother up.

"Dad is on the kitchen floor," I said. She jumped out of bed, came into the kitchen, and knelt down.

"Henry, Henry," she wept, "don't *be* like that! Get up!" She stayed there awhile, holding him, the prayers flowing out of her.

I called 911 and my siblings to tell them the news. The emergency workers walked in the door before I had blinked. They tried to revive him, but I knew he was gone. We went to the hospital together in the ambulance and I stayed in the waiting room. Some time after that, the doctor came out and told me that my father had died. I knew that already, but I guess he had to make it official.

Before long, the rest of the family showed up. We said one last goodbye to our father in the hospital. He looked so majestic lying there. Just an hour before, he had been on his way to the garage to warm up the car to take me to the subway. It had been a rapid and sudden exit.

Within twenty-four hours we arranged for the funeral, which is the custom for Jews. I remember that it was a freezing cold day when we were all together in the funeral home. Before the ceremony, the rabbi took the five of us into a small room. He pinned a little black ribbon on each of our lapels, made a small snip with a scissor and then tore the ribbon. This is a tradition that harkens back to ancient times when Jews ripped their clothes as part of the mourning ritual. There is something about that sound of the ribbon tearing that helps the grieving process to start. It is a powerful moment.

It is ironic that so many people showed up at Dad's funeral because he placed very little value on friends. He never bothered to cultivate friendships, and yet everybody liked him. The funeral parlor was filled with so much love, so many good people – our cousins, aunts, uncles, and friends. Just my mother's enormous family was enough to fill a room. They had always loved Uncle Henry and were honored to be there to bid him goodbye.

Everything about the funeral was a high level experience of great unity. Like the cold day, the entire room seemed to be in ultra-sharp focus. My clearest recollection is of my brother Steve standing up front, delivering the first eulogy, which was so simple and heartfelt:

Dad – Thanks for the good start and the help along the way. Thanks for the good direction and thanks for making mistakes, so that I never really had to be too perfect to keep up. Thanks for slowing down once in awhile and thanks for always being there…even now.

In the cemetery, the coffin was placed in a family plot where a dignified headstone bore the family name, *Freeman*. My father was buried next to his parents. Later he would have his own headstone on which we would have the carvers replicate his handwriting with the closing he always used on greeting cards: *All my love*. Years later, I recreated that scene in my book, *Grandmother Mary*, by saying, *His family buried him in a quiet green place and on his grave they placed a stone with an inscription, "All My Love."* Mom knew that when her time would come, she would not be able to be buried in that plot because she was not Jewish. She made a provision for herself by buying a grave in another cemetery. But we would not have to face Mom's death for many years.

After my father's burial we went back to our house and received guests. What a strange custom that is when you are mourning, having to think about pots of coffee and platters of food! But the company is good and the companionship of familiar faces and voices helps to ease the crippling pain of loss.

That night, Joe and I slept in the same room. Some time after I had fallen asleep, I awoke to the sound of him crying. I crept onto his bed and held him and we both cried.

"Our father is *dead*," he said, as if it had just occurred to him. It was a new idea for us. We were in our thirties and had never lost anyone close.

As a family, we thought we were going to mourn and receive guests for seven days, but after three days we simply closed the door and knew that it was over. Now was the time for all of us to just be together without any other socializing. We sat around the house talking about Dad, remembering and reliving so many good years. There was so much we did not know about Dad, for in some ways he was a private person. But curiously, right after he died, we found a diary in the top drawer of his armoire. He had started writing it within the last year or so, I suppose in an effort to look at his own life. There, in his own handwriting, were the accounts of how he had grown up in East New York and then Bensonhurst, and how he had met and married our mother. We thought it odd indeed that the last line of the diary read, *It couldn't be better*. It was wonderful to learn that he thought of his life that way. This was a very special time; we were gathered in a unique way that was not to happen again. We had a chance to talk and dispel some of the pain in a safe place. And shortly after that, we knew that this, too was over.

My father's sudden death put me into another state of mind. I had stayed home from work for one week, and when I returned, I was glad to hear my boss say, "This job is too stressful for you now that you have had a loss. You can still work here, at the same salary, but you will work at the other end of the office and you will not have a boss. You will just take the overflow from the secretaries who have too much work."

This sounded like a much better situation. I guess he knew that he had been too hard on me and that we both could not continue in this way. So in a sense, my father's death delivered me from this situation, which is a good thing, since I did not have the courage to deliver myself from it.

I had a desk at the other end of the corridor and became completely anonymous and invisible. I reported to no one, answered no one's phone. In the course of the day, work would arrive at my desk — letters to type, papers to file. Sometimes there was nothing to do but wait. And so it did not take long for me to realize that this was not the way to spend each day, and I started my quest for the next job.

* * *

In my search, I recalled an important conversation I had with my father six months before he died. When he had the first heart attack, I had thought *that* was the end. I went to the hospital to see him. There really was nothing to say because I had a good relationship with my father and there were no unspoken words. Still, I wanted to tell him one more time that I loved him.

I stood at the foot of the hospital bed and started to cry.

"What's the matter?" Dad asked.

"I am afraid you are going to die."

"And if I do, so what? I've lived a good life and everyone I love is fine."

"I'm not fine, Dad," I said. "I don't know which way my life is going to go."

"You?" he said. "I am not worried about you. You always land on your feet. You have a good head on your shoulders. There is nothing to worry about."

I was amused that my father thought I was fine because I had so much uncertainty about my life and about what lay ahead. I wondered if I would ever be able to put everything back together. But my father could see something I could not see, and I believed him. It may have been the confidence he had in me that allowed me to take the next step. Even though Dad was gone, his words stayed with me.

Out came the New York Times and my search began. In looking for a job, I used to search the classifieds under the key words *Travel*, *French*, *Education*, and *Translation*. Now I had a new skill. I had been an executive secretary, and could add that to my choices as I looked in the paper. Amazingly, I saw an ad that read:

FRENCH SPEAKING ASSISTANT
For International Businessman

I answered the ad and a few days later I came home from work to find a message my mother had scribbled, saying a gentleman named Michael Badger had called in reference to the resume I had sent.

What followed was perhaps the easiest entry I have ever made into any job. I called Mr. Badger and had a brief conversation with him. In his crisp English accent he told me he had been living in Europe and would now open a New York office for his own company. He invited me to come for an interview.

The office was right down the block from where I was working. I rang the bell and the door opened. Mr. Badger, a very tall, handsome, good-natured man was standing there with a big smile and a warm greeting for me.

"Come in, come in!" he said, as though we were good friends. I suddenly felt shy. It might have been the contrast with the meanness and coldness of the environment in which I had been working – I had grown unaccustomed to this kind of cordiality.

The office was small – just three rooms, and had NOTHING in it but two desks and two chairs. Everything was brand new and ready to be launched. Mr. Badger had just arrived and whoever was going to be his assistant was going to build this business with him. The interview was easy.

"I assume you can type," he said.

"Yes, of course."

"You speak French?"

"Yes, fluently."

"*Vous parlez vraiment couramment?*" (You really speak fluently?)

"*Oui, bien sûr.*" (Yes, of course.)

"That's good, because I do a lot of work with France. And I travel a lot. In fact most of the time I will be traveling and you will be here alone," he said, as if I already had the job.

"Fine."

"Do you know how to use a computer?"

"No, but I would be happy to learn." (I was actually a little scared of this.)

"And how much money do you need?"

"$20,000 a year." (I was quaking. This was SO much money to me.)

"Well, I think that sounds all right. When could you start?"

"In three days."

"Great. You see, I have more furniture and computers coming in three days, and you could help me set everything up. I think we should do a deal."

"Me too. Thank you."

We shook hands and that was it. I had a new job for more money, working for a nice person in a place where I could use my French. I went back to the office and quit, giving two days' notice.

I stayed with Mr. Badger for four and a half years and never had one unpleasant moment. He always treated me with respect, never raised his voice, and was fun to work for. He was reasonable, lighthearted, interesting, and smart. We made a great team and became good friends. I would still be working with him today if I had not suddenly gotten the idea be a librarian. I sometimes think it was the peaceful and healing environment of our office that allowed that idea to surface. Because the job was not stressful, it gave me a chance to get to know myself again and re-evaluate what I wanted from life.

But the really important lesson of the experience was something I always keep in mind whenever I am in a bad situation: there I was in my last job, suffering at the hands of a cruel boss and his even crueler secretary, when right down the block, a two-minute walk, the perfect job was waiting for me. I only had to find it. This idea comes back again and again when people tell me that their job, their boyfriend, or their apartment is the ONLY one and they have to put up with some kind of misery to stay in it. No, it is NOT the only one. It is just the only one you're in. And it is very possible that a short distance away, in time or space, there is something much, much better.

* * *

That same year, Joe and I went to Europe together. We had lost our dad in the deep midwinter, and now it was early fall, when the sun is still strong and the air is cool. A few days before our trip, Joe flew in from California, and we spent some time tooling around New York, exploring some places on the list of things "to do and see," which we had been accumulating since his last trip.

Right before we left for London, we went to Dad's grave. Now the earth had settled, and there was only a small mound to show that this was a recent death. The grave is in a little courtyard of its own, enclosed and secure in feeling. In the pale sunlight of that autumn day, we sat there and visited with Dad. I, in fact, lay down right on the soft earth and gazed heavenward, feeling the love I had for my father.

And now Joe and I would go to London and Paris to do the same things we liked to do in New York – walk around, gather ideas and inspiration. Joe had never been to Europe. I had been there several times, but this was the first time for me after a hiatus of seven years, for I had been spending the last few years going back and forth to Brazil.

Walking around London and Paris with my brother was like some kind of dream from which we did not awaken for two weeks. We needed very little sleep or food and were nourished by everything we were seeing – the stately streets of London, the brilliant white row houses with their shiny façades, the shops selling envelopes and paper, threads, postcards, all those tiny things we collect. The air was clear and dry, and the urban gardens were in bloom. We stood in St. James's Park, which is expansive and green and full of little lakes and glades, and we fed the little birds that came to eat right out of our hands.

Then we went to Paris for another kind of inspiration, for Paris and London are very different. Paris is like a shimmering jewel box full of treasures. Its graceful, flowering trees ennoble even the most banal street. And what is more legendary that the Eiffel Tower, which sits elegantly in a park and calls to mind a Paris of prewar times?

I think Joe and I walked every street in Paris, letting all the images soak into our brains, marking us for life. In one sense, being in London and Paris added something to each of us, but in another sense, it brought out something that was already there, waiting to be awakened.

Joe never went back to Europe, but what we saw on that trip was essential to our development. If one only gets to Europe once, perhaps a week in London and one in Paris is the perfect small dose.

* * *

During the first year that I worked for Michael Badger, my friend Alexandra, whom I had met in Texas, came back to New York. She invited me to her family home, and that is where I met her mother, Joan. Alexandra was right; Joan and I had an instant rapport, as if we had always known each other. The moment we started to talk, we had so much to say, as though we were making up for all the time that we *should* have been friends. In time, I became friends with the whole family and would spend weekends at their house, eating, talking, and walking in the countryside.

Joan was the director of a large library on Long Island, and it was she who pointed the way to my becoming a children's librarian. Since I returned to New York, I had been wondering what profession to enter, where to go to school. I had thought I was going to go to business school and use some of my foreign languages, perhaps to do something like international marketing. I even went so far as to apply to business school and take the Graduate Management Admissions Test, a long and difficult exam that determines whether or not the school will accept you.

I did well on the exam and was just about to start the fall semester when my path changed. One night when Joan and I were eating dinner, a thought popped into my head, seemingly out of nowhere. I turned to her and said, "I know it's too late now because I was already accepted to Baruch College, but if I could do what I *really* want, I would become a children's librarian."

Her eyes opened wide. "Why don't you do *that*?" she asked. "It's *not* too late!"

"It *is*," I said, sadly. "I'm already thirty-one."

"That's not too old!" Joan protested. "I think you'd make a wonderful children's librarian! Please...just call Queens College and ask. Will you do it for me? Please?"

To appease my friend, I called the school and submitted the papers they asked for. A day or two later I got a call from the school office, imploring me to enroll in their library science program. But I told them, "No, I just did this to satisfy a friend. I am going to business school."

The head of the department did not like this answer. He said he wanted to meet me in person and discuss this idea. I really didn't want to waste his time or mine and said no, but he insisted. And so to appease *him*, I agreed to meet at the public library for fifteen minutes.

In the hall of the somber Forty-second Street Library, we sat on a marble bench and talked. I explained that I really had other plans and would not be going to library school. But he would not be discouraged. Then he said the magic words: "You really have everything a person needs to be a children's librarian. Please come into our program." And at that moment, something in me shifted and I changed course, abandoning my other plans.

I started library school within a couple of weeks and felt from the start that I had found my true path. It was as though I had entered a world made for me – one filled with books, art, languages, children, research, ideas, and interesting people. For the entire three years that it took to get my degree, I loved all the courses. But most important, I felt I had finally found the way to a profession of my own, which was something I had been seeking since I graduated from college nine years earlier.

* * *

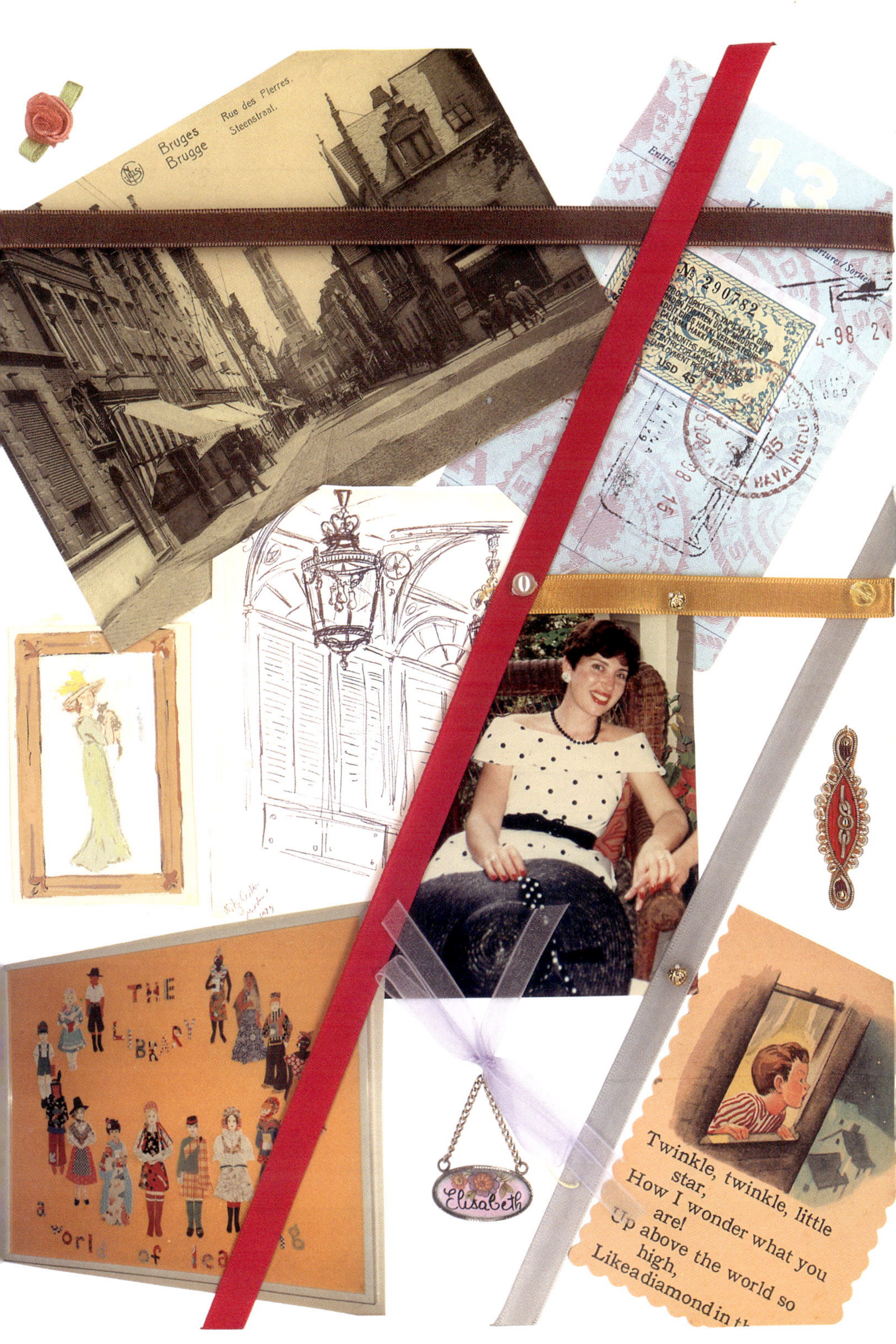
Bruges Brugge
Rue des Pierres.
Steenstraat.
THE LIBRARY
a world of lea[...]g
Elisabeth
Twinkle, twinkle, little star,
How I wonder what you are!
Up above the world so high,
Likeadiamond in th

Part Eight: A New Beginning

During one of the summers that I was attending library school, I spent a month taking a children's literature course in England. There is no better place to study children's literature, I think, because so many good children's stories came out of England: *Mary Poppins*, *Winnie-the-Pooh*, *Peter Rabbit*, and many others.

The setting for this course was a college campus right on the edge of London. There were rolling hills with deer, lush gardens, and right outside the gates was my favorite city, London. We were fourteen students, most of us American, who all had an interest in children's books. It was an extremely compatible group despite a great variation in ages and geographic origins. It was wonderful to see people between the ages of twenty-five and fifty-five who were able to laugh together, learn together, and become lifelong friends. Perhaps this is because we all had one common interest – children and their books.

The beauty of the program was that we had a chance to see the actual places where English authors had lived and worked. We took a bus trip down to Surrey to see the Hundred Acre Wood that Milne wrote of in *Winnie-the-Pooh*. We ventured up north to the Lake District to visit the farm and home of Beatrix Potter, the author/illustrator who created Peter Rabbit and all the other books in the series. We breathed in that moist and fragrant English air and watched the velvety countryside roll by outside the bus windows.

When I was just six years old, my sister, who was already a grown-up, had given me given me Potter's book *The Tale of the Flopsy Bunnies Bunnies*. I still have the copy with Eleanore's inscription, dated 1958. Beatrix Potter was an Englishwoman from a well-to-do

London family. She had no intention of becoming an author, but rather, decided to be a sheep farmer. A twist of fate led her to write a series of letters to a sickly child whom she did not know. To make the letters more intimate, she decorated the margins with little drawings of her own farm animals – bunnies, mice, owls, and ducks. These letters later became famous classic children's stories. Every child knows Peter Rabbit and his mischievous deeds. And those of us who delved deeper into Potter's works know *Jemima Puddle Duck*, *The Two Bad Mice*, and of course, the *Flopsy Bunnies*.

Although the language of these books is quite out of date and somewhat starchy, the stories still have enormous appeal. The illustrations depict the dewy and lush countryside of England – the sweet, soft grass, tiny cottages, and rustic farms. A young American reader might wonder W*here is this delightful place? Is it real?* Indeed it is real, for it is the terrain on which the author herself lived and wrote. What an extraordinary experience, then, to visit Beatrix Potter's farm and to see the landscape she painted in her books! I nearly expected bunnies wearing aprons to come out of the woods. A sense of place is so important in writing, and seeing Potter's farm reassured me of this.

Most of the time we were on campus, which was beautiful enough. We lived in a dormitory and had all the pleasure of communal living – the laughter, the scurrying from room to room, sharing stories, experiences, and making new friends. We ate our meals in the spacious dining room, and the food was great and plentiful. And in the background of all of this was my personal knowledge that I was going to be a librarian one day, that I was going to work with children, read to them, explore their books, and build my own library. I had found my career.

* * *

Toward the end of library school, I prepared to write my master's thesis. We library students were allowed to choose any topic and write whatever we wanted. In a sense, this was the first "book" I had ever written, because I could focus on and develop something that had great value to me.

Having spent six months in Texas a few years before, I realized how different the culture of the Northeast is from that of our American

South. In just a short time there, I learned that the way southerners think is tempered by the history of their ancestors having lost the Civil War. Here in the North, we don't think much about the Civil War unless we are studying it or discussing the civil rights movement. But in the South, the topic is frequently brought up in conversation.

I came to realize that there is unfinished business in the South — the heartbreak of a lost way of life, abruptly changed values, and lost homes, either real or imagined. I concluded that these remaining thoughts and beliefs have certainly influenced the literature. And so I decided to write about children's literature of the American South. My job would be to read as much of it as I could.

It was a vast, overwhelming project, which took all my strength and passion, and it was successful. It pleased me to know that by some trick of nature, I had had a chance to live in the South, albeit for a short time, and could put that learning to use. I made a promise to myself that one day I would visit some of those cities that still held the feeling of the mythical "Old South," which is romanticized in literature and movies. Yes, I would do that some day.

In the meantime, I graduated from library school with good grades and a feeling of satisfaction. At the graduation, as I marched with the other students across the lawn of Queens College, I saw my mother standing off to the side. She appeared as someone in a dream; it was as though I had not seen her in a long time and she had suddenly come back. She was standing under a tree, watching for me in the enormous, winding stream of students in caps and gowns. We caught each other's eyes and smiled. She had encouraged me for the whole three years I was studying. She was proud of me and happy too, for she knew I had found the doorway to the next part of my life.

* * *

I may have found my path vocation-wise, but there were still two goals that I wanted to reach: to have a home of my own and to find a new mate. Between my two marriages I spent a lot of time with girlfriends, most of whom were trying to find boyfriends or husbands. My friends were very pessimistic. They kept saying that there were no single men who were good people, who wanted to have serious relationships that would last. But I didn't believe this. I had a strong feeling there was someone for me, someone *waiting* for me, *looking* for me. It was only a matter of our finding one another.

One friend who was important to me during this period was Karen, who would later go on to become my brother Steve's wife. We used to spend time on the phone or in diners, talking and laughing. I remember one evening when we sat at my mother's kitchen table chatting. At that time, neither one of us knew which way our lives were going. We were both in our thirties and in some ways we had both suffered some of the same woes, having been married to men with very keen intellects and strong personalities. We both welcomed the idea of life becoming fun, yet peaceful someday.

How clearly I remember Karen sitting across from me, saying, "I wonder what will happen to all of us."

"What do you mean?" I said.

"I just wonder," she continued, "what will happen, I mean, to you, to me, to Steve."

It all turned out much better than either of us could have imagined. Karen went on to marry Steve and shortly thereafter, adopted a baby boy. This child had a kind of magnetism that we all felt. I held him when he was a week old and knew then that we had a special connection, as if I had known him in some other life. And as he grew into a toddler, a child, a teenager, and then a young man, that feeling continued to grow.

I, too would find the right partner and get married, but first I did what some people do much earlier in life: I got my own apartment. I had to find a place to live on rather short notice, and, as most people will agree, finding an affordable, nice apartment in New York is a challenge, if not a miracle. I remember how worried I was, and how my mother eased that worry. "The right apartment is waiting for you," she said. "It is already standing, ready for you. You just have to find it."

I tried to imagine what that place would look like. I knew I wanted to be in Queens, not too far from where I had grown up. I wanted to be on the ground floor so that I could hear the sounds of people passing on the street. And I wanted to look out my window and see something pretty.

All my wishes came true. More than twenty-two years ago, I moved into my apartment, and have always been happy in it. It's almost like a small house, with its large rooms and lots of light. It faces the street and looks out on little row houses. The building was built in 1941, and although much of the original beauty has faded, you can see the remnants of a way of life that was once gracious in New York. There is one room that I use for my art studio. In this tiny space, I do all my writing, painting, studying of languages, and letter writing. It is the smallest room in the apartment and gets the most use. It is the creative center for my publishing house. Like a cat that has gotten used to a certain size basket for sleeping, I don't think I would be comfortable in a larger space. Everything is within reach here – paints, paper, scissors, reference materials, books, computer, and everything else one needs for a creative project. I like to be able to see everything I am working on, rather like the dormouse who, when he goes into hibernation, first prepares some nuts and seeds that he will find upon awakening. He sleeps curled up, but his little toes are touching the food, so that the moment he is roused from his winter slumber, he will not have one moment of anxiety – the food is literally at his feet.

When I moved in, I owned almost nothing. I had gotten divorced and had come away with very little. I arrived in my new home with a bed, a dresser, a small table, and four chairs. The rest was books and art supplies. The space was so big and there was so little in it that with its polished floors, it looked like Madame Susta's ballet studio. It was so wonderful to be in my own home. I could put whatever I wanted on the walls, in the refrigerator, and in my closet. I was on the threshold of a new part of life.

A year later I met my second husband, Doug, and the year after that we got married. We spent the next twenty years building our home together, and now it looks like a little museum. There is lovely furniture, a white piano, interesting artwork on the walls, and all the of art objects that we have collected from our travels around the world. Of course, many of the items in the house were gifts from people we love, and it feels so good to look upon them and think of those people. There is not one object in the house that we do not cherish. I have strong feelings about the concept *home* and I bring them into my books and stories, maybe because my own family home had such a strong influence on me. I waited a long time to have a place of my own and it only improved when I remarried and could share it with Doug. No matter where in the world we go, coming home is always the best.

In my book *Rainwalk*, the beauty of one's neighborhood is the main theme. All that happens in the book is that four different children take a walk in each of their neighborhoods. I wanted to convey to young readers that your neighborhood is the best place. Your neighborhood, your home.

Rainwalk was born out of my great affection for just that – taking a walk. I thought it would be valuable for children to have a book in which nothing in particular happens other than a child enjoying a walk near his/her own home. It is nice to think about just going out for the sake of enjoying what nature is offering – leaves, the breeze, a stray cat, a rain shower, the early morning fresh air. Our own neighborhoods change with the seasons, and it is pleasant to make observations as we walk around.

Since there are four different seasons, I decided to make four different children in four different neighborhoods, walking at four different times of day. The subtler message of this book is that things look different in different seasons and at different times. But it doesn't matter – the only really important message is that we can enjoy what's right outside our door.

* * *

Between my two marriages, I met a gentle young man named Michel, and we fell in love. He was soft-spoken and even-tempered, and wanted very much to get married. It seemed like a good idea. We started dating in the autumn and spent a lot of time in rural parts on Long Island, passing many a Sunday walking through the woods, canoeing, and meandering over the soft sand. All the fresh air, exercise, and affection were healing, and I began to feel as though much of the pain of what I had been through was starting to lift.

Just before the first frost came, Michel proposed. I was very, very happy, and grateful that I had fallen upon such good luck so fast. At least it seemed that way. But within a year, my feelings started to shift. Michel was the same sweet man, but I was undergoing deep changes. Suddenly, as we came to the end of the following summer, I felt uneasy about getting married. I didn't know how to tell Michel because I could not find any reason for my feelings. There was nothing wrong with him, and *his* feelings for *me* had not changed. I decided to seek the help of a professional therapist.

Jack was a low-key, older man who began the session like this: "Liz, what would it take for your life to work?"

That's a big question. I thought for a moment. *For my life to work?*

"Well," I said slowly, "I would be able to figure out why I don't want to marry the man who is in love with me. I have been through a first marriage and it was not easy. My first husband and I loved each other but could not solve our problems. Still, he was exciting and I miss some of what we had. But I don't want to be back in that situation. But I also don't want to be in *this* situation. Michel is very nice, and he would never hurt me. So why don't I want to marry him? What's the matter with me?"

"Liz, it sounds to me like this man is a little *too* nice. Maybe he is not exciting enough for you. Maybe when you got divorced you needed someone with whom you would be safe, but now that you are healing, you need someone with a little more *oomph*."

"But he's a nice fellow," I said. "In fact, I keep hearing this voice in my head every time I imagine myself breaking up with him. It says, *Don't be stupid! He's a nice fella!*"

"Whose voice is that?" Jack said. "It's not *your* voice. Whose is it?"

Whose is it? That's a good question. "It's my father's voice," I said, surprised at my own words. "That's what my father would say if he were here."

"That's fine, Liz, but he's not here. And only *you* know what's right for your life. You want to know what I think?"

"Of course."

"I think there are some traits that your husband had that you miss. You miss the intellectual challenge, you miss the city life because you have been spending so much time out in the country. Liz, I think what you need is someone who combines the interesting traits that Robert had with the gentle and kind traits that Michel has."

"Can one person have all that?" I asked.

"Of course they can. You talk like there are only two men in the world – your ex-husband and Michel. Did it ever occur to you that there is a *third* man, a new possibility?"

"What would he be like?"

"He would be the man in whom all these traits cross over. You just have to know that *that* is what you're looking for. Get out there now and find him!"

"Find him? How will I know when I have found him?"

"You'll know, Liz, the same way you know that you don't want to marry Michel. But you know what, Liz? Even if we didn't know all this, all that matters is that you don't want to marry him."

"But he's a nice fella!" I said, now purposely mimicking my father.

"It doesn't matter. Toots, you just don't want to marry him. And that's enough." And with that, Jack dismissed me. "You don't need me anymore," he said. "You know what to do."

I don't know if I knew what to do or not, but I knew what I *had* to do. I had to tell Michel as soon as possible that our engagement was off so that he could get on with his own life. And I did. It was not easy, for it is never easy to tell someone you don't want them. But I really had no choice.

Keeping in mind what had been revealed in my very short career in therapy, I would keep my eyes and ears out for that man who would fulfill both sides of the equation. As my mother might have told me, he was *out* there – I just had to find him.

* * *

Just after graduating with my master's degree in Library Science, I looked for a job. My precise wish – a weekend job as a children's librarian in a public library – was waiting to be granted. I called the library and had a fairly brief chat with the head of the children's room, who practically hired me over the phone. I could not believe how miraculous this was! The job would start the very next Saturday at the Great Neck Public Library. I could keep my position as a secretary with Mr. Badger while getting my feet wet in my new field of work.

The only question was – how would I get there? I was living in Rego Park and the library was about a half an hour away by car. But I didn't have a car, and I didn't drive! It didn't matter. I found a bus that would take me into Great Neck and from there I walked one mile to the library. I was so happy to be working in my new profession that any obstacles seemed minimal.

Once I started working, it did not take long for me to see that I did not know a lot about children's literature. The learning would take place on the job. There were sixteen other children's librarians and we all shared our expertise, learning from each other. Finally, I was able to work with children and use my art skills. I was in heaven.

My mile-long walks to and from the library didn't last long, because the same weekend that I started at Great Neck, I met Doug, who had a car. It seemed as though everything good was happening at once. After so many disappointments, I easily and effortlessly met this terrific man. I had been thinking, *How great it would be to meet the right partner, just about now.* I had run out of ideas about how to meet potential mates, so I decided to answer some personal ads in New York Magazine. In those days, there was no Internet or online dating, so answering an ad had to be done with a pen and paper. I saw an unusual ad one day and thought it could offer some possibilities. It read like this:

> ***Serious and Intense****, but warm and cuddly, successful entrepreneur, 39, seeks brunette with big brown eyes and her own career, 32-35, maybe half-Jewish, for commitment in the arts, meditation, photography, tennis, singing, and romance.*

I thought this little piece of text was just charming and was intrigued that someone would be looking for a half-Jewish girl! I sat down and wrote a note saying I was fairly sure I was the girl he was looking for – except that I had green eyes. After addressing the note and stamping it, the next thought I had was, *This won't amount to anything*, and I threw the note in the trash. But then I thought, *Well, I already stamped it, so I may as well send it.*

About one week later, Doug called me. I did not recognize the name, so he reminded me that I had answered his ad.

"Are you the guy who was looking for the half-Jewish girl?" I asked.

"Yes," he replied.

We had some kind of conversation that I cannot remember *at all*, and made a date to have breakfast that weekend. And when we did meet, I was nervous. But the date was relaxing and easy, and we felt good together.

How remarkable it was that this man came into my life, into my home, with his beautiful singing voice and his guitar. I, who came from a family in which there had always been singing, piano playing, and dancing, had now met someone for whom music was a natural part of life. I remember a day when Doug came to my home with his guitar in hand. There was so little furniture in the apartment, but there was a piano. We both played and sang, and at one particular moment, I thought *How did this happen? We are both here, playing instruments and singing, as if we have always done this.*

It was not long before Doug asked me to marry him. He was an officer in the air force, and so we had a military wedding, crossed swords and all. My three stepdaughters were our flower girls, and my good friend Maria, with whom I had gone to college in Montreal, sang the wedding march in her glorious operatic voice. As I walked down the aisle on the arm of my oldest brother, I just wept, not for any sadness, but from the sheer miracle of this moment in my life.

At the reception we had one long table that formed a horseshoe. Doug and I each took a turn to get up to speak to the guests, telling them that we loved them and appreciated their coming to our wedding. Then several people got up to make toasts – Doug's father, his brother, my brother Herm, and my mother. Her toast was especially noteworthy. She said that while we had voiced our love for the people gathered together that day, she wanted us to remember that "...we all love *you*." That was twenty years ago, and much has happened since. It was a good way to begin married life.

Learning about each other's families has been an ongoing process, for all families are layers deep with stories. Doug is the son of two immigrants, both of whom lived life with great courage. Doug's father, Hank, whose real name was Henry, left Germany when he was just seventeen, and came to America. He said goodbye to his mother and grandmother, knowing he would not see them again. He had known at a young age that he wanted to leave Germany because he could see nothing to look forward to. "I looked to the future," he told me, "and there was nothing there but a bland life in a poor country."

When he arrived in New York in1929 it was the time of the Great Depression. This was a worldwide problem and had had its effect on Germany. Hank had stories about years back in Europe when there was nothing to eat but turnips.

Hank was lucky and clever – he had learned a trade in Europe and was able to get work in the States as a baker. He knew how to make European-style bread, rolls, plum cake, and Christmas *stollen*, fragrant with lemon zest. For awhile he earned a living from that. He knew no English when he arrived, but learned to speak by going to the movies and listening to the language.

When Doug and I met, it was amusing to learn that both our fathers were named Henry and both were born in 1911. Our dads had something else in common, although they never met each other — their attitude toward God and religion. Both were spiritual men who did not subscribe to organized religion but felt a connection to God. Our mothers had something in common, too. They were both Catholic women married to men who did not share their religious beliefs. Each of them had to experience their relationship with God alone, and not as part of a couple.

I liked learning these things about Doug's family. Although we came from such different backgrounds, we did have some extraordinary little details of life in common. We were both named after famous people instead of relatives. Doug was named after General Douglas MacArthur, with whom Hank had fought in the Second World War. And I was named after Queen Elizabeth II, who was crowned in 1952, the year I was born.

In our first conversation, Doug told me that his mother, Iris, was Australian. Hank had met Iris when he was a soldier in the Pacific during World War II. He went to a dance one night and saw this beautiful, dark-haired girl, fresh as the first daffodil of spring. He moved through the crowd, strode over to her and said confidently, "I'm going to marry you."

"Oh no you're not!" she replied. "I'm engaged."

"Baby," he said, "you don't stand a chance." And that was it. He won her over, married her, and brought her to the United States.

Iris was the youngest of three girls and had never been out of Australia. Only twenty-three, she had to make the journey by herself across the Pacific on a boat in which all the passengers were war brides. Then she had to cross America from one coast to the other by train to get to her new home, a small apartment in New Jersey.

Iris told me that the ship out of Sydney, Australia sat in the harbor for three days before departing, and for those three days she had to wrestle with the most painful feelings of separation. She was being wrenched from her family, although voluntarily, and going to a world of which she knew nothing. I try to imagine her standing on deck on a moonless night, thinking about the decision she had made. It must have been a relief when the boat finally pulled out onto the high seas.

Two years after the war, in America, Doug was born. Doug, an all-American boy, the son of two foreigners who made their home in the U.S. A few years later, Hank and Iris had another son, Dennis, and the two boys grew up in New Jersey doing all those things American boys do.

During the war, Hank had learned to be a photographer. He had the kinds of adventures that adventurers dream of – visiting "primitive" societies and gathering data, as an anthropologist would. He was young, handsome, and fearless. When he came back to the States, he opened his own photography business, earned his own living, and supported his family.

With the passage of time, Hank lost his connection to his German relatives, and in fact did not even know who was still alive back in Europe. When Doug was a college student, he suggested that his dad write to an uncle whose address he had kept, to ask if anyone were still there. And that's just what Hank did – in fact, the letter said *If you're alive, write back*. Soon a letter came back saying, *Yes! We're here! Please come*. And so Doug, his brother, and his parents all went to Germany to reconnect with the family.

During the Second World War, Germany had been carved up into two Germanies, and Hank's family was living in the East, which was under Communist rule. Hank, Iris, and the boys had to get special visas to go across the border. Doug described this to me, saying how frightening and somber it was. Everything was bleak and grey, the people looked so sad and hopeless.

On one of the trips to Germany that Doug and I would make *after* the dismantling of the Berlin Wall, we went to see where Hank had grown up. When Hank was a child, his hometown was called Chemnitz. With the onset of Communism, the name was changed to Karl Marx Stadt. And after the fall of Communism, when we went, it had gone back to being called Chemnitz. I had always wanted to see the Eastern part of Germany, so we went to the jeweled cities of Dresden and Meissen and then took a side trip to Chemnitz. As we walked around, Doug recognized almost nothing of what he had seen with his parents.

Anyone who comes from Chemnitz and goes back to visit probably would recognize very, very little of it. It was terribly bombed during the war and so little of what was old and beautiful is there – just a few small pieces – a church steeple, a town hall, that's all. Everything else is modern and ugly.

This was just one of several trips we made to Germany. Our first was at Christmas, when we attended a reunion in Frankfurt for Hank's family. This was 1987, when East Germany was still living under Communism. For Doug, it was a chance to revisit the many relatives who had been confined behind the Iron Curtain. By this time, things had loosened up a bit and East Germans were able to travel to West Germany for a day. It was a great moment for them when they could cross the border and see something of how the rest of the western world was living.

We got to Frankfurt on an overcast morning in mid-December and were greeted with all the gaiety that the holiday season could have. There is no Christmas quite like a German Christmas. There are markets with thousands of ornaments in baskets – miniature manger scenes rendered in glass, wood, or plaster; ceramic tree decorations that look like real gingerbread cookies; glittering, silver shooting stars. There are small angels with gold foil haloes, and silver filigree snowflakes. The market just goes on and on, block after block, coiling around the church and into the square. The shop windows are also splendid, with walls of cuckoo clocks all swinging, clicking, and hooting at once, and giant gingerbread houses frosted with white sugar "snow."

It was wonderful to meet Doug's extended family, to speak German with them, and hear the family history. There were so many relatives! The reunion was a gala affair that was held in what used to be a splendid *Kurhaus*, or spa of old time Germany, where people came to "take the waters" for health reasons. It looked like the set of a 1930s movie with fabulous Bauhaus architecture and Art Deco furniture. Hank's cousins must have saved up for decades to sponsor this party, which featured champagne and food that was served from 11:00 in the morning until the early evening. There were relatives who had not seen each other for many years; there were speeches, poems, laughter, and songs.

A white-haired woman sitting across from me clutched a gift about the size of a small detergent box, wrapped in shiny blue paper. She looked very excited.

"Aren't you going to open it?" I asked.

"I don't have to," she said, squeezing the firm box. "I know what's in it. I get this every year."

"Really. What is in it?"

She smiled, and drawing the gift even closer, lifted her shoulders slightly, leaned toward me and whispered, "A pound of coffee."

This small exchange gave me such perspective about the kinds of deprivations people suffer that we in the United States just do not know. Even in my years in Brazil, where I had observed grinding poverty, I had not really come in close contact with it as I had in this moment with the East German woman, whom I shall not forget.

* * *

By the time I married Doug, I felt I had satisfied the three major elements of life. I had a home of my own, a new profession, and a wonderful husband. I thought back on how, some years before, I had made the choice to not stay in Texas, but to come home to reconstruct my life. And I had done it. I had gone back to my parents' house, started all over again to find work, to find a place to live, and to get married. I had accomplished three important goals and I felt content and grateful for everything. Some of it was not easy, but I had had a lot of support and made some good choices. And now I would continue.

I saw an advertisement for the position of librarian The Chapin School, a well-respected girls' private school on the Upper East Side of Manhattan. When I went for the interview, I knew I was entering a world I had never been in before – one of ease, fortune, and gentility. I had come from midtown, where so much of life was a struggle, with people being pushy, mean, and competitive. This was a welcome change. I was hired by the headmistress (a word I had only read in books) after my first interview. With both reluctance and exuberance, I left my job as executive secretary and moved full time into my new-found field.

The library was on the fifth floor of a beautiful old building. Generations had passed through Chapin, and the school's walls were decorated with photos of school life in days gone by – demure girls in white eyelet dresses with sweet smiles. *Who are these people?* I wondered. *Where have I been all the time that they were living their lives?* This was a branch of New York society I had never touched upon before.

The job was ideal, at least for the first two years. The library was quaint and cozy, its shelves filled with well-preserved volumes that many small hands had held. Everything I had wanted to accomplish as a librarian was possible now – building the collection, making the library a welcoming place, and getting to know each child. The students were polite, bright, well-to-do girls. They were children of great privilege, who lived in large, luxurious apartments and had country houses too. Many of their mothers had gone to Chapin and wanted their daughters to have the same experience.

There was one student with whom I had a special relationship, which has lasted into the present. A sixteen-year-old named Christina wanted to be a writer. We used to spend a lot of time in the library talking about ideas, stories, her life, my life. We liked each other, and when she graduated and went on to Boston University, we kept in touch through letters. Now she is an adult in the working world, and we are still good friends.

* * *

During my tenure at Chapin a new area of creativity opened up for me. I call it my "Japanese Period." How could I have predicted that in marrying Doug, I would have a chance to go to the Orient because of his career in the U.S. Air Force? He was given the opportunity to do foreign tours of duty in Japan and I was able to go along.

Each of our trips to Tokyo was for a two-week period, and the experience was certainly one of the most extraordinary and unexpected in my life. Doug would work at the American Embassy all day, and I was free to wander around Tokyo, which is a safe and friendly city. You don't have to know Japanese to get around Tokyo – everything is explained with pictures and maps, and you can make your way easily without the use of language! Words are not a good medium for describing Tokyo because our western concepts of color, shape, and form do not apply in that environment. Despite all my previous travels, in Tokyo I saw colors I had never seen before – muted greens and pinks that were the color of tea with milk; yellows that were paler than lemon ice. Perhaps it is the light.

Things are topsy-turvy for a westerner once they are in Japan. Ideas to which we attach mental pictures, such as "department store," mean something else there. A Japanese department store is nothing like Macy's or Bloomingdale's. It is more like a museum of everything you never saw before, in which every item is for sale at an astronomical price. There are little surprises everywhere: you may be coming down the escalator, and on the opposite wall are many tiny television screens all playing different films of butterflies flitting around in nature. You may wish to get a drink or a snack, and there, in what Americans would consider a space too small to use for anything, is an entire restaurant with tiny chairs and tables, a kitchen and counter, and a full menu. And then, as you are seated in this doll-sized but comfortable place, you may hear a whirring noise behind your head. And you turn around and find that embedded in the wall behind glass, there is a miniature village through which a train is passing. And you have to wonder if you have landed on the other side of the rainbow. You step outside into a mishmash of vertical neon signs of letters and colors. And so many people in the streets! And yet Tokyo is not a chaotic place, but rather, an orderly environment.

There is no question that it was essential for me, as an artist, to have had this Japanese experience. I was used to visiting Europe, where everything was left over from a world that was long gone – old cafés, faded streets, crumbling monuments, majestic but somewhat tired looking opera houses, parks, and gardens. But Tokyo was happening right *then*, right at the moment when I was there. For once in my life, I did not feel that I had arrived too late.

The first time we went to Japan, it was cherry blossom season, and the trees were fluffy with flowers. How dreamlike it was to walk up and down the alleyways under a canopy of pink blossoms. In the marketplaces topped by red paper lanterns, vendors were selling hair ornaments like crowns of silver with dangling flowers and slender reeds of metal; ceramic chopstick holders in the shape of butterflies, lily pads, barbells, fans, cows, or tiny teapots assembled like cupcakes, each painted with a different design. In the park, toddlers were skipping around with pinwheels or flying kites shaped like dragons with long tails. Children were walking alone in the street carrying their miniature umbrellas, backpacks, and lunchboxes. This is Tokyo. The sky, the shadows in the small side streets, the brilliance of the flashing neon – that is Tokyo too.

* * *

Just as I was coming into my third year at The Chapin School, I started to think about change. Although I was grateful to have had the opportunity to be a real school librarian so early in my career, I had a strange feeling that somewhere, another population was waiting for me – a population of children with whom I could make more of a difference. And I was right.

I answered an ad for a library position at a school for physically disabled children. Since I had been looking for a more meaningful mission, this seemed appealing. The morning I got the phone call, I just knew that the next step of my life was coming, and gratefully accepted the invitation for an interview.

The Human Resources School was out on Long Island in a suburban neighborhood. The moment I walked in, I felt a sensation that was absolutely clear; there was great love in the place. I spoke for a while with the superintendent, who then offered to have someone take me on a tour of the school. As I walked around the building, I passed classrooms in which all the children, although in wheelchairs, were happily engaged in learning. There was an extraordinary atmosphere, as though everyone were there for a common mission – to make life easier and more meaningful for these children.

When I returned to the superintendent's office, I said quite plainly, "I want to work here. I want you to hire me; I will do a good job for you." He smiled and thanked me for coming out.

Within a day or two I got a job offer, which I accepted. Thus I began the next part of my career as a librarian. At Chapin I had been working with children of great privilege; at The Human Resources School I worked with children who were greatly disadvantaged. Some had such heartbreaking conditions – no arms, no legs, terrible terminal conditions. Others had just been in bad accidents that had marked them for a lifetime of disability. But somehow, the school was not a sad place. The children were just as enthusiastic and excited about life as other children, wanting to be astronauts, basketball players, and ballerinas. Their disabilities did not seem to dampen their zest for life. And they loved to read. They came wheeling into the library with bright faces, eager to see the new books. Yes, they were just like any other children, except that they could not walk.

I worked with people who genuinely loved children and had

patience such as I had never seen. The superintendent who had hired me was a young and vibrant man who made work a pleasure. I think what anyone wants in a job is to work for someone who appreciates your talent and lets you use it. Work is not just about money, prestige, or advancement. It is about feeling that what you are doing has meaning for yourself and others. Without this kind of satisfaction, most jobs eventually become boring, routine, and depressing.

At Human Resources, everything I knew how to do was useful. My background in music and art was called upon when it was time to prepare for a Christmas show or special event. My love of books, children, and storytelling was in great demand and every day was meaningful. And no one could tell me that I was not in the *real world* (wherever that is).

At Christmas we put on spectacular shows. Imagine that – a show with music, dancing, singing, and acting – but with all the children in wheelchairs. We had a team of four faculty members who brainstormed. We were so excited, laughing, visualizing, using our imaginations to produce a show that would be a great experience for the children and would amaze the audience. It is astonishing what people can do when they all have the same goal. I kept thinking, *I am so lucky to be here, right now, with these people*. And this is *work*! I couldn't believe it was a day of work.

In the library, I had an assistant who made a tremendous impact on my life, although she died during my tenure at the school. Marilyn was unique, and I could not believe my good fortune in having her as a companion. She was a peaceful presence, whose good humor was not affected by her having a terminal illness. We developed a deep friendship in a short time. Marilyn loved the children and they felt the same way about her. Perhaps her best quality was that she only saw the highest and best in everyone, never finding fault or judging anyone.

When the doctors told Marilyn she might only have only six months to live, I asked her how she felt about that. She told me, "Well, if all I have is six months, I will be very happy if I can spend them here in the library, with you and the children." That is almost how it ended, but not quite. Marilyn needed to go to the hospital and within a few weeks, she died there.

In this job, I finally got the glass case I wanted, like the one I had seen as I walked by the Jamaica Library that day so many years before. The school library had two glass windows that looked out on the hallway. They were *mine*, and I could do anything I wanted with them. Every month, I mounted a display made of detailed paper figures. Yes, I finally got to make those paper figures I had wanted to make as a teenager! I enlivened those windows with figures of Pilgrims, cartoon characters, children in their 'round-the-world costumes. People would pass the windows to see what was new, just as people used to pass the windows of our family home to see what my mother had done. I was indeed lucky to have my chance to share my artwork that way.

When Marilyn passed away I used the windows as a place to display a memorial – a silk flower wreath with a small hand-painted plaque on it saying *You Will Always Live in Our Hearts*. Perhaps that was the best use of those windows.

It was a privilege to work at Human Resources, which is now called the Henry Viscardi School, after its founder. Henry was a charming and charismatic man, who, in the 1960s, gave himself the mission of bringing disabled children "out of back rooms." He created a school in which these children could be with others like themselves and where everything would be accessible to them. Henry had grown up with a tremendous handicap but had great parents, and he knew that with enough support, a disabled child might have a decent and meaningful life. I believe it was this core mission that penetrated the thinking of the employees and made it possible for us to do our jobs.

The time came when I had to leave The Henry Viscardi School. I did not want to leave, but I had to. As much as I loved the work, the people, and the children, I had to make more money. And I could not deny that without Marilyn, something had gone out of the job for me. I left suddenly, in the middle of the school year.

In a way, my experience at HVS was like a compressed lifetime of library work; I had the satisfaction that people seek after decades of dedication to an organization, but sometimes never find. I had made good friends and had the chance to use the talents I had never been able to share before. Soon after I left, the other members of the "creative team" left also. This is something I have noticed about life – sometimes we are part of a team, group, or family that has its own special energy. It may last a long time or be short-lived, and we never know how long we will have the privilege of enjoying it. In this case, it was just three years, but how I remember those years and cherish them.

* * *

During that splendid time at HVS, Doug and I bought a house in New Jersey. We kept our apartment in New York, but added another dimension to our lives by changing environments on the weekends. Doug was not a city boy and found Queens to be too urban. He felt he needed something to balance out the frenetic nature of New York life. We drove down to New Jersey one November weekend and within two days, bought a sweet little house near the beach.

I have never really been a big fan of the beach because of my beach experiences as a child. Those days were good ones, but with the awareness I have as an adult, I would not want to relive them. We kids used to go with Dad to Jones Beach, which was a fair ride from our house. Nowadays people go to the beach with all kinds of equipment for their comfort – toys, rafts, lotions, food, chairs, umbrellas, and enough drinks for the whole day. We did no such thing. We had an itchy army blanket to sit on and no food at all, because Dad liked to buy lunch at the concessions on the boardwalk. As we got into our suits and prepared to trundle into the car, Dad had a little ditty he used to sing to get us in the mood:

To the beach! To the beach! To the beach,
CockDECKtal, yitz-ka-da-BOOM-bah!...

Then there was another song for the road, although this one was more suited for picnics, for its lyrics included a kind of inventory:

Did you bring the pickles, pickles, pickles?
Did you bring the mustard, mustard, mustard?

But that's all I remember of that. Anyway, we didn't bring anything to eat. No tidy little plaid bag with sandwiches and a thermos for us. We were going to rough it.

We usually made this trip without Mom, and before lunch Dad used to say, "Let's eat all the things that Mommy wouldn't want us to eat." This meant hot dogs, pizza (whose thick end crust we called the *golden crunchy*), and ice cream, specific to Jones Beach, called Mell-o-Roll. To say we were eating things Mom would not have wanted us to eat was to ascribe to her traits that she did not have, because she of all people loved to indulge in food. So in that sense, my father was assuming a pseudo-personality, like that of a television father. We played along, knowing it was all a game.

There were no ocean waves that were too high for my father. He loved to dive into the rough, crashing sea and taught us to do the same. He taught Herm and Joe how to ride the waves all the way to the shoreline, and taught us how to duck a terrifying, oncoming mountain of water by simply surrendering and going under it. When we'd had enough of the freezing water and being tossed about in the violent surf, he'd say "Let's go in." I thought the use of the word "in" was curious, as we were really going *out* of the water, but that's the way we all said it.

Getting a sunburn was a normal part of a day at the beach. So was riding home in the car on the uncomfortably hot flannel seats of the Chrysler (and later on the scorching hot vinyl seats of the Pontiac) our suits all full of sand, our skin all red. There were showers at the beach, but that was for *other* people, people who had money to waste on such trifles. In our family, showers were something you took at home.

When we did get back, the solution to all discomfort was Noxema skin cream smeared everywhere and about three days of suffering. That's how it was. This may be why I was not too enthusiastic about Doug and me getting a house at the beach. Those Jones Beach days were fun, as long as they were a memory.

But buying our beach house proved to be a very smart move for us because every creative person needs some kind of retreat from daily life, and what is more soothing than the ocean?

* * *

Doug and I always loved to travel, and made many, many trips together, too many to write about here. We would usually go to

London at least once a year; we had wonderful friends there whom we used to visit. Sometimes London would be the final stop for us after we had made a longer trip, say to Germany or France. No matter where we had been, we always felt we were coming home when we got to London and to our friends' house. They lived in a cozy little flat that seemed to be waiting for us. We would still be going there today if they had not decided to move to Spain, which is nice too, but not comparable with England.

One of the trips we made was to France to see the home of my favorite French author, Colette. Colette had written about her childhood home so tenderly in her book *My Mother's House*, a collection of essays about growing up. She speaks of the cats, the neighbors, the garden with its mysterious pathways, the trees she climbed to look over the garden wall. *My Mother's House* is Colette's only collection of childhood memories, but it contained enough reminiscences to inspire me to go and see the house in which she lived.

As we drove out of Paris, we went from the highway to a four-lane road, to a two-lane road, until the street got very narrow and we were in Colette's hometown, Saint Sauveur-en-Puisaye. It was October and the light was just right for making a literary and nostalgic journey. I wanted to see the house as Colette described it: "...the street rose steeply, which meant that the stables and shed, the hen-houses, the laundry room and the dairy were obliged to huddle around a closed courtyard at the bottom of the slope."

It was not hard to find the house because the town is so small. Indeed, it does stand at the top of a steep street. A small, blue enamel plaque on the front states that Colette lived there, but apart from that, it is a private residence. That's OK. I did not want to see the inside but rather, the surrounding areas where Colette had run and played as a child.

Colette's childhood was nothing like mine, but I feel a kinship with her. Though we lived a half a century apart, our literary minds and hearts meet in that place called *home*.

* * *

In my quest for a new position with a higher salary, I took one

Sunday afternoon to look at the jobs in the New York Times. There I saw an ad for a law firm that was looking for someone with a librarian's skills. But the job was not in a library. It was doing research with trademarks, and required someone who could think like a librarian and could work in more than one language. I answered the ad and soon heard from the law firm, which was in midtown Manhattan. Not long after that, I was hired.

Well, I did get that money I wanted, but it took me quite some time to get used to the idea that there were not going to be any children in my workday. *Where are the kids?* I kept wondering. The job was difficult for me; I had been used to running a library, reading stories, having a very varied day. This job, like many jobs, consisted of just one activity all day long. While the people in the office were bright and sharp, the work was mono-dimensional and the day seemed endless.

The artistic side of me was not getting nourished, so in order to keep it thriving, I decided to learn a new language. It didn't matter which language, as long as I could get to my lessons on my lunch hour. I opened the *Yellow Pages* and looked under "Language Instruction." There were lots of schools in the midtown area. I called a few, but none of them had time slots that fit my schedule. And then I saw a *tiny* listing that said "Greek Language Center," with an address right across the street. I called and spoke to the one and only person working there – Trifon Tsifas, the owner, director, and teacher. I made an appointment to meet with him.

The school was in one of the last remaining small buildings in the midtown area. A low, brownish building, about one hundred years old, it actually had an elevator that was still operated by a human being. I went up to the third floor, stepped out in the dim hallway and rounded the corner. And there was the Greek Language Center – a frosted glass door with gold letters. I knocked and walked in, not knowing that a very important chapter of my life was about to begin.

Mr. Tsifas was a very polite gentleman with a calm demeanor. I explained to him that I wanted to take private lessons for no purpose other than to keep my mind happy while I was in this law job. I signed on to take lessons twice a week, at noon.

From the first lesson, Trifon was delighted with the ease with which the language took hold of me. He had trouble believing that I was not at least part Greek. But I knew the secret of this magic – I was in love with the language. I enjoyed making the sounds needed to form the words and was intrigued by the way everything fit together. And so began my love affair with Greek. I got a notebook and carried it everywhere with me – to the beach, on the train, into bed at night. I would leave my office at lunchtime and go flying to my Greek lesson as though I were meeting a beloved friend, and indeed I was, for I loved Greek, and I loved my teacher. He was learned and refined, generous and good-natured. There, in that teeny tiny classroom, with a cup of espresso, I sank into a world of higher, better thoughts – of literature, language, and life itself. As my ability with Greek improved, I was able to tell Trifon stories about my own life – but in Greek! Most delicious were hot summer days when a thunderstorm would erupt. Inside the little classroom, we'd have the air conditioner on and behind its rumble was the sound of the storm – I loved that – the hot, horrible day outside, bursting at its seams with rain, and Trifon and I inside, in the cool serenity of the classroom, with our coffee and our Greek.

* * *

I stayed with Trifon for seven years, even after the law job ended. Then one day I knew it was over. I had learned all the Greek I could learn from my teacher and I would have to go out on my own. Doug and I decided to take a trip to Greece to give me a chance to "try out" what I had learned.

Although many people in Greece speak very good English, they are thrilled to find out that an American has gone to the trouble of learning *their* language. How many times during that trip I answered the question, "Why did you study Greek?" which was almost immediately answered by the asker himself, "Are you married to a Greek?" or "Do you work for a Greek company?" These are reasonable guesses, but of course, they are not reasons. I would just say that I did it for pleasure, which is even more amusing to the person asking the question.

But whether or not one speaks Greek, Greece is a place worth visiting. In fact, Doug and I went twice within a three-year period, once to see the magnificent city of Athens and the island Santorini, and the next time to see the island of Mykonos and then back to Athens. And a few years after going to Greece, I wrote *Beginner's Greek*, textbook in which I incorporated everything Trifon had taught me and perhaps a little more. Having studied so many languages, I wrote the textbook I had always wanted, one that would teach the language in a logical sequence. I took great pleasure in assembling all the notebooks and papers I had accumulated over the seven years with Trifon, and rolled them into one large work. For the cover, I made an illustration that is a composite of several Greek streets, choosing the components I like best – the white houses, hanging gardens, the solitary cat sitting in the sunlight. In a sense, I created my own ideal street. How rich, how important was that decision that I had made seven years before when all I needed was some nourishment for my hungry soul. It was not so much the language that added to my growth and development. It was the whole episode, and the relationship with a master teacher who opened a portal for me.

* * *

During my time at the law firm, I always had a thought at the back of my mind that I was going to go back to library work. One day I got a call from someone at a large Catholic high school in Queens, saying that they wanted to interview me for a library position. To this day, I don't know where that school got my name and resume, because I never applied there. The invitation for the interview just seemed to come out of nowhere, and I took it as a sign that it was time to make a move again.

When I showed up to meet the principal, I was kept waiting a while in the outer office. I used this time to study the photos on the wall – there were pictures of the most recent graduating classes and the current senior class. Standing near me were some senior girls who were also looking at the photos. I asked them if they were in the graduating class, and they said they were, giggling with excitement. We chatted for a bit about how their senior year was going and what their plans were for after graduation.

Then the principal, a tall, friendly man with brilliant white hair, came out to greet me and ushered me into his office. This was an unusual interview, because this gentleman was not as interested in my qualifications as a librarian as he was in my rapport with the students. He said he had been watching me from his office and noticed how easily I spoke to those girls. He continued, saying that this was the quality he had been looking for in a librarian – someone who liked kids and enjoyed interacting with them. He hired me on the spot. This little story illustrates one of the principles of life that I hold very dear: you never know who is watching and how your behavior speaks about you.

A few weeks later, I started at the school, immediately going to work to make the library as pleasant a place as possible. It was a sun-filled room with very high ceilings, and at first glance, was very impressive. But on closer examination, it revealed a problem one often finds in school libraries: no new books had been purchased in a very long time. Just looking at the collection, one could guess the last time that the library was really functioning was in the late 1960s. It all looked quite neglected, as though reading had gone out of style.

Over the next few months, I freshened up the shelves with new materials, threw out old books, and made the library a welcoming place for the students. I loved my job, despite many obstacles which I don't even want to think about, much less write about. I tried, while I was there, to learn as much as I could about myself and life at the school. Not all of it made me happy, which is to be expected almost anywhere.

I did make some good friends, both among the faculty and students, and also had a chance to flex some muscles that had not been used for awhile. There were courses to teach and clubs to run, and I took these opportunities with pleasure. This gave me a chance to get to know more kids and help them to bring out some of their talents.

It's something of a shame that shortly after I started working at this school, the principal who had hired me announced his upcoming retirement. I was sorry I had only gotten to know him at the end of his career because we liked and respected each other. The principal who replaced him was a totally different person and I don't think she appreciated inheriting me. Although we liked each other as people, we had different work styles, and it was only a matter of time before she found a reason to ask me to leave. I saw this coming, and sure enough, in the middle of my third year, the job came to an abrupt end. And while it is never pleasant to lose a job, one can look upon such an event as a way to go to the next level of the talent you need to express. This closing out of my library job signaled to me the start of a new era in my life, one in which I would no longer run libraries or work again in the traditional sense.

* * *

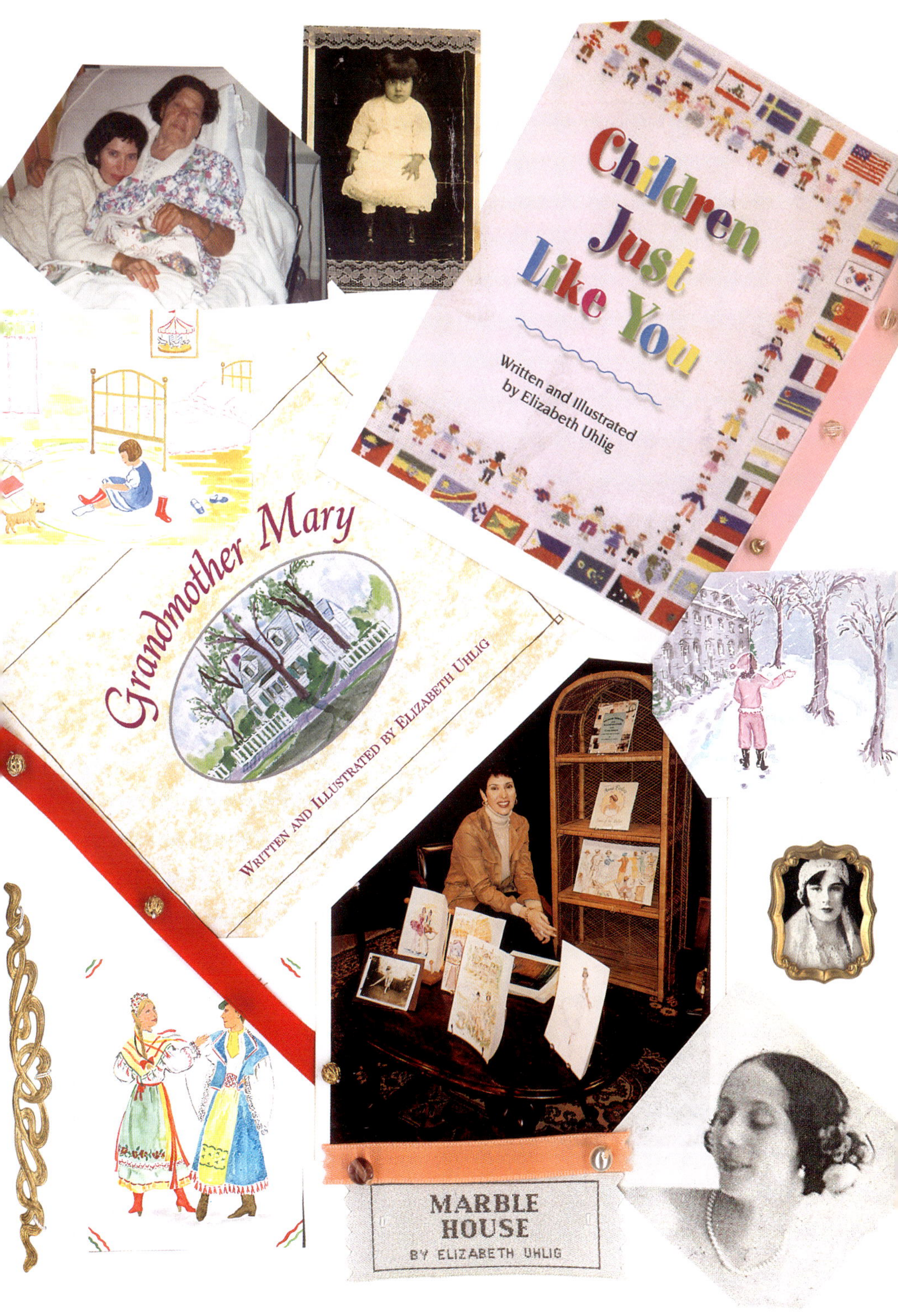
Children Just Like You
Written and Illustrated by Elizabeth Uhlig
Grandmother Mary
Written and Illustrated by Elizabeth Uhlig
MARBLE HOUSE
BY ELIZABETH UHLIG

Part Nine: Full Flower

I had the idea that I wanted to start my own business using all the skills and knowledge I had acquired over the years, and created a service offering publishers translation and illustration of children's books. I started with a mailing to many large publishers, making them aware that I was a specialist in children's literature who could also speak a number of foreign languages. In a very short time, I was contacted by a few companies looking for this service, and I got right to work.

At the same time, I got a few offers to do some illustration work, and so the two services I had wanted to offer were in demand. In the first year, I was quite busy and extremely happy. I was doing exactly what I wanted, creating my own schedule and being my own boss. I could work in the style that I preferred, being as organized and efficient as I had always hoped everyone else would be, and was able to deliver work I was proud of. I worked very, very hard, but enjoyed it, and watched my little business grow.

I was flabbergasted that at the end of the first year I had made $10,000, only from the work of my own hands. The second year, I made $15,000. I had made something out of nothing and was successful. Once you are in your own business, it is hard to imagine ever working for anyone else again. Even though business goes up and down and requires risk-taking and faith, it is so gratifying that you cannot ever imagine being confined again to a "regular" job. I was lucky that I had the perfect conditions in which to take such a risk, but I also have the personality and the drive to do so. Doug, who had done the same thing several years before, encouraged me and stood behind me as I kept asking, "Am I doing the right thing?"

"You're doing everything right," he'd tell me. He believed I would be successful and never said one discouraging word.

* * *

Then one day, after having illustrated and translated other people's books, I decided to write and illustrate my own. Children often ask me why I became an author, and they frequently use the word "inspired," as in "What *inspired* you to become an author?" I answer them thus: You don't have to be inspired to write a book. You just have to have a story you would like to share with other readers. I guess it's great to feel inspired, but I wouldn't advise waiting for that. How would we know that we were inspired anyway? What would that look like? A lot of energy or excitement? Feelings of confidence that we are going to be successful? Anticipation of other people applauding our work?

Instead, I recommend that you find a topic or story you like, that you think other readers will like, and that you can tell about in a way that no one else has before. That's not so hard. We all have something we like, and surely we can find an audience who will also like it. And since each of us is unique, we can tell our story in our own way without closely mimicking someone else's work.

A good place to start is in our own families, where there are loads of stories. The further you reach back in your family, the more interesting the stories get because they blossom out of a world you did not live in. My first book, *Grandmother Mary*, is the story of my mother, her unusual childhood during World War I, and her subsequent life events. I chose my mother's story because I liked it and because I knew it had a good lesson for children.

I was not sure how I would construct the story, but there were some texts that served as models for me. When I was in the first grade, Miss Hallock read us one of the all-time great picture books, *The Little House*, by author/illustrator Virginia Lee Burton. I commend my six-year-old self on being so astute as to realize that this book had such an important message. In fact, the book's message is even more significant today as we watch forests and countryside communities disappear and become ugly cities and suburbs.

The title character is a small house, not unlike the one I grew up in, located in a bucolic country setting in the early twentieth century. The author/illustrator uses the first few pages to explain how very happy the little house is to be out in the country, watching the change of seasons and the rhythm of country life. Burton herself lived in Vermont and had close ties with nature. Her illustrations reflect her skills as a textile designer in their repeating patterns of suns and moons across the open sky.

But then city life starts to encroach on the little house's environment. On the horizon, the reader can see just the slightest hint of urban life starting to rise up. And then one day an *automobile* ventures out into the country. The little house knows something is changing. With the turning of each page, the basic scene is the same, but with the addition of more elements of the city. The little house, though, still sits in the middle of each illustration. Eventually, the house is all but obscured by the downtown's elevated train and the darkened, dirty sky, which blocks out the sunlight.

As readers, we share the house's sadness at seeing the disappearance of her natural environment. We feel her sense of abandonment at now being uninhabited, forgotten, and broken down. But then relief comes as a woman passing the house recognizes it as the one her great-great-grandmother lived in so long ago. She arranges for the house to be lifted out of the city and brought to the country, to sit once again among the flowers and the open, green spaces.

As a child, I was touched by the story, and felt a deep sense of nostalgia. I worked this theme into *Grandmother Mary*, in which my parents' house is just as much a character in the story as any of the people are. Toward the end of the book, the narrator mentions that the grandchildren of the family "... would go out walking to find hidden, magical places their parents had known years ago. Some of the places weren't there anymore." This refers to the constant building and changing that was going on in our neighborhood with the construction of St. John's University. For years and years we witnessed the disappearance of the woods where we used to go sledding, and the giving way of small, quaint shops to sterile, new ones.

I don't know if *The Little House* started me on this kind of thinking, or if the seeds of it were already there and the book helped them to sprout. It doesn't matter. This is one of the roles that books play in our lives – to make us more aware of what we may already know. At any rate, *The Little House* is indisputably one of the most relevant books today, with our ever-growing cries against hideous urban sprawl that is making our country lose its regional character and depleting resources and habitats for animals. Could Virginia Lee Burton ever have known, when she wrote this affectionate tale of country life, that her message would reach through so many future generations of readers? I wonder if my books could ever do the same.

There was another text that served me: *Miss Rumphius*, by Barbara Cooney. In the story, the title character is followed from childhood through to old age. But the story is circular – we meet the character when she is already old, and then flip back to her childhood and start the journey forward. That is how I got the idea I could write about my own mother, who was eighty-four at the time.

Using *Miss Rumphius* as structural model, I wrote *Grandmother Mary.* It was not easy to choose what to put in and what to leave out, as I was tempted to tell everything. But we cannot do that in a memoir. It is best to choose a theme and write only that which supports the message. The theme of this book is that a person can have a less-than-perfect childhood and still grow up to be a solid human being, a loving parent, and a wise adult. My mother had many hard circumstances as a child, but she made good choices and had so much courage and gumption that she was able to live a healthy, rich, and long life.

Her story was much bigger than the one I would write, so I had to assemble everything and then select what would be included. It all started in Connecticut. Right up to the last days of her life, Mom responded to the word "Connecticut." At age 94, she had so little vocabulary left and could remember almost nothing – you could say the names of her children, her husband, her dog – they were meaningless to her. But if you said "Connecticut," her eyes became bright and a smile came to her face. Sometimes she would also volunteer the words, "*I* come from Connecticut!"

She had only lived in Connecticut until she was twelve. As I have mentioned earlier, my grandmother had placed my mother with Aunt Theresa, who had lots of money and no children. Theresa proposed that she give little Mary a privileged upbringing. This childhood, rife with luxury but bereft of love, lasted until Theresa was killed in a car crash. This turn of events eventually sent my mother back to her own mother, whom she barely knew, and who had had many more children in my mother's absence.

It would have been tempting to write a long, long story about my mother, but I wanted to write for children. I extracted from the story of her life only those pieces that contributed to my theme, and carved away the pieces that did not. Then, working from old photos and other reference material, doing research on the clothing, hairstyles, and backgrounds, I made the illustrations.

As part of my research, Doug and I went on an outing to Brooklyn, seeking out some of the places that are in the story. We had a tiny white convertible at the time. We sat Mom in the front; I, holding the map of Brooklyn, sat in the back, and Doug was at the wheel. We rode with the top down, and as we drove in and out of the streets of Bushwick, Mom had perfect recall about what had been on this corner and up that street. Even though she had not thought about these landmarks for decades, she pointed out buildings and shop fronts that were the places of her youth, with no problem. She *certainly* did not need the map.

We found the street where she had lived when she met my father, the corner candy shop where she had known the owner, the old brick building and adjacent church that had been her school. She pointed out the house she was living in when my father had rolled the big wooden crate up the front lawn and she had invited him in to see the new baby. The house was quite dilapidated, but I used my brain like a computer, rolling time backwards to imagine what that house might have looked like back in 1930 when my mother was a teenager. Later, when I made the illustration, I depicted it as it had been in those early days.

I had no idea how this book was going to get published, but I did not let that stop me – I just forged ahead with my idea, full of passion and energy. Once the manuscript and pictures were ready,

I started to contact publishers. I was willing to send the book around for six months and knew that rejection would be part of the experience. At just about the six month mark, a small publisher offered to take the book, and I took a chance and gave it to her. But alas, this turned out to be a wrong move, for this publisher was not legitimate. She held on to the work and after numerous delays, produced nothing. After three years of waiting, I withdrew the book.

Quite discouraged, I was about to abandon the whole idea of being an author, when Doug said, "No, we have come so far, we're not giving up now. We'll publish the book ourselves." He reasoned that we had at least as much on the ball as this "publisher" did, plus we had ethics and business sense. We spent our own money and had the book printed up – 2,400 copies. Now we had formed our own publishing house, which we called Marble House Editions. The name came from Steve and Karen's little son Danny, who was about five years old at the time. When he used to come and visit me at my apartment, he would play with a glass bowl of marbles and therefore "named" my home "Marble House." I thought it was an elegant name for my company.

I shall never forget the moment when the boxes of *Grandmother Mary* were delivered. I walked in the door that day and Doug handed me the first copy. It was so beautiful to hold! Its glossy dust jacket on the firm hardback cover, the shiny paper that held the story and the lovingly painted pictures are unforgettable.

I sent samples around to bookstores and libraries and managed to sell a few hundred copies. But as a small publisher, I needed to find a way to sell more books and reach more readers. I sent letters to one school district in New York asking if I could come and visit the children and share my book. I was not asking to be paid, just to read my story and show the students the original artwork, which the general public never gets to see. I offered the school the opportunity to buy the books at a discount, or have the students buy a book, if the school would permit that.

My mail campaign resulted in invitations to forty schools, and by the end of the school year, all the books were gone. *Grandmother Mary* is now a collector's item. But best of all is that many, many children enjoyed the story and I got to express myself as an author and artist.

My mother was amazed that modern-day children would find her life story interesting. But I was not surprised, because when a story has universal value, it does not matter when or where it takes place. Many children could relate to a child having been separated from his or her mother, or having grown up without a father. It did not matter that the story took place almost a century ago.

Each of us has stories in our families that could be interesting and educational for readers. I always encourage young authors to look into their own family circles, to listen and to ask questions, for there are many good stories hiding there. Even the most hideous or sad story can be meaningful if the author extracts the message and makes it palatable for readers.

* * *

Sometime after the publication of *Grandmother Mary*, I asked my mother, "Whatever happened to your father after your parents got divorced?"

"He got married again, to a woman named Louiselle who had just come from Italy. They had two children, Steve and Rosemarie."

"Really? Where are Steve and Rosemarie?" I asked, new excitement building.

"They're up in West Haven, Connecticut."

"Why didn't we ever visit them?"

"What for?" she asked. "I didn't have much of a relationship with them. I only met Steve a few times. I don't know much about Rosemarie."

I wanted to have a relationship with them, though. I had not been able to have one with my grandfather, but I would find a way to have one with his son, my uncle Steve. And I would find out whatever pieces of my mother's story were missing.

I called Information and got the phone number of Steve Simeti in West Haven. It was late to be calling someone's house, but I did not care. A woman answered.

"Hello," I said, "my name is Elizabeth, and I am looking for Steve Simeti, son of Christopher Simeti."

"Yes, he's here," the woman answered in quite a friendly voice. I explained who I was, and she quickly said, "Steve, your niece is on the phone." That was all there was to it. My uncle came to the phone and I explained that I wanted to know him and anyone else to whom I was related.

He did not waste any time. "Yes, I remember my sister Mannie," Steve said. "I always liked her. She always had so much *class*. You'll have to come up and visit us." And we made a date. It was that easy.

I took the railroad, as I had done so many years ago with my mother when I went in search of my grandfather. The train stopped at precisely the place on the platform where Uncle Steve and his wife Jo were standing. I knew Steve at once, for he looked exactly like his dad. And just as I had melted into the arms of my grandfather, so I did with my uncle.

We got into the car and drove to their house. On the way, as we drove along the coast road, in one particular spot I got a familiar feeling, but said nothing. Then, just as we rolled past that spot, Uncle Steve said, "Right there, where we just passed, that was where my Aunt Michelina's house was." *Michelina. The little house with the gnarled trees and the gold stars in the window*. I had *felt* it when we drove by. It was something about the light, the distance from the water, and the mood. She was not there, the house was long gone, but something remained, even after more than thirty years. It was eerie and wonderful.

"Michelina was your aunt?" I asked. "Explain the relationship to me."

"She was my mother's sister," Uncle Steve replied. Then I put it together. Michelina, the maid of honor at my grandparents' wedding, introduced my grandfather to his next wife, Louiselle. She was Michelina's sister, newly arrived from Italy. Louiselle and Christopher got married and they had Steve and Rosemarie.

I can't help but wonder: was my grandfather so shocked by my grandmother's having fallen in love with Alfred while he was at war that he turned around and married someone he barely knew, the sister of a family friend? How happy could this new marriage have been?

When we arrived at their home, Aunt Jo, sensing immediately what I had come for, said, "I know you want to see these," and brought out some old photo albums. Walking me through the pages, I saw faces of people I had only known when they were old – my grandfather, my uncles, and some people I had never known. Aunt Jo peeled a well-preserved photo of Christopher from its page. "Here," she said. "You'll want this."

As I visited with Uncle Steve and Aunt Jo, I heard them and their three grown children talking about "Grandpa Chris." These cousins of mine had had the benefit of a grandfather close at hand, a grandfather who did all those things that kids love – teasing, telling stories, going for walks. Not that I had missed anything in my childhood, having the parents I had, but it seemed odd and disturbing to me that my grandfather had only been a short distance away in Connecticut, with a whole other family. Yes, I would have liked knowing him as they had.

Then more revelations came: I learned that I still had relatives in Sicily. My grandfather's brother, Nick, the baby of the seven children, was *still alive*. And amazingly, although infuriating, was learning that until I was about seventeen, I had had a *great*-grandmother living in Sicily. Wouldn't I have *loved* to have known that! My great-grandmother was still living at the time that I met my grandfather.

This was astounding news to me. How could my mother have had so little interest in her family? I had to know, and I asked her when I got home.

"Did you know that your *grandmother* was still living in Sicily when you were already a grandmother yourself?"

"I didn't CARE!" she answered.

"Why NOT? I would have loved to know that I had a great-grandmother!"

"I was busy living my life!" she said. "I had no relationship with my father. He and my mother separated when I was a baby. Why would I care about a grandmother in Sicily?" It was no use. I just could not make the past come back. It was too late.

I had a similar conversation with Doug once, after his cousin Peter came to the States. Peter is the son of one of Iris's sisters back in Australia, and grew up with the benefit of the family that Iris had left behind. There were cousins and "Nana" and "Grandpa." So Doug, like me, had grown up without that close relationship with his grandparents.

I never gave this a thought until Peter came to visit. Walking into our apartment and seeing the antiques, the lace curtains, and the old-fashioned furniture, he said, "You know what place this reminds me of?"

"I can guess," I said. "Your grandmother's house?"

"Yes," he said. "That's right. My Nana's house."

Nana's house. Did Doug ever see Nana's house, eat there, know what Nana was like? No, just as I had not ever eaten anything or played in either of my grandmothers' houses.

"You missed out!" I said to Doug. "You had a grandmother over in Australia but you didn't know her."

"I don't feel that I missed anything," he said.

But I felt that I had missed something. Not that I could ever get it back, but just for curiosity, we decided to just go to Sicily and see who and what was still there. One of my cousins, who had already made the trip, gave me an address in Pacheco, a small suburb of Palermo. I wrote to my relatives but didn't receive a reply. So we just decided to go.

We flew to Palermo, rented a car, and drove along the western edge of Sicily. It is a place of such astonishing beauty, unrivalled in the drama of its coastline and the character of its ancient streets. Doug, undaunted by the steep roads and windswept terrain, drove us down to Pacheco. This was a small urban village with two and three-storey houses, so old that they must be haunted by ghosts of Sicilians past. We found the house – a stucco row house, like the others, but painted a soft mint green. I approached the door. There was the name plate: Simeti. I felt a pang of awe at finding a lost homeland, one in which I had never lived.

I rang the bell, but no response came. I knocked. Nothing. Then a woman wearing an apron and holding a broom came out on a balcony next door. She waved her hand as though she were shooing something away.

"Those people went away!" she shouted in Italian.

"Where?" I asked.

"I don't know. Maybe Francesca knows. Wait!" And she disappeared for a moment. She came out of her front door, the broom still in her hand, and motioned to us to come across the street. Inside that house a vacuum cleaner buzzed. She banged on the door. "Francesca! Open up! Francescaaaaah!!"

The buzzing stopped and the door opened. A small woman with a cleaning rag in her hand stood there. "What is it?" she asked.

"Francesca, these people are looking for the Simetis. Where are they now?"

"Simetis? They went away."

"I know, but where?"

"I think they went to Marsala."

"Hmmm."

When I explained who we were, the case became a serious one for them. "Let's go ask Maria!" Francesca said. "*She* has a phone number." And so we followed these two women with their cleaning equipment through the little street until we reached Maria's house around the corner.

Tiny Maria answered the door. She looked very happy to see us, which is interesting, since she had no idea who we were or why we were there. Like my Italian cousins, just happy to see us. Francesca explained that I was the granddaughter of Cristoforo, who had left so many years ago to go to America. I had now come looking for the family.

"*Sì, sì*," she cried, "I have the phone number and we will call them in Marsala. But first, let's have some coffee!" She proceeded into her doll-sized kitchen and removed a minuscule espresso maker from the shelf. I felt like we were playing house.

As we waited for the coffee, Doug and I looked around. This was a very old stucco house, somewhat gloomy inside and rather dark in midday. It also felt a bit dank, which made sense, since the walls of the house were as thick as those in a medieval castle. We noticed a few decorations in the room. Of course, there was Jesus with his sacred heart glowing, some souvenir plates from places not too far off – Agrigento, Cefalù, the Isle of Capri. Some wedding photos, recent ones in full, garish color, and others that were quite old. There were photos of the generations gone by – two sepia faces side by side, probably Maria's parents. No smiles there. Her own wedding portrait from when she was a fresh-faced bride, her veil flowing from a crown of orange blossom.

Maria returned with a tray that held the little cups and a large sugar bowl and set it down on a table. We had the coffee and chatted. Doug did not mind that he couldn't understand a word. He was enjoying the surreal experience of having coffee with a total stranger in her home in Pacheco, where we had never been and knew no one.

Then Maria dialed the phone and spoke in a VERY loud voice: "MARIA? It's Maria here! *Sì, sì*, Maria from Pacheco! Your relatives are here from America – here!" And she handed me the phone.

I was terrified. I did not know to whom I was speaking, except that her name was Maria. A very soft voice greeted me. It was my Uncle Nick's daughter (my mother's first cousin). My mother had never mentioned any cousins in Sicily. I explained that we had come to meet her, Uncle Nick, and anyone else we could meet, that I had written a book about our family and wanted to learn more. Reluctantly, she told me they were now living in Marsala, not too far away. Because Uncle Nick was not well, Maria's brother had advised her, "Just lock the door of the house in Pacheco and come here and stay with us." This was a vast disappointment to me, for I was dying to see the inside of that little green house with their name on the door.

Maria informed me that their apartment in Marsala would be hard to find. I thought she was discouraging me.

"If you don't want to meet, that's OK," I said. "I understand. After all, we did not give you any notice."

"Oh no!" she cried, repentant that she had made me feel unwelcome. "It's not that...it's just that Uncle Nick has had a stroke and is lying in bed...but please come." She gave me the address and told me again that it would not be easy.

When I got off the phone, our hostess, who understood *exactly* what had taken place, said, as my mother might have said, "Listen, you go there, you get yourself a place to stay. You take your time, don't rush. See Marsala, and then, if you FEEL like it, you go and find her." Then she said something that was the rough equivalent of *Don't knock yourself out.*

We drove down the coast to Marsala and arrived as dusk was gathering and the rising autumn moon was glazing the sea. As we walked slowly along the *Lungomare*, other visitors and locals were out for their evening stroll, enjoying the soft air and the view of the water. Then night closed in. We had dinner and went to our hotel room. Tomorrow we would continue our quest.

Cousin Maria was right. It was not easy to find the place. Though only a short distance away, the apartment was in a newish, poorly kept complex. Unlike tidy little Pacheco, with its succinct numbering system and approachable houses, this monstrosity was totally impersonal. In the spaces between the large buildings there were pieces of broken concrete, smashed bottles, trash blowing around and stray dogs picking through it. It looked to us as though the builder or perhaps the landlord had run out of money and just left the tenants to fend for themselves.

We drove around the complex looking for the number of the building. Whatever system they were using was not decipherable to us, and it appeared that all the buildings had the same number – like in a nightmare. Suddenly I got tired and didn't want to continue. "Let's just forget it and go on," I said.

"No," Doug said, "Not when we have come so far (the same thing he had said about publishing the book). We know she is somewhere around here. We can find her."

Then at that moment, I saw the postman, leathery-faced little *postino* on a motorcycle. *He'll know*, I thought. I showed him the paper on which I had written the address, and explained how we had made this trip to meet our family. As he nodded and smiled, the skin around his sapphire blue eyes crinkled up.

"Do you know these people?" I asked, wanting confirmation on that smile.

"Of course!" he said, grinning to show what was left of his teeth. "Follow me!" he commanded.

Like the president of the United States being escorted by a motorcade down Fifth Avenue, we drove slowly behind Carlino on his *motociclette*, his mailbag dangling from his shoulder and bouncing around his hip. Over a small walkway and little bridge, down a winding gravel path, we followed him up to the *one* building we had not seen.

He parked his vehicle and, taking a step back and tilting his head up in order to throw his voice to the third floor, he bellowed, "Maria!! Your relatives from America are here!" Then confident that someone was about to appear, he turned toward us, nodded and smiled as if to say, "There, it's *done*," and he disappeared.

A moment later a woman appeared on her balcony, black eyes flashing with anticipation. "I'm coming!" she shouted, with a warmth in her voice that was not there the day before. Imagine if we had not shown up. A minute later, the front door opened and Maria stepped out, embracing us both, a babble of Italian effusing from her lips. We went upstairs and into her apartment. You would never know from the outside of the building how lustrous and elegant the inside would be. There was highly polished, lavishly upholstered furniture, glass tables, pictures in gilt frames, and lamps with small crystal pendants.

We spoke for a few minutes, explaining how we had met the relatives in Connecticut and how they had led me to know of our family in Sicily. Maria listened, enjoying every word. Then she said gently, "Would you like to see Uncle Nick?" Yes, we would. We certainly would like *that*.

We walked down the maple-paneled hallway and into Nick's room.

He lay in bed, a ninety-two-year-old man who was obviously getting very good care from his daughter. Clean sheets with that sweet smell of fresh laundry, a pale light entering through the half-opened Roman shades. I noticed that above his bed hung a large portrait of the Madonna, the same print that was hanging above my mother's bed.

Maria bent gently toward her father. "*Papà, Papà*," she whispered, "Remember when your brother Cristoforo left to go to America?" she asked, as though she had been there when it happened back in 1900. Uncle Nick nodded. "Well, you remember that he married Lucy and had a little girl named Mary? This is Elizabeth, Mary's youngest child. She came here to meet you, *Papà*. She wants to know you."

A papery white hand emerged from under the covers, and a voice that also seemed papery said, "*Piacere di conoscerLa*," as a way of telling me he was glad to meet me. I took the hand. It was soft and cool. Great Uncle Nick, ninety-two years old. Back in New York, his little niece, my mother, was eighty-nine years old. This is how it is when the siblings span more than one generation.

Then I said, "This is my husband, Doug. He wanted to meet you too."

"*Piacere di conoscerLa!*" Uncle Nick said in a strong, manly voice, which was accompanied by a strong, manly handshake. For Doug, a *man*, Nick summoned the strength. I found this to be *very* Italian of him.

We sat in the room and talked, and then, as I might have predicted, Uncle Nick got tired and wanted to rest. That was fine. We had had our visit, we had accomplished our goal. I knew it was time to leave. Just before departing, I asked Maria what happened to the little green house in Pacheco. Was it still in the family?

"*Oh, sì*," she said, "But when my father had a stroke, my brother told me to just lock the door and come here. Too bad. I know you would love to see what I have there…all the old photos and keepsakes." *Yes, I would. I certainly would.* "You see," she continued, "That was my mother's mother's house. When my parents got married, my father got the house as a gift from them. It was not always two floors. It was just a small house, one storey, and my father built the second storey as he became more prosperous."

So much history. There was not one piece of it I was not dying to hear. But I had gleaned a lot and was satisfied.

"Maybe next time," I said. She smiled. Yes, maybe next time.

Maria was all set to make us spaghetti, but we were off to our next destination. We promised to write and so did she. I sent her a copy of my book and she sent a little note and a Christmas card. Curiously, I got a Christmas card several years in a row from the *other* Maria, the one who had made the coffee and the phone call for us. The next time I would hear from Cousin Maria would be a few years later when Uncle Nick would die peacefully in his bed. I wonder if she went back to Pacheco to live in the little green house. Perhaps she is still there.

When we got home, we shared all of this with my mother. As I suspected, she was not all that interested. But what shocked her was seeing the videotape Doug had taken of Palermo, with its shaded boulevards and centuries-old buildings.

"*That's* Sicily?" she said, almost wincing, as though she had the sudden realization of having been told a pack of lies by her family. "I thought Sicily was a backwater!"

"Yes, that's it," Doug said. "It's no backwater, Mom. It's overwhelmingly beautiful."

"Hmm," she said, no doubt thinking, *That's not what they told me.*

* * *

When I next visited the Simetis in Connecticut, they filled in a missing piece of the story. Uncle Nick had lived there with them for seventeen years. He had come to the States to be with his brother (my grandfather) and worked as a cobbler. He spoke perfect English! Maria had not alluded much to this during our visit, except to say that her father had "gone away" for a while, leaving her with her mother and brother. Back then, it was not unusual for Europeans to go to America, make some money and go home again.

So now I had more to think about. Not only had my mother's father been so close by, but his brother had, too. All those years, the two of them were in West Haven together, and their mother back home in Sicily.

What had happened to my grandfather's five other siblings? Two of the boys had been Italian soldiers during World War I and had not come home. The girls, well, I never found out. I had asked Maria, "Are there other Simetis here in Sicily?"

"Yes," she said, "and we are all related. If a person has the name *Simeti*, they are family."

"Do you know them?" I asked, afraid of her answer.

"No," she said. "I never bothered." Like my mother, she never bothered.

* * *

With *Grandmother Mary*, I had reached my goal of writing and illustrating my own book and sharing it with teachers and children, thus fulfilling my dream. I suppose I could have written a bigger book, but I had great success with this first book just as it was. It went into many libraries and schools, and gave rise to a lot of projects for schoolchildren. The irony is that my mother was already in her eighties, and I was concerned that I would have a book about her and she might not live long enough to see the results. But it did not turn out that way. Instead, the book sold out within a few years and *she* lived well into her nineties!

This experience brought such joy that I thought about my next book, and came up with the idea to write about Anna Pavlova, a famous, now long-gone ballerina. I didn't want to write a book about ballet itself, but rather, a story about someone who had a dream and made it come true.

Pavlova lived most of her life in England, and as part of the research for my book, Doug and I made a trip there to see Ivy House, where Pavlova had lived and taught. We went in the dead of winter when England is dark and wet. What an unforgettable experience it was to find Pavlova's house on that cold December afternoon! Ivy House is not a museum, just an old house with a blue enamel plaque that states *Pavlova Lived Here, 1913 – 1938*. You cannot go in, and no one is there to give you any information, so we just walked across the grounds and "felt" her presence, sitting on a stone bench in her garden where she had once sat to gaze at her pet swans. I took some photos and made some sketches that would find their way into the book.

When *Anna Pavlova, Jewel of the Ballet* was finally published, I wondered if boys would buy it, even though it was about a ballerina. I should not have worried, because equal numbers of boys and girls bought the book and loved it. Having had good results with both *Grandmother Mary* and *Anna Pavlova,* I continued to build Marble House Editions and started to take on other authors and author/illustrators. Sometimes we collaborate – the author has the story and I make the illustrations and then publish the book. This was the case with *The Magic Lunch Box* and *Not Another Christmas*, both written by Joan Fitzgerald, a retired art teacher. These books are now out of print, but in their time they were very popular.

The first is the story of a little boy who lives half of the year in New York State with his parents and the other half in Mexico with his grandmother. As a result, he feels does not have a real home. With the help of his grandmother and a little magic, he finds friends and the true feeling of belonging.

The second is a tale about the year Santa decides he does not want to distribute gifts, but would rather go to Florida on vacation. Perceiving that today's children don't "need" him, Santa feels he will not be missed. All goes well until his Florida tour bus takes a detour through a poor neighborhood in Miami where Santa's eyes are opened to how much he really is needed. A mad dash back to the Pole is in order and thank heavens he *does* make it. Just thinking about the ending of this book makes my eyes tear up, even though I have read it hundreds of times! I had great fun illustrating it, painting the interior scene of Santa's cottage at the North Pole. Since none of us has ever been there, we can portray it any way we imagine.

Joan Fitzgerald went on to write three more books, this time for teenagers: *The Iris House, Dark Towers,* and *Merry-Go-Round*. These are chapter books, thrillers in fact, one involving time travel and the other two merely suspenseful. They have good messages for young adults, and although the author crafted them to be mysteries, she embedded good role models and important lessons in her stories.

Then another author, Joan Eiseman, came along. She could not only write but could also illustrate, and her story, *The Tale of Jackie Berry*, had so much potential that I wanted to publish it. I just knew kids were going to love it. It did so well that Joan went on to write and illustrate *Ricardo and the Fisherman*. Adding these authors' works to the Marble House collection gave me a richer, broader assortment of work to offer young readers. Since I don't write fiction, I am glad to have another genre to present, and I think it is interesting for children and teachers to hear about how a publisher selects stories. I look for stories that have a lesson that can be of benefit to kids. The story can be true or not, sad or funny, as long as it teaches the reader something about life. I think I can recognize a good story the minute I read one, and get terribly excited when I have found something of value to bring to my audience.

The next author to come to me was Evelyn Rothstein, for whom I have published four books. Evelyn had written her stories years ago and could not find a publisher. When she saw *Grandmother Mary*, it sparked an idea in her head about a story she had written about her own mother. This was *My Great Grandma Clara*. Evelyn shared the story with me and I loved it, offered to illustrate and publish it. Kids loved it and teachers did, too, so much so that we ran out of the first printing in the middle of the school year and had to send it to press again! We followed this with the story of Evelyn's father, *My Great Grandpa Dave*, and followed both of these with sequels. *Clara* is the story of how a young girl from a rural village in Russia decides to leave her home and come to America. It takes place in the early part of the twentieth century, a time period that I love to illustrate. Using materials from the library and my own personal storehouse of knowledge, I created the mood of the time and place in which Clara lived – the clothes, the streets, the interior of her rustic wooden house in Russia. These are the artist's conception, of course, because the author had no visuals for me to work with. But part of being an illustrator is enjoying the research, creating the characters, their faces, expressions, and gestures.

The *Dave* story takes place during the same time period, but on the Lower East Side of New York. Dave's problem is that at age seven he must leave school because he has a contagious rash. Being a resourceful child, he goes out to work. But even after he is cured, he does not return to school. His dedicated sister Lena teaches him at night so he does not lose ground with his education. When he is caught by the truant officer at age twelve, he is marched back to school and, despite his age, he is placed in the second grade. Dave's goal is to catch up with his peers and graduate on time. Again, everything had to be created – Dave, his mother, the school, and all the other characters and backgrounds.

The sequel to this story, *Dave the Boxer*, is about Dave's teenage years, when he tries his hand at amateur boxing. Always ready to make more money to support his family, Dave is willing to venture into the arena, but soon learns that he is better suited for other things.

Evelyn has lots more stories in her head and I have lots more pictures, so we expect to produce many more books together.

* * *

One day my phone rang and a new author entered my life. Frima Laub had heard about me from a mutual friend and told me she had a story about being a child during World War II. "Are you the lady who writes the books?" she asked. (I loved being referred to that way.) When I answered *yes*, she went on to say "I have a story, but I cannot write it. I can only *tell* it to you."

I invited Frima to come to my home and tell me her story. That afternoon an elegant lady entered my apartment. She looked like one of my ballet teachers of days gone by: slim, with dark hair pulled back in a bun, and wearing lovely clothes. First we sat and talked over a cup of coffee. We were lucky – we felt a great rapport. Then Frima sat on my couch and I sat on the floor with my notebook. I listened as she told me about being a five-year-old girl from a well-to-do Jewish family in Poland, and how the war swept into her life and changed everything. I was spellbound as she described being close to death more than once and how her mother had left her behind with a family as she fled Poland. I tried to picture this sophisticated woman as a brave little girl fending for herself through the harsh Polish winter, with soldiers everywhere.

As Frima talked, I took notes. I understood how she could not write her story, for it was so real to her as she spoke, she could not stop to write it down. But I could, and I knew this would be a valuable book to bring to children. I had an important question for her: "Where did you hide?"

"Between the shadows," she answered. And with that, I knew what the title of her book would be. I offered to write the story and illustrate it for her.

Frima's story was far too cruel and frightening to be told to children exactly as it happened. Frima, who is called *Feema* in the story, was on a death march with her mother and sister and was saved by a miraculous move her mother made. But I did not want to even use the words "death march" in the book. I had to find other ways to describe some of the war's ugliest details without horrifying a young mind. Essentially, it is a tale of gratitude, not one of self-pity or anger. Even though this child endured tremendous hardships, her message as an *adult* is that she was lucky, and in the end, appreciative that her life went in the direction that it did, to America. This is the challenge of memoir writing – to take a real story and modify it for the intended audience. Were the readers adults, I would have told it differently. But because it is for younger readers, the language had to be carefully chosen while still preserving the story line.

When I planned the pictures, something told me to do them in grey ink. It must have been the atmosphere of the 1940s, the war, the nature of the story that dictated this. Using my own reference material from trips I had made to Poland, Hungary, and the Czech Republic, I depicted the Eastern Europe of the author's youth. I had no pictures of Frima's mother, so I just "invented" a 1940-ish looking woman. When the author saw the pictures, she was touched, and said, "How did you *know* what my Mama looked like?" Of course I did not know. I was merely feeling my way through the story. If I did not have a feel for the story, I would not have taken it on.

Marble House published *Between the Shadows* in 2007 and it was immediately met with great approval from readers. The author, who had had no previous experience with writing a book, was delighted and somewhat surprised by this. But I was not. What child would not want to hear such an amazing story of a little girl who survived on her own? And the fact that the story is true makes it all the more valuable.

And so the creation of books continued. One book was born out of my experience as a dance teacher. It had come to my attention that the children I worked with knew nothing about folk dances from other parts of the world. In fact, it appeared that children only knew one kind of dance, contemporary dance. They did not have any idea about the many other kinds of steps and movements their bodies could make.

As a dance coach, I got the idea to write a book on this topic, and later wrote and illustrated *The Whole World is Dancing*. A little rhyming book, it takes the reader on a 'round-the-world journey to twenty-eight different places. There were various influences from childhood that affected the illustrating of this book. One was my doll collection. Knorr, a company that makes powdered soups, had a campaign back in the 1950s in which they promoted dolls in costumes of the world. Each month they offered a special gift: if you mailed them a fair number of box tops from your purchases, you could get a male and female pair of dolls dressed in the costumes of their country.

I had to have all these dolls, as I loved costumes and the very notion of foreign countries. I had no idea how I was ever going to get to all the places in the world I longed to see, so these dolls kept me satisfied while I waited. Actually, underneath the clothes it was all the same doll; just a cheesy plastic doll whose eyes opened and closed, but the costumes were great and full of detail. There was the Dutch doll with her gaily striped dress and delicate pointed lace cap; the Italian doll, who wore a Neapolitan gondolier's costume, and others I cannot recall. These dolls represented for me the world that I would someday explore. As I look at my illustrations for *The Whole World is Dancing*, I see hints of the little Knorr dolls.

Another influence was more subtle. When I was young, I used to see advertisements in the back of children's magazines offering a whole envelope of assorted international stamps for fifty cents. I guess the appeal was that the stamps were small and had finely detailed art on them. I realize now that my attraction to foreign stamps was the seedling stage of my interest in art, foreign countries, and languages, which developed so fully later on.

There was a stamp that kicked off the entire collection. It was from Bulgaria and showed a young woman dressed in folkloric clothes with a wreath of flowers in her hair. Many decades later, "she" would show up as an illustration in *The Whole World is Dancing*, such a deep impression did she make on me. Part of the mystery and beauty for me as a child was that no one knew anything about Bulgaria – it was behind the Iron Curtain and was totally inaccessible to us westerners. I daresay that even today the average person has no idea where Bulgaria is or what the culture or language is like.

Each illustration in *The Whole World is Dancing* was accompanied by a set of two rhyming couplets, and with this rather economical use of language, I included something about the dance itself, its meaning, the costume, and music. I wanted children to see that the dance, its dancer, and his or her clothing all have significance.

All 1,000 volumes sold out in one year. By producing this book, I felt I was able to open young readers' minds to an important message: people everywhere and at every time in history have danced. It is just part of being human. I was so happy to learn that some schools used the book as the centerpiece for dance festivals, projects, and reports.

My delight is to bring as many good stories as possible to children and to speak to as many children and educators as I can. And so it has continued – Marble House has produced more than twenty-four books and I have broadened my scope of schools, now having gone outside New York to some distant places and to all kinds of venues. I never know when I am going to get a good idea for a story or when someone is going to offer me one. I keep my eyes and ears ready and my sketchbook handy.

* * *

Sometimes when the wind blows a certain way and the light is just right, I can remember what it was like to sit in the kitchen in my mother's house. We used to make a pot of coffee and talk, never running out of ideas. We loved each other's company, and it was always painful to say goodbye. It was just around the time I was completing my first book that I felt that the hour was drawing close to say goodbye to her for good.

There was a winter day on which Mom had to go to the emergency room. This was going to be the beginning of many problems, which would eventually lead to her decline. But this emergency was a short-lived one.

There were not enough beds in the hospital that day, so she was put on a gurney in the hallway for many hours. All of us in the family showed up to be with her, but as night fell, it made more sense for everyone to go home. I decided to stay with Mom, as she was frightened of being in the hospital. Having been blessed with radiant good health her whole life, she had not been in a hospital since she had given birth to me forty-five years earlier, and the modern facility was cold and alien to her. She had been a patient back in the days when nurses like herself wore white dresses, crisp little caps, and navy blue capes. Hospital rooms in Mom's day had immaculate, tiled walls and glossy white wooden cabinets with little glass doors. So on the day of this hospital visit, all the modern stainless steel and cold-edged equipment was scary to her. She did not want to be left alone there.

I was not prepared for a night at the hospital. As the hours wore on, a staff member rolled Mom out of the hall and into a small room. It was getting late. I was so tired, but Mom was wide awake. I thought it best to simply crawl onto the gurney and lie there with her, side by side, and talk. It was very cold in that room and the lights were very harsh. I thought, *If we are going to stay here all night, I am turning out the light*. So I did, and to mitigate against the cold, I took my long, orange wool scarf and wrapped it around her head several times and then around mine. This way, we were bound together, our faces almost touching.

She looked at me at such close range, and I could see the love in her tender eyes. "You're going to be famous one day," she whispered. I have no idea what made her say that, except that she must have felt such love and appreciation at that moment that she thought surely the rest of the world would too, one day. I thought it odd, since being famous is not a goal of mine. It was as though she could see something I could not see. I chuckle to myself whenever I am in front of a large audience that is cheering and clapping, and I wonder – is this what she meant?

* * *

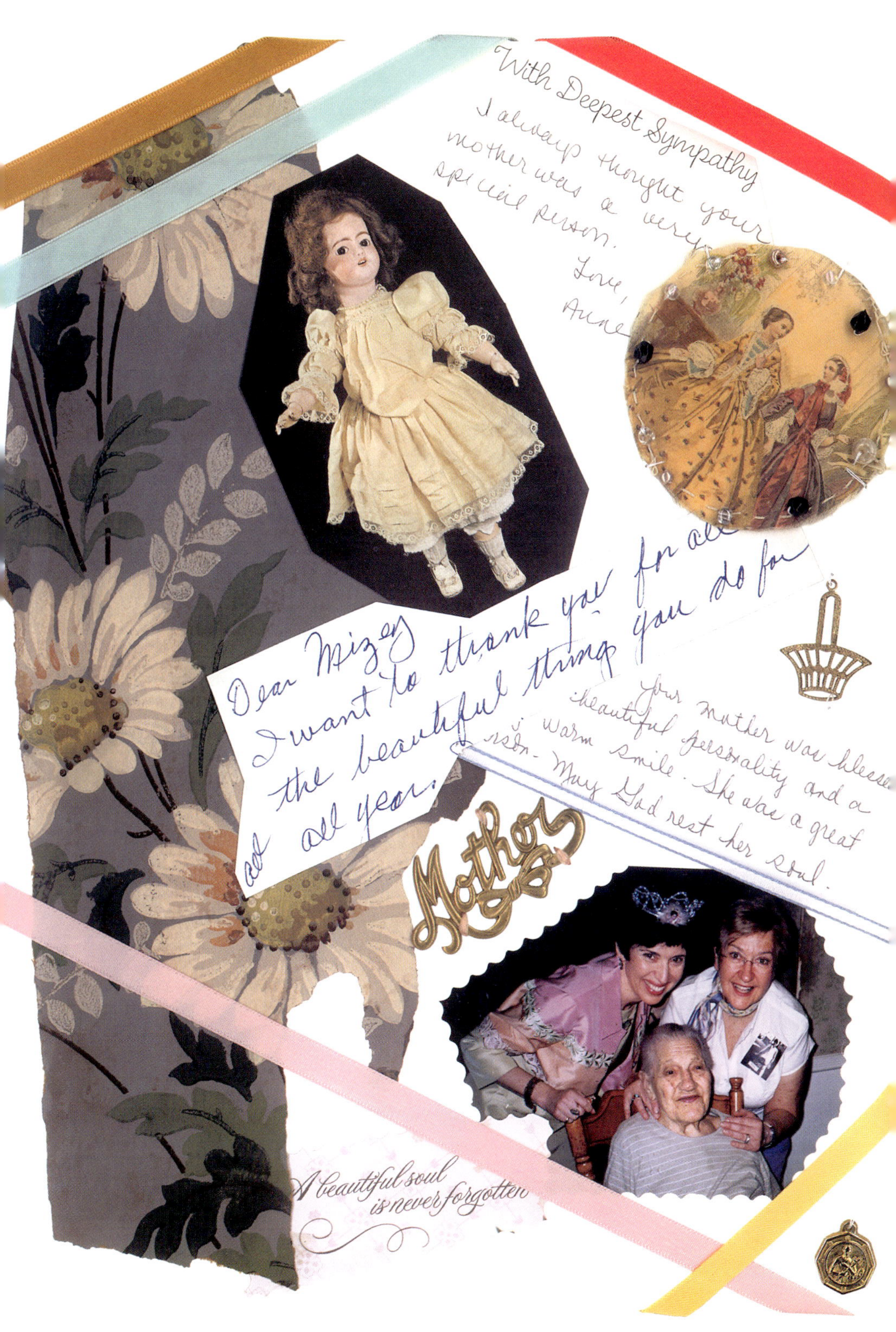

With Deepest Sympathy
I always thought your mother was a very special person.
Love,
Anne
Dear Mizey
I want to thank you for all the beautiful thing you do for all year.
Your mother was blessed beautiful personality and a warm smile. She was a great person. May God rest her soul.
Mother
A beautiful soul is never forgotten

Part Ten: Farewell

Over the next six or seven years, Mom declined very, very gradually. At first she was still able to be alone in her house and needed some assistance with chores. She had friends who dropped by regularly, and even had someone whom she imagined was a kind of boyfriend. She had acquaintances in the park who were dog lovers, neighborhood children who came to visit her or see her pets. She still liked her quilting and sewing, her books, piano, and her television shows. Like a lot of old people, she did not always eat properly, so we all kept an eye on that.

Her pets were still important to her, almost right to the end. When she was younger, Mom had raised dogs with my father, and when I was a child, we had always had cats at home. There was just one cat after the other. We did not take them nearly as seriously as people take pets today. They just lived with us, frequently became pregnant and had litters of kittens. Somehow, there were always people who wanted to adopt those kittens, but any cat that did not get adopted just stayed with us until it became interested in living somewhere else.

If a cat ran out in the street and got killed, or if we determined that it had run away, my mother would just call my father at work and say, as if she needed an extra quart of milk, "Can you stop by the ASPCA and pick up a cat on your way home?" And that night, he'd walk in the door with some small furry kitty in his hand. We'd give it a name and it just blended into the household immediately.

Long after we were all grown and out of the house and my father had gone to heaven, my mother still had a cat. She also had a series of dogs, and they all coexisted peacefully, as though they were living on a farm out in the country instead of on a busy street in Queens. She had so many pets that she ran out of names for them and called the last cat *Kitty*. Her last dog, whose name was *Brandy*, she eventually called *Baby*, which was the name of the dog she had before Brandy. The two dogs had been in the house simultaneously and then Baby died, bequeathing her name to Brandy.

The story of Brandy coming into my mother's life is one I have used frequently to show children that a "story" doesn't have to be anything long and involved, but rather, just a little vignette in which something *happens*. Mom was outside one autumn day raking the leaves when a little boy walked by the house. A small honey-colored dog was following him, and as he passed by, my mother said, "What a cute little dog you have there!"

"Lady," the boy said, "this is not my dog! It's just following me home and I know my mother won't let me keep it! I don't know what to do."

"I'll tell you what," my mother said, "leave it here and I'll post some signs in the neighborhood saying I have found this dog. If someone comes to claim her, I'll give her back. If not, she can live here." No one did come to claim her, so she became a member of the household, instantly bonding with my mother. Brandy fiercely defended Mom from her imaginary foes, like *me*, when I came to visit. The animals were such good companions for Mom. For us as children, they had been no more than household pets, but for her they were almost human.

And so Mom's life continued pleasantly for several years, and we knew we had an extraordinary situation. But in time my mother got so old that she could no longer be alone. It happened suddenly, like a slate shingle slipping from the roof. All at once, she could not keep track of her medicines and would forget to eat. She was not making sense on the telephone and did not know what day it was. Someone had to be with her. But who? We did not know where to turn. My parents had always prided themselves on not *belonging* to anything, not *joining*. They never joined a church, a synagogue, a country club, or any kind of group. So now we were adrift with no place to tap into when we needed help. And we needed help immediately.

Joe was coming home from California for a visit, and we were glad to have an extra set of hands. We had been taking turns staying with Mom while we searched for someone to be her companion. One day, as I helped her back to bed from the bathroom, she asked, "Is this my room?"

"Mom!" I answered, "Of course this is your room! Where else could you be?"

"Well," she said quietly – perhaps embarrassed because she knew she was confused – "I didn't know if it was my room or a *picture* of my room." I thought this comment was surreal. What was she seeing? And where would we go from here?

When Joe came to stay with Mom, I stayed at the house with him. The two of us slept in the room upstairs, as we did when we were children waiting for Mom to call us downstairs on New Year's Eve. We had a small intercom system so that we could listen to Mom in her bedroom downstairs. She was having a conversation with her dog that consisted mostly of, "Yes, that's my baby! I love you. Yes, Mommy loves you, yes I do!" Then there would be a silence. "Joie? Joie? Where are you?" Then another silence. Then she would sleep and so would we.

But in the morning she was up early and started talking again. One of us would go downstairs and find her sitting on the edge of the bed. "Go back to sleep, Mom," Joe pleaded, but he could not get her back into the bed.

"Joie," she said. "What should I do now?" We were so tired.

Someone else came that day to relieve us; I was so exhausted I don't remember who it was. We had to find a solution. We could not expect ourselves to do this much longer. I went home that day and sat down to think. I had called some friends to ask if they knew anyone, but no one seemed to be available immediately. There was only one thing to do. I lay back on my bed and put my hands over my head, as if in surrender. *Please God*, I begged, *please send us the right person. I am giving this to You.*

The same day, that person appeared. Steve was visiting Mom when a man named Luis came to deliver the Meals on Wheels. This time he brought his wife, Marcia with him. Steve explained to Luis that we were looking for someone who could look in on Mom in the morning and at night, prepare a meal, and clean the house a little bit. Luis turned to Marcia and asked her in Spanish if she would like a job. She nodded her head *yes*.

She began immediately. She spoke very little English, but knew exactly what was needed. She used to call my mother *Miss Mary*, and treated her with the utmost respect. She worked for us seven days a week for the next seven years, even staying on when the situation became more serious and Mom needed more medically skilled assistance. She was the constant, ever-present help that we needed, never getting sick, never failing to show up, and always keeping the house clean. She was the clearest demonstration of a prayer answered that I had ever experienced.

Mom had made us promise not to remove her from her home, and so we arranged to have a series of aides come in and care for her. She had long ago run out of money, and we accomplished a small miracle by collectively getting through the morass of the Medicaid system to get her 24-hour care at home. But while *we* thought this was an amazing stroke of good luck, it made Mom so angry that she stopped talking, except to complain. She did not want "strangers" in her house. She then stopped all the activities she had so cherished at home – no more sewing, painting, playing the piano, cooking. In protest to the terrible thing we had done, she just stopped.

And then it was only a matter of time before her mind stopped too, and she did not know any of *us* anymore. We would visit her regularly and try to make life more cheerful. She liked to be taken out in the car for a ride, go out for ice cream, or go around the corner to visit her friend, but it was somewhat painful to be with her. She kept on asking, "Who are you?"

We all had different ways of coping. For some, it was to keep busy with her house, mowing the lawn, fixing small broken things; for others it was to talk a blue streak and hope that the time passed as the afternoon stretched out endlessly in front of us. Eleanore, for whom all challenges are fun, used to seek out new places and people for Mom to visit. Steve would take her to the park with the dog; he did not mind driving around with a panting dog in his car, dander flying everywhere. He said it was better than sitting in the house with her, feeling sad.

What made it so hard? She wasn't the same person anymore. She could not remember anything, so we could not reminisce with her about the many decades that had come before, those decades filled with family parties, holidays, trips, marriages, babies…I used to try to jog her memory by taking out her scrapbooks and looking at the pictures and clippings she had archived over the years, but no, she could not make sense of anything.

She had loads of postcards from all of us, from all our travels. Wherever I went, I sent her one every day. She saved them all. Going through her scrapbooks and files, I found all the pieces of correspondence and gathered them together. I wanted so much to sit with Mom and look at them again, read them, and remember the places from which I had sent them. But by that time, she was past knowing that these scrapbooks, which were a chronicle of her life, belonged to her. In fact, she did not even know she was in her own house. Although Mom appeared to be *looking* at a card or picture, she really did not see it. So this kind of visit was a very solitary activity.

I took the postcards home with me one night, and sat and read them all. Some were from England, from the places I visited that I knew she'd love. There were postcards from my stay in Brazil, my journeys to Japan, from my sketching trips to Germany and Austria. Some of the cards were from a time I went alone to Italy to attend the International Children's Book Fair when I was studying to be a librarian. It was Easter season then, and the shop windows were lush and full of oversized chocolate eggs, each covered in different colored foils – glimmering pale blue, brilliant gold and silver, with big shiny bows. There were small candy eggs with little scenes inside – tiny chicks and ducks, a miniature cottage, all made out of sugar. And the shops in town with their hundreds of cheeses, candies and pastries, harlequin masks with bizarre expressions. It was all too much and I wanted Mom to see it.

There were postcards from my Montreal days, from my summer at school in Paris, from the many voyages I had made with Doug. We had dipped into the heart of Eastern Europe and seen Prague, with its pastel colored, swirling seventeenth century buildings; we had sat in high-ceilinged cafés with walls of gold paneling, glittering mirrors, and frosted glass windows. We had shared in writing the rush of excitement we felt when leaving the rainy towns of northern England and saw the brilliant colors in Ireland – the famous doorways of Dublin, painted teal green, butter yellow, cobalt blue, and crimson, and crowned with lacy Edwardian arcs; the inns and houses near the seaside dressed in bright coral, pistachio green, warm pink, and deep red. And a row of houses that went from burnt orange to cherry to ochre to pale yellow, all on the same block.

We had loved seeing Italy, with its terra cotta landscape dotted with cypress trees, and had the breath knocked out of us when we saw Venice, the floating city, adorned with colored glass lanterns, everything tinkling and glowing in the moonlight. And Spain! Madrid on a cold night, when the *tavernas* are full of literary types, their woolen scarves about the necks, their voices full of passion as they discuss art and music while drinking syrupy liqueurs and eating olives, spitting the pits with full force into small plates. The streets of Málaga, so narrow that the balconies of opposing buildings practically touch one another. The quiet solemnity of Mexico City, where so many walls are tiled and whole families gather in the giant and cavernous Café Tacuba for a night of singing, eating, and laughing. And news of all this we sent home to Mom.

An old photo taken on a family vacation shows Joe and me standing on the border between Vermont and New Hampshire. There is a sign designating the demarcation line between the states. I like this idea of standing at the "edge" of the world. We know the world really has no edge, since it is round, but there have been a few times when I have had the pleasant sensation of being at the crossroads of two parts of the earth. One winter Doug and I went to Australia to visit his mother's side of the family. Of course, it was summer there, since Australia is on the other side of the world. We stayed with Doug's ninety-year-old Auntie Olga, who lived for a long, long time in a tiny house at the tippy top of a hill overlooking the sea. On New Year's Eve, the end of one year, the beginning of another, we stood right at the summit of that hill and could feel the two-sidedness of everything – one year giving way to the other, *one* side of the hill, the *other* side of the hill, even one wind blowing in and the other blowing out. Everything was being experienced in pairs. I tried to explain this to my mother in a postcard.

We had explored the American South – the cities resplendent with antebellum grace – New Orleans, Savannah, and Charleston, the places I had wanted to see when I wrote my thesis on southern children's literature. We saw the decaying white mansions with their peeling columns and fading green shutters, the giant live oak trees, their thick branches reaching out and up, covering an entire yard. We had walked along the shady streets of Savannah to see the intricate and well-preserved row houses lined up like cakes in a bakery window, decorated with wisteria and bougainvillea.

On a trip to Brazil I showed Doug where I had lived and we visited with Anna-Maria and her family. We took a ride out to the country to taste again the Brazil I had known twenty years earlier, the Brazil of small towns and steep streets, of modest houses painted mint green, pale coral, and cool blue, each with its windows displaying lace curtains, crocheted, no doubt, by the women from the North who sit under trees and spin beauty from white thread.

Everywhere I went, I wanted to share it with Mom. But what was most striking to me was that every card ended the same way: *Mom, I am so happy. I am happy every minute. I love everything here.* How she must have enjoyed getting this message over and over.

About everything I ever liked, my mother used to say, "You like it because it's *you* looking back at *you*." She believed that if you responded to something out in the world, it was because it was already residing in you. That was how you were able to recognize it. Hence, she often said "It's good to want things." She thought that this was a sign of good mental health – to feel the desire to see, to be, to do, and to have things. This is why she indulged our every whim, our every creative impulse.

When I turned forty and realized how young twenty was, I asked my mother, "How could you have let me go to school in Europe alone when I was so young?"

"I had to," she replied. "I knew you would not be able to become the person you needed to become if you did not do that."

* * *

Looking through my own photo albums now, I see that I collected the same images over and over, and in my sketchbooks I drew the same pictures. It was as if I could not get enough of certain pieces of the world and tried to capture them, somehow hoping to internalize them. Here they are again and again – the open-air markets, the shop windows and storefronts, the garden gates, the doorways, the children playing in the park. There are those old houses – sometimes made of wood, painted white with colored shutters; or they are villas of Germany or Sweden, with slate roofs, walkways, and paths leading through gardens of big blue hydrangeas; or tidy row houses of Holland, which one might think are inhabited by dolls, they are so small. And the merry-go-rounds! The little ones in the streets of Paris, whose horses can only hold a child of six, the ornate carousels of Deauville with their mirrored panels that give the rider the sensation of moving through multiple worlds; a German carousel, curiously standing in an amusement park in Tokyo, elaborately outfitted with Venetian boat-shaped seats that rock, and overhead, carved figures of scantily clad females holding long clarions, the entire machine illuminated by many small electric bulbs; the good old-fashioned, familiar merry-go-rounds of American boardwalks, whose horses had big, carved wooden roses cascading down their long necks. These photos and sketches appear decade after decade, as if I had been photographing my own children as they grew up. I cannot help but ask myself, *What have I been looking for, and how many times have I already found it?*

Now when I sit alone with my photos, I think of what it was like to try to breathe life into these pictures as I talked to Mom. Once, in her younger days she did not even need a photo – her powers of visualization were tremendous. She only needed to hear words and she understood what you meant – she could see it with you. But at this late date, no words and no pictures could bring her memory back.

Sometimes I would step out into the backyard and just stand there, imagining all the events that took place on that one plot of land. I can hear the early summer-morning sound of my father hammering, our voices as we celebrated some happy event, the stillness of a winter evening when the yard was deep under snow. I can hear that unique sound of Dad's yellow hand lawnmower as it sliced the blades of grass and released that fresh smell in the early spring twilight. I am called back, seeing Dad with one of his many tools, working in the little vegetable patch he tried to cultivate, which never yielded anything but a few puny ears of corn and some undernourished cucumbers. Sometimes he is walking behind the wheelbarrow, in which a tiny me is a passenger. All around the periphery of the yard forsythia bushes crowd together, and next to the white façade of the house, pale pink globes of peonies, which Dad planted, stand in fragrant beauty.

Our backyard was like an ever-changing theater set. At varying times it had a tree house that Dad built in the forked branches of a large mulberry tree, a life-sized doll house that my uncle built for me from masonite and plywood. For a number of years there was a stone fireplace for outdoor campfires, and through the years, an assortment of outdoor grills for the many late night barbeques and Fourth of July celebrations. On these occasions, we would plunge dry branches into the fire to create batons with glowing tips that we'd swirl around, writing our names in midair. On such a night as that, hot, muggy, and inky-blue, we'd see hundreds of lightning bugs turning their tiny lamps on and off.

The year I turned twenty, I was interested in opera and at the same time was getting ready to go to school in Paris for the summer. For my birthday in April, my father made me a party with the theme "April in Paris at the time of *La Bohème*," to which all guests came dressed in their *belle époque* costumes. The lawn was covered with small bistro tables with red checkered cloths, and guests strolled around with parasols and long-handled cigarette holders, the men in fake moustaches.

In and out of these years, the yard would be the reception area for two family weddings. This meant crepe paper streamers, outdoor lighting, a large tent. And at other times, the yard was bare sand – no grass – because Herm and his neighborhood friends would use it as an athletic field. By contrast, other people's yards had a static quality, with backyard furniture always in the same place, the grass consistently lovely, and everything just so. But not at the Freeman house – no, the yard could be whatever you needed it to be. Long after anyone used it, it just lay there peacefully. Not a trace of any of the earlier activities was apparent. It is all a memory now, a vanished garden with its abandoned flowerbeds.

Yes, visiting Mom was a solitary activity. Oh, the joy of coming to the house and seeing another car in the driveway! *I don't have to do this alone*! Or to be inside already and hear the lurch of the screen door and know someone else was there. It didn't matter who it was – anyone was welcome. Another person to add some stimulation to the afternoon. Mom never really understood that we were there anyway, for in the middle of a visit she'd ask, "Do you think anyone is coming today?" I used to wonder if she was confusing our time together with the time when I lived in the house with her, and so she did not count me as a visitor now.

Little by little, our mother faded completely from us. She spent all day with her aides – they were godsends – and she believed them to be her best friends. They were gentle, loving women who cared for her as though she were their child, combing her hair, keeping her clean and well nourished. Leila, the daytime aide, used to speak of her childhood days in Guyana. I loved to listen to her narratives, and felt it was a shame that Mom could not understand them. Her speech was so very much her own, inimitable. She used to talk about the Riceland, where she lived with her amazingly capable grandmother whom she helped with the rice harvest. One story began like this: *Sometimes when I'm asleep in my bed at night, my soul travels back to Guyana to those places I knew in my small days.* Leila's Guyanese accent was so thick that even if Mom were able to understand the concepts, she would not have been able to make sense of the speech.

As time went on, Mom had less and less to say. Her vocabulary whittled itself down to "I love you," and "You're beautiful." I thought it odd, yet tender, that this phrase remained. She had always told us she loved us and it was no different now. She did not know us, but she knew she loved us.

Once a month, a priest from the local church used to come to give

Mom communion. Then one day she asked him to give it to the dog. He got disgusted and never came back. Having heard that Father had not been to the house in some time, Eleanore decided to bring Mom over to the church, to use this as a destination for an outing. She took Mom out in the wheelchair and walked her over to St. Nick's, Brandy trotting alongside them. The priest was in, and Eleanore asked him to give Mom communion.

"I can't do that," he replied. "Your mother is senile. I can't give communion to someone who is not aware of what is happening."

My sister was outraged. "Father!" she said. "If someone brought you a child who was retarded or brain damaged, would you deny them communion because of that?"

"I can't DO it!" the priest said. "Do you know that the last time I went to her house she asked me to give communion to the DOG?"

"Father," Eleanore said gently but firmly, "I'll have you know that THIS is a very holy dog. This dog stays with my mother, sleeps in her bed, and protects her!"

"I can't do it," the priest replied. "I am not giving the communion to your mother and I am NOT giving it to her dog."

With that, Eleanore whirled the wheelchair around, strode down the aisle of the church and in loud voice said, "That's IT! I'm burying you in the Jewish cemetery."

* * *

People would say how lucky we were to still have our mother at this late date, all of us grown up, some of us grandparents already. We knew we were lucky. Somewhere, other old parents were lying in hospital beds with tubes and medicines, and our mother was in her own home eating ice cream and being taken out for fresh air. But this did not make it any easier. In fact, it may have made it harder because we did not feel entitled to grieve. Our mother was still here! She just didn't *know* she was here.

Once in awhile, a little more speech would emerge. "Are my babies OK?" she would ask. We didn't know if she meant *us*, her children, whom she was imagining as babies in our cribs upstairs, or if she was concerned about the dog that had morphed into multiple dogs in her mind. We just will never know.

We loved Mom. We loved the person she had been and loved her as the tiny, white-haired lady she was now. She had come to look like her godmother, Michelina. But what was she still doing here? *When would Dad come and get her?* I used to wonder. I felt as though she had been left behind, like a student who had not graduated with the rest of her class. Then one day in the autumn of 2007, she refused to eat. She opened her eyes that morning in her soft, warm bed where she had slept for decades, and told her aide she did not want breakfast. Then she closed her eyes and left for good.

Two days later we had a magnificent funeral for her. There must have been about one hundred people there. The feeling in that room was palpable, as though the room were pulsating with the excitement and exhilaration of being together to celebrate Mom's life. Fifteen different people got up to speak, to sing, to pay tribute. For most of us it was not a sad day. It was the culmination of all the years of love, all our years of life together. Eleanore made the first eulogy, which was long and full, touching on all the relationships Mom had with each member of the family and community. I love the way it ended:

In closing, let me say, as Mom would say, thank you, God, for giving me such a wonderful mother, for the blessing of her long life, and the gentle way she passed – in her own home, in her own bed, with her own friends and family. I love you, Mom. You're beautiful.

* * *

I was wondering how I was going to finish this book, but it seems to have come to a natural end with my mother's death and the dismantling of our family home. In that home were all the seeds of my artistic beginnings and from that space and from my parents arose all the yearnings that inspired me to do everything I have done.

Shortly after Mom died, we started to clear out the house and get it ready for sale. Being practical people, we did not delay in addressing the inevitable – the disposal of the place that had housed so many events and had seen so much history. But none of us wanted to live there or own it – we all had our own homes –

and so we had to prepare it for the next family that would live there.

We could never have known the quality of this experience when we started the task in front of us. We were about to embark on a journey of discovery that would reveal secrets about my mother that were, until now, hidden from us. Working together also taught us so much about how different we are in the way we go about things. We had always known we were individuals – our parents had encouraged that. But it was not until we had to cooperate and collaborate on this project that we realized our styles are so varied that they might sometimes clash violently. We were all trying to survive, grieving whether or not we knew it, and yet addressing the huge job in front of us.

Steve, being pragmatic and no-nonsense, was keen to empty the house as fast as possible. Eleanore, slow to change and more outwardly sentimental than Steve, wanted to enjoy the process, savoring each step. Two very competent people with opposing methods. Herm and I went with the flow of whatever was happening. Joe was totally absent, wrapped in a cocoon of silence in California, not participating at all.

We were going to have to move pieces of furniture that had never budged from their original spots. There were windows that had not admitted light in more than a decade because they were blocked by huge armoires. So many places in the house were hidden, obscured from view because my mother was a collector, and by the time she died, the house was filled to the brim with furniture, art supplies, sewing supplies, books, dolls, china, and various and sundry items. And we had to dispose of all of it.

The project coincided with Thanksgiving. We had one last Thanksgiving dinner in her house, thanks to Herm and Phyllis, who brought in elegant food that we ate off paper plates. We told each other what we were thankful for and then enjoyed a nice meal together. And then, painful though it was, we got to work.

We removed Mom's clothes from her drawers first. She had lovely clothes and in better times she had enjoyed wearing them. For the last six years or so she wore mostly practical clothes – soft, stretchable tops and pants that made her life easy and comfortable.

Occasionally, say, for one last Christmas or wedding, her aides would dress her in a pretty party "frock" (as she used to call them) with some nice scarf or jewelry. The aides thought Mom was their little doll and they loved to primp her. But for the most part, Mom did not use most of the clothes that were in her closets and drawers.

And so we set about extracting all this apparel and packing it up to pass on to some useful cause. As Eleanore and I went through each drawer, we found all Mom's dainty, lacy, ladylike things – nightgowns, hankies, blouses, silk scarves – tucked between layers of tissue and sprinkled with talcum powder. Everything smelled so sweet and clean, and had an essence of *her* about it. In every pocket we found religious medals and rosary beads, as though she had been a squirrel tucking nuts away for the winter.

There were pocketbooks, fine leather gloves, and jewelry boxes hidden in drawers. Mom did not have much valuable jewelry – mostly beads of all colors. There were items we had given her for Christmas. As Mom got older, it became a little more challenging to find gifts for her; she had always loved clothes, but then she really didn't need and couldn't use very much. The choices were fewer and fewer. She liked religious articles – medals, statues, and rosaries. For a long time she liked books, usually spiritual books, but after a time, she couldn't read anymore. Her eyes were fine but she had lost the ability to decode words. But there was one thing she always liked and could always use – Oscar de la Renta perfume, soap, or powder. Thank heaven for Oscar, for he supplied me with an idea for a lifetime, and all because of the little jaunt Mom and Dad had taken to his house so many years before.

We found clothes that Eleanore had sewn for Mom that even had her own label on them – *Made for You with Love by Eleanore*. You could tell that so much time had gone by because the clothes were way bigger than Mom was when she died. Once, she had been a plump woman, but in time had gone down to a much smaller size. We were lucky we did not see our mother wither away to a twig-like state. She was not sick, apart from her dementia, and she always had an appetite. These clothes spoke of another era, now long gone.

Then came the task of excavating what we called her "little room." This was a bedroom that Mom used as a quasi-antique shop. Late in life she developed a collection of armoires and antique dolls, and they were all kept in that room. In the years before my father died, Mom had put so much stuff into that room that it became impossible to pass through it. But now we would remove everything and see what was really there.

What was there? Everything anyone had ever given her for a gift and anything she had collected on her own: doll clothes, doll furniture, scrapbooks of cards, photos, postcards, clippings, and letters. Then there were her paints, her palette and brushes, paintings that she had done and that Herm had made as a child. There were Christmas decorations and her book collection, which fell into a few categories: English country life, spirituality, antiques, and dogs. In other parts of the house were her cookbooks, her glassware, chinaware, silverware. Then there were lamps, pots and pans, tablecloths, teapots, records, tapes, hair ornaments, and more photo albums and greeting cards.

We could not find the dolls. Sometime during her seventies, Mom started collecting good antique dolls, some costing hundreds of dollars. She had said that she wanted to "create heirlooms" since there were none in the family. Ironically, no one really wanted those dolls, not even the granddaughters or great-granddaughters. Anyway, we could not find them.

And then one day, when there was finally space to maneuver the furniture in "the little room," we pulled one more armoire away from the other, revealing the back of a piece we had not noticed before. We swung this last piece away to expose its doors. I opened them up and there were the dolls – about ten porcelain dolls, all dressed in clothes that Mom had made for them – little velvet frocks, plaid dresses, fur-trimmed capes, straw hats, lace gloves. Their glass eyes looked out at me as they all lay there together in the closet. Their tiny painted red lips had the serious expression of Victorian children in old photographs. Here were the "heirlooms." How long had they been buried there? We placed them in a suitcase and tucked them away for safekeeping, at least for the moment when we could decide how to find homes for them.

Over a period of a week or so, everyone in the family came and took whatever they wanted. Eleanore, by her own admission, wanted everything, but only out of sentiment, and did not mind conceding to someone else if they wanted the same item. In fact, she even placed baskets on the piano, each labeled with our names, and as the clearing out project progressed, she would deposit items in each person's basket. These were things she had unearthed in the house that she thought each of us might like to have. It became a kind of game to go to the piano and see what Eleanore had put there. Perhaps it was a toy soldier that had once belonged to Herm, an odd sketch of mine that fell out of a book, or an ashtray for Steve to remind him of our dad.

There was so much to go around and it was amazing to see what people chose! What was hideous to one person was a delight and treasure to the next. Doug wanted a small blue pitcher and some blue and white Chinese porcelain figurines. One of the great-grandchildren wanted a Christmas ornament from the White House. The smallest boy in the family, only five years old, took a basket and with his tiny hands, went into one of the many breakfronts and took some delicate objects that he fancied – a small silver box with a blue enamel lid and some other minutia that only he found valuable. Eleanore, his grandmother, offered him a tiny needlepoint pillow that Mom had made – it had a rather crudely stitched billy goat on it. He took it and, holding it to his pearly little cheek, said, "Oh, it's going to be so cozy in my bed tonight with this."

For every granddaughter there was something they had always longed to have. Who knew? Who knew that one of them had always loved a certain lamp or desk or piece of china? Danny would inherit the white silk bow tie from my parents' wedding day in 1935. It seemed that there would be a home for every item in the house. That is, until all three generations took everything we wanted. And then there was still so much left over. The piano. The twin beds upstairs. The dining room table.

For Steve's son Michael, now a doctor living in rural upstate New York, we put aside all the record albums. He had his own relationship with his grandmother, and it included music. He picked up the albums some time after the house was sold, but it was only after Christmas that he got to play them. Having done this, he sent me this email:

I took a personal day today and have spent time enjoying the stacks of Gram's record albums, and am spinning them. It is a very eclectic cross section, from Viennese waltzes to Charlie Pride, to an artist I never heard of named John Prine. WHO listened to him? There must be a story I am missing. Is it an Uncle Herm thing? After today they will be sorted, but to keep them in the state I found them in, maybe I'll mix up the jackets. I have never been truly depressed but I think the night I listened to the Ed Ames album while taking down the Christmas tree, I came close to knowing about how people suffer.

* * *

We had an estate sale, and then real revelations took place. People came from far and wide to buy something from the house. We discovered that Mom had had many more friends than we knew. People showed up and identified themselves: "I loved Mrs. Freeman. I used to come and sit on the lawn with her. I'm sorry – I did not know she passed away." And that person would look around the house and find something to buy. Then there were people who had known her and wanted huge pieces of the house – one friend bought the dining room table and some armoires. "These will be living in Brooklyn," she said, "and you can come to dinner at my house and eat on your family table." That friend brought her brother, and he bought Dad's yellow lawnmower, pitchfork, snow shovel, and metal rake. Dad's tools. They had such lovely, smooth wooden handles.

"I have a farm," he told me, "and that's where I will use these."

"A farm?" I asked. Dad had always fantasized about having a farm. "And where is your farm?"

"In Brooklyn!" he answered, big white teeth showing. He was thrilled to have the sixty-year-old tools.

After the first weekend, a great part of the contents of the house was sold, but there was still a lot left over. I spent the next few days at the house with Steve, and together we sat and waited for the last customers who would help us empty the place of its remaining pieces. There we sat in the living room, which looked like an antique shop. Thanks to Eleanore, the house never degraded into a rummage sale, for she would place all the odd bits in nice arrangements before leaving for the day. She'd take the remaining bead necklaces and position them daintily in porcelain bowls and silver trays, giving them the dignity that she felt they deserved. The large carving knives and other kitchen tools were laid out in an open drawer, tastefully awaiting a possible buyer. Whatever pitchers, dishes, vases, and baskets were there were placed on a table for maximum appeal. Never at any time were things heaped in boxes to face an ignominious end. No, that would not do. These things had belonged to our parents.

And Larry kept raking the leaves and cleaning up the acorns. It was late autumn and even though Mom had died, her trees had not stopped their natural function. The leaves fell and fell, and Larry kept bagging them and putting them out at the curb. And so the house never would have the look of one that had been abandoned. The grass did not grow tall and the windows were not boarded up, like "the house with nobody in it" that is spoken of in the Kilmer poem. Christmas was coming and Eleanore put a few sweet decorations in those long windows – small, sparkling festoons and little trees all dressed for Christmas, the way Mom would have done, to say to the passerby that the holiday is here and I am glad of that.

When the house was nearly empty, Steve was hit with a wave of emotion, not because the end of owning the house was near, but because he was seeing it as it had been when he, Eleanore, and our parents had moved there back in 1945. The house was new then, so beautiful in its pristine, fresh state. He took me to the top of the stairs, and from the landing we stood and looked into the two bedrooms, now empty, with the pale winter sunlight coming in.

"This is what I meant," he told me. "Look how beautiful everything is – the moldings, the windows, the space and light. This is how it was when I was four years old." And he experienced the sadness of such a long-ago memory and deplored the fact that the house had come so far from how it had once been.

One day, when Eleanore and I were minding the "shop," a man walked in and bought a few books. Then he spied the piano. It was marked $500. His eyes lit up. “A piano!” he said.

“Do you play?” I asked.

“No,” he said, “but I would love to get that for my wife and children for a Christmas surprise.”

I sat at the piano and played a little for him. I wanted him to hear that this piano was old and out of tune. He thought it sounded beautiful. He took a $50 bill out of his pocket and said, “This is my deposit. I will be back tomorrow with the rest of the money.”

The next day I was there with Steve. A woman walked in and saw the piano. “I knew Mrs. Freeman,” she said. “But I did not know she played the piano! I would love to have that piano. Hmm. $500. I just have to go to the ATM.”

“The piano is sold,” I told her. “I’m sorry, but the man who is supposed to come for it has not called yet.”

“That’s OK,” she said. “Here is my phone number. If he doesn’t buy it, call me. In the meantime, I’ll get something else.” With that, she picked up my mother’s oil painting palette, now encrusted with decades-old dried-up paint, my mother’s brushes, her paints, and some pastels. “My children are very creative,” she said. “I would love for them to use Mrs. Freeman’s paints.”

Why did we not know this person? When had she had a relationship with Mom? We had all visited Mom so often, but none of us had ever met these unknown friends.

Then the man came back for the piano. He was so excited; he drew the $450 out of his pocket and handed it to me. “I have arranged for a piano mover to come this weekend,” he said. “But my family does not know about this surprise.” *They’re going to know about it soon*, I thought.

That weekend, two strong men showed up and removed the piano. By that time, many of the largest objects were gone. I had always thought that the house would look sad and naked when empty, but that is not what happened. Without the clutter, it clearly had much more majesty. It even had a kind of royal quality about it. In fact, the more vacant it got, the better it looked. The fireplace and mantle, where we had enjoyed many a log fire on a cold night, looked like a grand dame, clean and white, crowned by the large mirror. The dining room, which had always seemed so cramped, was now spacious and open.

Strangely, the house never seemed devoid of my mother. Perhaps it was because the wallpaper was still up, creating a familiar backdrop. I wandered into her empty bedroom. There was nothing in it. *Where are you, Mom?* I thought. I had slept in that room with my parents until I was five years old. I remember when that room was being built. It was added onto the house because our family had grown so large. Two years old, I was standing on the grass as the lumber was being moved onto the construction site. *Someone pick up the baby!* a concerned voice had cried out.

Now the room had served its purpose. So had the house. And as the poet has said…

…But a house that has done what a house should do,
a house that has sheltered life,
That has put its loving wooden arms around a
man and his wife…

Yes, our time in it was over. It would have a new life with a new family.

* * *

A few weeks after the house was sold, I decided to drive by and see it. I anticipated, as I turned the corner, that I might have to endure some suffering, seeing it for the first time since it had changed hands. But that's not what happened. I saw a truck in the driveway and knew that someone was inside working on the house. Perhaps they were putting up new wallpaper or repairing some of the broken, worn-out spots. Curiously, I was neither sad nor happy. I felt as my mother must have felt that afternoon when she asked me, "Is this my room or a *picture* of my room?" It was as though I were looking at a *picture* of the house instead of the actual structure. It was as though the house had receded to a two-dimensional state.

As I continued driving down the street, I looked out the car window to see the other houses and shops in the neighborhood, some that have always been the same, some that have changed, and some that *will* change as time goes by. I had the thought that the world is really the same *all* the time. It is a surface upon which things come into existence and then disappear. We watch people, places, and things come and go, but really, we are watching the same screen all the time, one on which the pictures change slowly or quickly. And as we watch the pictures, the world just keeps spinning through space.

* * *

Now it is time to continue my journey as an artist, to benefit from everything I have seen and will see, to use what I have gleaned and inherited from the rich experiences of my past, from my parents, my family, my friends, my work, and my travels. I am still carrying my sketchbook, and I am still taking notes. I wonder what will happen next.

* * *

Postscript

Just as I concluded writing this book, the tenth great-grandchild in our family was born. Finley Gray Freeman, the daughter of Ian, that one blond child who was born when I was living in Brazil, and his pretty blonde wife, Justyn. With the loss of our mother that we had sustained in the fall, it was so good to know that a new little life was in our midst. And so the story will continue....

- *Elizabeth Uhlig, July, 2008*